EROS IN MOURNING

Eros in Mourning

HOMER TO LACAN

Henry Staten

THE JOHNS HOPKINS UNIVERSITY PRESS

BALTIMORE AND LONDON

© 1995 The Johns Hopkins University Press
All rights reserved. Published 1995
Printed in the United States of America on acid-free paper
04 03 02 01 00 99 98 97 96 95   5 4 3 2 1

The Johns Hopkins University Press
2715 North Charles Street
Baltimore, Maryland 21218-4319
The Johns Hopkins Press Ltd., London

Library of Congress Cataloging-in-Publication Data will be found
at the end of this book.

A catalog record for this book is available from the British Library.

ISBN 0-8018-4923-3

For my father, *Henry Jeffery Staten*
In memory of my mother, *Aurora Paez*
And for my BEL VEZER

Our souls
Are love, and a continual farewell.

—W. B. Yeats, "Ephemera"

We die with the dying:
See: they depart, and we go with them.

—T. S. Eliot, "Little Gidding"

Contents

Preface

$\mathcal{T}$HIS BOOK IS NOT ABOUT THE PROCESS OF MOURNING AS SUCH BUT about the entirety of what I will call the *dialectic of mourning:* the field of movement of all affective phenomena determined by the mortality of a love object, as this field is articulated in certain influential texts of the Western tradition. The mourning process *strictu sensu* will come into the center of focus at times (notably in the essay on the *Iliad*), but this process characterizes only one moment in the dialectic with which I am concerned. The dialectic of mourning begins with the process of attachment to, or cathexis of, an object, without which mourning would never arise,[1] and includes all the moments of libidinal relation in general (the moments of libidinal approach, attachment, and loss), as well as all the strategies of deferral, avoidance, or transcendence that arise in response to the threat of loss—strategies by which the self is "economized" against the libidinal expenditure involved in mourning.

The phenomena I treat under the heading of mourning are those commonly treated today under the heading of desire; yet, for the religious-philosophical tradition in which Western literature is rooted, mourning is the horizon of all desire. In a study of this tradition it is thus not only possible but necessary to transpose the problematic of desire into the key of mourning. As soon as desire is something felt by a mortal being for a mortal being, eros (as desire-in-general) will always be to some degree agitated by the anticipation of loss—an anticipation that operates even with regard to what is not yet possessed. This anticipation calls forth the strategies of libidinal economization I mentioned above, and in particular the strategies of idealization and transcendence associated with the massive historical phenomena of Platonism and Platonizing Christianity.

As we will see, what motivates the classical project of transcendence of mourning at the deepest level is the fear not of loss of object but of loss of self. This is so not only for the obvious reason, that the loss of the beloved is a loss of self, but because the very object that is desired and whose loss is dreaded may become itself dreadful if it assumes the aspect of unmediated presence, which may be fled like death itself. Hence the thanato-erotic anxiety that determines the functioning of the "supplement" in Rousseau, according to Derrida's analysis: "The supplement has not only the power of *procuring* an absent presence through its image; procuring it for us through the proxy of the sign, it holds it at a distance and masters it. For this presence is at the same time desired and feared. . . . Thus, the supplement is dangerous in that it threatens us with death, but Rousseau thinks that it is not at all as dangerous as 'cohabitation with women.'"[2] Whatever its status may be in epistemology or ontology, unmediated presence plays a crucial role in thanato-erotic anxiety. Such, at least, is what we read in certain texts that loom large in the dominant tradition of the West, the tradition I struggle with in this book.

The same question will always be at issue everywhere in this book across the apparent shifts of emphasis: a question concerning the most fundamental stance that a human being might take with respect to the pouring-out or gashing-open of the self that is caught in the rapture of the beloved's allure. This is the rapture stigmatized, depreciated, or at least subordinated as vulgar or mortal eros by the tradition of transcendence.[3]

Is it really unthinkable, as the idealizing-transcendentalizing tradition insists, to pour out all one's being toward merely mortal objects precisely as mortal, with no thought of any transcendence of any sort beyond that which is mortal love itself, of love for what is mortal precisely *as* mortal and because it is mortal? Would such love as this set off unbearable grief, a despair that would (as Plato argues in the *Republic*) unsettle the very grounds of possibility of rationality and of a community based on rationality? (No doubt the onset of AIDS has made our culture in general more vulnerable to thanato-erotic anxiety in its most concrete form than we have been since the conquest of gonorrhea and syphilis. All the more reason to peel away every transcendental mystification of our erotic and organic fate.)

Yet the thought that the Platonic-Christian tradition declares unthinkable remains always close by the thought of transcendence as its inescapable shadow, as the ever-present possibility that calls forth the project of transcendence, as though mortal and immortal eros were themselves locked in an unbreakable embrace. It is thus only with and through the same texts that declare the unthinkability of nontranscendence, its inferiority to anything that could properly be called thought, that the thought of nontranscendence can be articulated and developed. (Whether it can be *lived* without these texts, immediately and inarticulately, is a question I do not know how even to approach.)

Acknowledgments

I OWE A SPECIAL DEBT OF GRATITUDE TO THOSE READERS WHO SUF-
fered through the entire manuscript of this book at various stages of its
development: Robert Caserio, Donald Marshall, and Charles Altieri. It is
hard to imagine what the finished book would look like without their
criticism.

I am also especially grateful to various readers of whose expertise I
availed myself on particular chapters. Gregory Nagy, whom I have never
met, was extraordinarily generous in consenting to read the chapter on
the *Iliad*, and his criticism and encouragement have been invaluable to
me. Barry Weller read almost the entire Greek text of the *Iliad* with me,
and we discussed its grammar and interpretation sentence by sentence—
an unusual and scintillating experience of collegiality. And behind my
entire encounter with Homer stands Gareth Morgan, whose amazing
intensive Greek course twenty summers ago at the University of Texas
opened a path for me that would otherwise have remained forever closed.

My special advisor on the Gospel of John was Kathryn Stockton, who
also helped with the first chapter; on Dante, Tom Stillinger; on Shakespeare, again Barry Weller; on Milton, Norman Council and, yet again,
Barry Weller; on Conrad, Karen Lawrence. Charles Berger, Lee Rust
Brown, and Srinivas Aravamudan read and criticized various portions of
the manuscript. To all these colleagues I extend my affectionate thanks.

Toula Leventis was responsible for producing the typescript of the book through several incarnations. I am warmly grateful to her for her skill, patience, and good humor throughout this arduous process.

Last and above all, I am grateful to the person who reads me most closely and with the most exigent standard. Jeri Schneider has been the final arbiter of the style and argumentation of this book; whatever felicity these may have are due in no small part to her, and I thank the accident of destiny that has given me such a reader.

A good deal of the work on this book was done during sabbatical and faculty fellow leave granted by the University of Utah from fall 1990 to spring 1991.

A slightly different version of chapter 1 appeared in *New Literary History* (Spring 1993) and of chapter 2 in *Representations* (Winter 1993); an embryonic version of chapter 7 appeared in *Critical Inquiry* (Summer 1986).

I am grateful to the University of Chicago Press for permission to cite from Richmond Lattimore's translation of the *Iliad,* copyright 1951 by the University of Chicago.

CHAPTER ONE

The Argument

THERE IS IN EUROPEAN INTELLECTUAL HISTORY A STRONG, PERHAPS dominant, tendency that pushes to transcend all merely mortal loves, loves that can be lost. There are other points of view represented in the vast panoply of texts since Homer; but none that is organized and institutionalized in such a way as to effectively counterbalance the push toward transcendence of Platonism, Platonizing Christianity, and their descendants and derivatives. Much of what appears on the surface to be exterior to this idealizing-transcendentalizing tradition turns out on examination to be seeking other routes to the same end—the end of avoiding a certain terminal conflagration of flesh.

Our single most important point of reference with respect to the tradition of transcendence will be Plato's *Symposium,* and specifically the doctrine of eros articulated in the speech by the prophetess Diotima of Mantineia, as reported by Socrates. By means of a method of questioning of which Socrates is usually the practitioner but to which he is here subjected, Diotima gradually unfolds for him the inner essence of desire, its aim at the absolute, time-mastering presence of the desired good:

Diotima: Then may we state categorically that men are lovers of the good?
Socrates: Yes, I said, we may.
Diotima: And shouldn't we add that they long for the good to be their own?

Socrates: We should.
Diotima: And not merely to be their own but to be their own
            forever?
Socrates: Yes, that must follow.
Diotima: In short, that Eros longs for the good to be his own
            forever?
Socrates: Yes, I said, that's absolutely true.   (206a)[1]

Diotima/Plato's logic seems irrefutable. It seems that desire must aim
at the continued possession of or proximity to what is desired, such that
the loss of the loved thing, or even the anticipation of its loss, is necessarily the destruction of the happiness of the desiring subject. Conceived
in this way, eros is the *origin of idealism.* Nothing short of perfect possession can satisfy its craving, for the desired good is either all there or it
isn't; any flaw in the absoluteness of its presence is a wound in the
substance of the lover. And what flaw could be more decisive than that of
mortality? The lover knows that his possession of a mortal object is
temporary, that it is slipping away from him at this very moment; hence
the Renaissance Neoplatonist Leone Ebreo will draw from Diotima's
doctrine of the desire for continuity of possession the inference that there
is "always some lack" of the thing possessed, that there is no difference of
essence between desire of an absent object and love of an apparently
present one.[2]
      Even though Plato/Diotima never mentions the question of mourning
in this speech, it underlies the logic of the entire argument, as will become evident in later writers. Marsilio Ficino, the great Renaissance re-
discoverer of Plato, for example, posits a "hidden and continual grief" at
the core of human experience as a consequence of the transitoriness of
temporal things.[3] Ficino's analysis is of course as much Christian as it is
Neoplatonic; Augustine, that great early synthesizer of these two streams
of thought, also locates mourning at the heart of every libidinal investment in created beings.[4] "I was unhappy," he writes in the *Confessions,*
"and so is every soul unhappy which is tied to its love for mortal things;
when it loses them, it is torn in pieces, and it is then that it realizes the
unhappiness which was there even before it lost them" (4.6).
      The distinction between mortal and transcendent eros in the *Sympo-
sium* is not an isolated or isolable moment in the text of Plato; it is
consistent with the system of Platonism as a whole.
      We should keep in mind that what Diotima does in her speech is to
eroticize the mental processes of abstraction and idealization, of ascent

from empirical particulars to ideal universals. Here is how she prescribes the steps of the lover/philosopher's ascent:

> First of all . . . he will fall in love with the beauty of one individual body. . . . Next he must consider how nearly related the beauty of any one body is to the beauty of any other, when he will see that if he is to devote himself to loveliness of form it will be absurd to deny that the beauty of each and every body is the same. . . .
>
> Next he must grasp that the beauties of the body are as nothing to the beauties of the soul. . . . And from this he will be led to contemplate the beauty of laws and institutions. . . .
>
> And next, his attention should be diverted from institutions to the sciences, so that he may know the beauty of every kind of knowledge. . . . And, turning his eyes toward the open sea of beauty, he will find in such contemplation the seed of the most fruitful discourse and the loftiest thought, and reap a golden harvest of philosophy. (210a–d)

In terms of her parable, every act of mind that can be classed as philosophical or as on its way toward the properly philosophical participates to some degree in divine eros, whether the thinker knows it or not. And since divine eros is rooted in mortal eros, since, before it is the love of Ideas, eros is the sexual attraction of bodies, Plato/Diotima's eroticization of thought points toward Freud. Plato makes similar arguments elsewhere; notably in the *Phaedrus,* but also in the *Republic* (402–3), Plato binds the question of the sublimating of sexual love very tightly to that of the ascent to the ideal.[5]

It is arguable that even when it is not explicitly brought into view, the conflict of mortal and divine eros is nevertheless always implicit in Plato. Every time Socrates shows someone how to pass from the diversity of particulars to the ideal he is teaching the sublimation of eros, its liberation from the realm of the body.

That this sublimating or sublating movement is also the overcoming of mourning is made explicit in the *Republic.* Underlying and motivating the famous critique of poetry as imitation of an imitation in *Republic* 10 is its condemnation on the grounds that it foments turbulence in the soul—above all, the turbulence of mourning. The analogy with painting in book 10 allows Socrates to speak of poetic representation in terms of proportion and perspective; thus the "imitative poet" is said to gratify the "unthinking part of the soul" that "does not know the difference between greater and less, but which believes the same thing to be now great and now small, by imaging things very far away indeed from the truth" (605c).[6] But this derangement of cognition is not in itself the ultimate violence that assaults the substance of rationality: the ultimate violence is the unmeasured affect, the "wailing," "lamentation," and "brooding" that are unleashed in the man who fails to perceive, not indeed tables and beds, but his afflictions, in their proper proportions—as the small and insignificant things that in reality they are. "A decent man . . . whose fortune is to have lost a son or something he prized very highly" will, Socrates argues, be "moderate in his grief," because "reason and law" tell him that "nothing that happens to man matters very much" (603–4). Conversely,

> the part which the poets feed up and delight is the very one
> which . . . is forcibly restrained in private misfortunes, and hungers
> to be satisfied with tears and a good hearty cry, being by nature such
> as to desire these things; the naturally best part of us, since it has not
> been properly educated by reason or habit either, relaxes the guard
> over this lamenting part, because it is a spectator of the sufferings of
> others; it feels no shame for itself in praising and pitying another
> man who, calling himself a good man, weeps and wails unseasonably.
> (606a–b)

Poetic mimesis is thus most dangerous because in a badly regulated city it could set off an epidemic of uncontrolled grief.

Grief is of course not the only affect that is stimulated by mimesis and that needs to be "dried up": the same goes for "sex and anger, and all the appetites and pains and pleasures of the soul" (*Republic* 606a). But Plato gives grief a (negatively) privileged place in this series. His remarks in book 10 return to a theme he had developed in book 3, where the passages Socrates wants censored from Homer are primarily those that stimulate the fear of death, both one's own death and that of the loved one (386–87). It is clearly the "weepings and wailings" of Akhilleus that Socrates criticizes in the following remarks (the interlocutor is Adeimantos):

> "We say, I take it, that the good man will not believe death is a
> terror for his comrade, who also is a good man."
> "We do."
> "Then he would not lament for him as if he had suffered some-
> thing terrible."
> "He would not."
> "Moreover, we say that such a man is most self-sufficient for living
> well, and least needs the help of others."

"True."

"Then it is least terrible for him to lose a son or brother, or wealth or any other such."

"Yes, least of all." (387d–e)

What we begin to see in Socrates' critique of poetry, and specifically of Homer, is that mourning, as the agitation that is set off in the soul by an illusion, deception, or untruth that magnifies the importance of losing what we love, is philosophical unwisdom in general.[7]

The underlying issue in both the critique of mourning in the *Republic* and Diotima's doctrine of eros is the proper management of what Freud calls libidinal investment, or cathexis. The doctrine of transcendent eros of the *Symposium* is a doctrine of libidinal investment that cannot fail, in which the substance of the lover will be preserved against all possibility of loss and thus of unmeasured bereavement. It is thus the alternate route to philosophic calm from that which is touted in the *Republic,* the science of objective measurement. In either case it is a matter of learning how to extract one's libidinal substance from the mortal or losable objects in which it could be trapped.

This process of anticipatory detachment of libido will be the explicit focus of meditation for the later Roman Stoics. Nothing better exemplifies this aspect of the Stoic *askesis* than the following passage from the *Enchiridion* of Epictetus:

> In every thing which pleases the soul, or supplies a want, or is loved, remember to add this to the (description, notion); what is the nature of each thing, beginning from the smallest? If you love an earthen vessel, say it is an earthen vessel which you love; for when it has been broken, you will not be disturbed. If you are kissing your child or wife, say that it is a human being whom you are kissing, for when the wife or child dies, you will not be disturbed.[8]

"What is the nature of each thing?"—this is the fundamental question of classical philosophy. But in this remark Epictetus reduces this question to its bare libidinal nucleus; the essence of the essence of any worldly object is its transience or mortality. To know *this* essence is to be forearmed against mourning.

The history of the Christian reading of the Stoic meditation on mortality and attachment is complex; in particular, the Stoic emphasis on the self-ruled and self-sufficient character of the soul clashes with the Christian doctrine of dependence on God's grace.[9] But the "stoic" element that is already present in Socrates' stance toward mourning and which is then intensified in Stoicism proper is reasserted in a new form by Christianity, once again in terms of a doctrine of transcendent eros. As Augustine puts it in his *Confessions,* the beauty of all earthly things declares the glory of the Creator (10.6), to whom all love must rise (4.12). Only in this way can the pain of loss be overcome—although Augustine confesses that, at least at the time of his mother's death, he had not quite mastered his mortal weakness in this regard:

> I CLOSED HER EYES, and a great flood of sorrow swept into my heart and would have overflowed in tears. But my eyes obeyed the forcible dictate of my mind and seemed to drink that fountain dry. Terrible indeed was my state as I struggled so. And then, when she had breathed her last, the boy Adeodatus burst out into loud cries until all the rest of us checked him, and he became silent. In the same way something childish in me which was bringing me to the brink of tears was, when I heard the young man's voice, the voice of the heart, brought under control and silenced. For we did not think it right that a funeral such as hers should be celebrated with tears and groans and lamentations. (9.12)

"I was deeply vexed that these human feelings should have such power over me," Augustine writes a little farther on; but he confesses that in the end he was unable to keep from weeping for his mother for a "small portion of an hour."

Augustine does not, however, limit his concern with the problem of libidinal investment to the grand attachments of love for a mother or a friend; the *Confessions* demonstrates that every motion of the soul can be interpreted as a problem of libidinal investment and defined at the limit by the relation to death and mourning. In the later books of the *Confessions* Augustine describes the infinite refinement of the *askesis* by which he turns his libidinal flow away from created beings:

> I no longer go to the Games to see a dog coursing a hare; but if I happen to be going through the country and see this sport going on, it may attract my attention away from some serious meditation—not so much as to make me turn my horse's body out of the way, but enough to alter the inclination of my mind. . . . And then there are all the occasions when I am sitting at home and my attention is attracted by a lizard catching flies or by a spider entangling them in his web. The animals may be small, but this does not make the thing

any different. I go on from them to praise you, wonderful Creator and Director of all things; but it was not this that first drew my attention. It is one thing to get up quickly and another thing not to fall down. (10.35)

For Augustine, as for Freud, the soul is libidinal in its very substance; the internal principle of movement of the psyche is eros, desire. Every slightest flickering of attention is the absorption of the soul-substance in the object of interest and thus a form of libidinal investment, and every libidinal investment is *either* a snare that death sets for the desiring subject *or* a movement of the soul toward the eternal and unchangeable, in whose bosom there are no farewells. Augustine thus goes even further than Plato in eroticizing mental activity, and it is no mere metaphor when he stigmatizes the love of this world as "fornication against God" (1.13; 2.6).

The fundamental terms of the classical problematic of eros are simple, though the logical and dialectical possibilities these terms open up are endless: one may love mutable, contingent beings *as such*, in which case one is subject to limitless mourning; or one may love such beings as a step on the way to the true, ultimate, and unfailing object of love, in which case mourning is mastered or at least mitigated by a movement of transcendence. In particular, the problematic of sexuality and of erotic intimacy is tangled in the antinomies of this structure, and the aporias of this entanglement define the dialectic of mourning across a large part of its expanse.

The sexual relation, and specifically the relation between male and female, will thus preoccupy us in much of what follows. But it is crucial to understand that there is no boundary of essence between the heterosexual relation and all other forms of erotic intimacy or of libidinal attachment in general. It is true that in classical antiquity homoerotism was to a considerable degree exempted from the anxiety attaching to heterosexual love; but this is only because, as Foucault has stressed, elaborate safeguards were devised to keep homoerotism free from the taint of physicality that was attached to love of a woman. From Plato to the Pseudo-Lucian in the early centuries of the Christian era, pederasty was "linked to philosophy, to virtue and hence to the elimination of physical pleasure"; in short, it was placed "under the sign of truth."[10] The very existence of the powerful imperative to idealize homosexual love, an imperative that persisted for centuries (in its sublimated form—as the ideal of friendship—for millennia) indicates a danger that is being kept at bay as much in homoerotism as in heteroerotism.

Conversely, heterosexual erotism can be idealized in such a way as to lift it to the same exalted status that homosexual love enjoyed in antiquity (though off the evidence of our history it appears difficult to do this without at the same time lowering the status of homosexuality). But once again the process of validation-by-idealization involves the attempt to bracket off the deathly organic element in sex, as we will see even in the case of so fervent an advocate of (married) sexual love as Milton.

Sexual relation is nevertheless only the most blatant instance of the deathliness that lurks in all libidinal relation to temporal existents; the profound, and profoundly anxious, philosophical mind understands that the snare is set for the soul everywhere it turns, that the movement toward death proceeds by minute, almost imperceptible, gradations of libidinal investment ("If you love an earthen vessel, say it is an earthen vessel which you love"). Mortal eros is thus conceived in this book in Platonic-Augustinian—which is to say, Freudian—terms as the relation to objects in general or as fornication with the world. Eros is another name for life, vitality, or soul; I privilege this term because it brings to a focus the principle of motivation, the *voluptas* that draws the self toward an object of desire, and which animates life or soul as its innermost essence.[11] The instance of *sexual* eros, in turn, for our own culture and apparently for many others as well, brings to a particularly sharp focus the dangers and excesses to which the motive force is liable. The special danger that the tradition, both classical and Christian, attributes to the heterosexual relation—almost always as viewed from a male perspective— can therefore serve as an allegory for the danger of erotic relation in general.

That the most dangerous erotic investments need not be heterosexual, however—nor even sexual, in the narrow sense of the term—is already abundantly manifest in the great poem of mourning that troubled Plato so much, the *Iliad*.

The phenomena of the dialectic of mourning all arise out of the affect of self-attachment that we could describe in Freudian terms as the narcis-sistic libidinal cathexis of the boundary of integrity of the self, or in Augustinian terms as the soul's desire for its own unity. Pain violates the boundary of integrity of the soul, whether in itself or, as Augustine describes it, in its connection with the body: "Neither voluntarily nor indifferently, but rather with hostility and opposition, [the soul] turns its attention to the suffering of its body, by which it perceives that its unity and completeness are, to its distress, being shattered."[12] On this account, the soul's desire is for its own most proper selfhood, and it reacts aggressively ("with hostility and opposition") to the disruption of its project of pleasurable self-unity. The limit term in the series of affronts to the soul's self-possession is of course death. "Even the righteous man himself will not live the life he wishes unless he reaches that state where he is wholly exempt from death, deception, and distress, and has the assurance that he will for ever be exempt. This is what our nature craves, and it will never be fully and finally happy unless it attains what it craves."[13] For Augustine the thought of death is the ultimate psychic pain, the ineliminable gap that keeps the circle of the self from closing against the intrusion of the not-self.

The aggressive reaction to the thought of one's own death is what I will call, on the basis of my reading of the *Iliad*, vengeful or resentful automourning. Akhilleus is overcome with grief for his own death, and must make someone pay for his suffering by making this person suffer, and preferably by making him or her grieve illimitably for his death.

Yet Akhilleus's grief of self-loss is also the most intense possible sensation of his own being or "self-affection" (Derrida's term). On the one hand, the thought of his own death arouses his anger or *ressentiment* at the injustice of this infinite self-loss. On the other hand, it opens the limitless flow toward his own self-as-lost of what Freud calls the "cathexis of longing" that in heteromourning is directed toward another. The sense of injury exasperates to the limit the grief, but also the pleasurable self-affection, of Akhilleus's autobereavement. Hence, when the loss of Briseis arouses his grief over the early death that lies in store for him, far from trying to palliate the absoluteness of this loss Akhilleus rushes ahead to absolutize it at a time when it is as yet reversible. Akhilleus not only rejects Agamemnon's offer to return Briseis untouched but invites him to complete his violation of her and of Akhilleus by having sex with her: "Let him lie beside her and be happy" (9.336–37).

It is true that the loss of Briseis is mediated through the injury to Akhilleus's honor, and he anticipates the suitable reparation of this injury by complete vengeance against Agamemnon. But it is precisely against the prevailing group interpretation of honor that Akhilleus refuses the offer of the emissaries, to their bafflement, preferring instead to cultivate another, more personal conception of honor that serves only to make limitless his feeling of injury and the dimensions of the revenge he fantasizes. Thus the invitation to Agamemnon to complete the violation does not express the unimportance of Briseis in and of herself; rather, it perfects Akhilleus's feeling of injury, a feeling from which he squeezes a yield of satisfaction so intense that he prefers it to the restoration of what has been lost.[14] The feeling of aggrieved vengefulness (*kholos*) is itself, in itself, "a thing sweeter . . . by far than the dripping of honey" (18.109–10).

There is of course a second phase to Akhilleus's anger. The greater loss of Patroklos stings him out of his enjoyment of *kholos*, and now he seeks compensation for his grief in a vengeance that would transcend all boundaries. But what emerges from both his lesser and his greater grief is mourning for his own death; loss of the object becomes the mirror of self-loss, and the various forms of vengefulness are rooted in the *ressentiment* of automourning.

If mourning for the loss of self is exacerbated by mourning for a lost object, it follows that the force of automourning could be at least blunted by the mastering of heteromourning. It is too late to master mourning once the beloved object is lost; it is necessary to cut off or attenuate the force of eros at its inception. Hence the Platonic-Stoic-Christian caution that no object that may be lost is to be loved in an unreserved fashion—that only a limited or conditional libidinal flow toward such objects is to be allowed, such that the self remains ready and able to retract its substance from the object before the unmasterable violence of mourning might assail it.

But because the passion of Jesus is central to Christianity, mourning occupies an essential place in Christianity that it does not hold in Platonism or Stoicism. Even if the ascent to the Absolute in orthodox Christianity tends to level out the intermediate difficulties posed by the passion of the mortal flesh, within orthodoxy there remains a powerful meditation on this passion that opens possibilities it does not completely develop. It was this tendency of Christianity to become attached to the mortal substance of Jesus that Hegel criticized as falling short of complete idealism, to the purity of which he attempted to raise it. I press in the opposite direction to Hegel's in my reading of the Gospel of John, toward the consummation of a thought of *absolute mourning*. Jesus by his divinity can call forth an unreserved libidinal investment from his disciples; he is an embodied being who can be loved as no ordinary mortal being can. But the disciples do not know that he will die, and soon. Jesus thus sets a libidinal trap for them that disarms all the usual strategies of economization of libido by which the force of mourning is anticipatorily moderated. Jesus' death hurls the *philoi* 'friends' into an abyss of loss nothing can relieve that does not belong to the innermost interior of the experience of loss itself, to the limitless pathos of the self-clinging that is the essential correlate of all object-cathexis. The essence of this pathos is fully manifest only in the unbearable sharpness of the pain of separation from the most loved and most loving being. (Isn't this paradigmatically the mother? It is her place that Jesus occupies.) Only complete trust in his love by the bereaved *philoi*, trust in the unreserved pouring-out of his substance toward them or on their behalf, can open the fountains of love in their own breasts. Any breach in this trust would arouse the anger and resentment of aggrieved automourning, the type of self-mourning that is still in rebellion against self-loss—that still reserves itself against the absolute expenditure it has begun to taste, because it has not yet grasped love as rooted in the unity of auto- and heteromourning. This enigmatic unity, so difficult to think along all its metamorphoses, is the matrix out of which all the effects of the dialectic of mourning are generated.

The commandment of love, together with the example of Jesus, enjoins the *philoi* to consummate their love by offering themselves up in death, and in this way shatters or deconstructs the Platonic distinction between mortal and transcendent eros. But this agapetic love is interpreted by Augustine and by the tradition in general in a Neoplatonizing and stoicizing fashion that within orthodoxy will block its most radical implications. Blameworthy desire or *libido*, says Augustine, is "the love of those things which a man can lose against his will" (*On Free Will*, 1.4), and all sins arise from this mistake (1.16).

As against Augustine and Christian orthodoxy in general I interpret Jesus' resurrection and his promise of eternal life as referring to this present life transformed by vision. Rudolf Bultmann seems to me to have gone a long way toward recovering the possibility that I read in John; but even for Bultmann there remains inassimilable the final element in the thanatoerotophobic complex: the organicity of life. Partly implicitly and partly explicitly, John thinks death all the way down to the dissolution of the body, and in this way sustains the thought of love in the face of that which the dominant Christian tradition has declared antithetical to all that is of the spirit.

But John nowhere touches on the question of sexual eros, that most intractable of forms of libidinal excitement and investment.

With the *fin'amors* discourse of the troubadours, we are launched on the distinctively modern quest for the reconciliation of (hetero)sexual love with the protocols of idealism. The troubadours, and in particular Bernart de Ventadorn, are thus the fulcrum on which the argument of this book turns. In a form of idealization that unbalances the tradition of transcendence, Bernart idealizes *foudatz* 'erotic folly' as an end in itself, the highest goal of aspiration. Yet the radicality of the troubadour project as exemplified by Bernart, Giraut de Bornelh, and Arnaut Daniel, was very soon recuperated for the purpose of transcendence by Dante. In so thoroughly sublimating sexual love into love of God, however, Dante backs away from the problem of how libidinal investment in general and sexual eros in particular can be approached without recourse to the transcendence of mortality.

As is well known, after Dante the tradition of courtly love finds its most influential development in the work of Petrarch, through which it spreads to most of Europe. I am only marginally interested in Petrarchism as a style; my focus is, rather, on the propagation of the erotic problematic associated with Petrarchism, a problematic the characteristic features of which are: the idealization of a woman, the maintenance of distance that preserves desire, the tendency for idealization of the woman to become denigration (because she is cold or unfaithful), and the detailed elaboration of the lover's own emotions of desire, resentment, self-pity, and joy.

The space of this problematic with all its transformations and permutations is very wide, as I attempt to show in brief accounts of *Hamlet* and *La Princesse de Clèves,* and then in an extended reading of *Paradise Lost.*

The continuity of the erotic problematic of *Hamlet* with that of courtly love is evident in the interplay between, on the one hand, Hamlet's idealization and denigration of Ophelia, and, on the other hand, his mourning. Hamlet's mourning for his father is disturbed by what he perceives as the infidelity of his mother, and the question of the fidelity of Ophelia in particular and women in general becomes an ontological abyss for him (as it had already at times threatened to become for the troubadours), a doubt that unsettles the ground of his being and throws him into an obsessive meditation on the identity of the body of love and the body of death (the meditation that culminates in the graveyard scene).

The question of the relation between mourning and erotic faithfulness is fascinatingly reconfigured in *La Princesse de Clèves.* In the case of Madame de Lafayette's novel, which is often said to be the first "psychological novel," the presence of courtly love is pervasive. These conventions are, however, presented in a highly reflective and critical fashion. *La Princesse* brings to light the reality of the woman's position in courtly love, a position that in the troubadour tradition was occulted by the idealization of the *domna.* Madame de Clèves refuses to be joined to her lover not out of cruelty or because she fails to reciprocate his love (as the lady of the troubadours is characteristically accused of doing) but because she realizes that his passion is sustained by the distance at which she keeps him and would disappear without it.

The problem that troubadour or courtly love does not address is the one that concerns Madame de Clèves: How can erotic passion subsist in the condition of full embodiment? Sexual consummation is not necessarily incompatible with love as conceived by the troubadours or by Madame de Lafayette, but it is incompatible with the full worldly entanglement of the self in a lifetime, or significant fragment of a lifetime, lived in intimate contact with one's mate.

It is in the interpolated de Tournon-Sancerre narrative that Madame de Lafayette outlines the problem of erotic unfaithfulness against that of mourning. Madame de Tournon dies and while Sancerre is in the first throes of bereavement he discovers that she has been unfaithful to him. This is the ultimate erotic-metaphysical nightmare, mortal love at its most undependable. The elements of Hamlet's discomfiture are here welded together into an unbearable unity; but in Madame de Lafayette's hands we see in the ambivalence of Sancerre's grief the reflection of the structural ambivalence of love in the courtly model, its tendency to slide between idealization and denigration of the woman.

This same ambivalence turns up in a mythic archetype in John Milton's account of the fall in *Paradise Lost*. Milton is one of the great early modern theorists of sex and marriage, and in his epic poem all the threads of Christianity, Platonism, and courtly love that I have been tracing converge.

In *Paradise Lost* sex is confronted directly in its identity with death, both as biological death and in Augustinian terms as the deathliness of drives that operate beyond the control of conscious volition. The problem of sexual drive is of course not a gender-specific problem, but in *Paradise Lost,* as in most of the textual tradition with which we are concerned, it is presented from a masculine viewpoint; thus the general problem of control by rationality over sexual passion is complicated and intensified by the cultural imperative of male control over the female. The disruptive otherness of the libidinal object that threatens the lover's self-possession is heightened both by the unmeasure of the erotic desire and pleasure aroused in Adam by Eve and also by the self-will and drive to knowledge of the "advent'rous" woman who belongs, beyond Adam's power of choice, to the interior of his libidinal economy.

Milton conceives the male in orthodox fashion as God's delegate, endowed with the measuring/idealizing faculty the function of which is to preserve the boundaries of self-identical life against the upsurge of passional drives that would transgress those boundaries and hence destroy life. Yet Milton also attempts to conceive as lawful what orthodox Christianity explicitly refuses, a complete erotic rapture directed at a creature of God rather than at God himself. What makes Milton's conception even imaginable as against the force of the tradition of transcendent love is the fact that Eve, though she is a finite, embodied individual, is immortal, so that the essential condition for the definition of what Augustine calls "blameworthy desire" is missing. But she then becomes mortal, and the moment she does so the force of mourning is unleashed. Eve's most compelling motive for giving Adam the fruit to eat is her fear that if she were struck dead he might not mourn her illimitably, that she would be forgotten:

> . . . What if God have seen
> And Death ensue? then I shall be no more,
> And *Adam* wedded to another *Eve,*
> Shall live with her enjoying, I extinct;
> A death to think.   (9.826–30)

"A death to think": in accord with the deep logic of the desire to be mourned, she thinks the unbearable death not as extinction itself but as the blotting out of this extinction, not her absence from the scene as such but the closing of the gap this absence would leave in the libidinal substance of her lover.

But now that death has been unleashed the force of mourning operates just as powerfully on unfallen Adam, whose substance, even though it is as yet immortal, is already wounded by death in the form of the unassuageable bereavement that Eve's mortality threatens:

> How can I live without thee, how forgo
> Thy sweet Converse and Love so dearly join'd,
> To live again in these wild Woods forlorn?
> Should God create another *Eve,* and I
> Another Rib afford, yet loss of thee
> Would never from my heart.   (9.908–13)

Rather than mourn eternally, Adam prefers to die with Eve, and he makes this choice before eating the apple. Adam's choice is not only motivated by love of a losable object, the love Augustine characterizes as the root of sinfulness, but precisely by the fact that she is losable. Thus when Adam says that, if Eve is mortal, death is to him as life (9.953–54), he affirms in the modality of sexual love what I have argued is affirmed by John in the modality of "friendly" love.

Of course Milton condemns Adam's choice, and Adam himself turns against Eve and blames her for their fall. The erotic affirmation I have described is glimpsed, rather than taken hold of, in *Paradise Lost*.

And even within Milton's closest approach to the affirmation of mortal love as such and in its totality, we only graze the question of organicity, which before the Fall is kept at bay by the exclusion of death from Eden and by the promise of an eventual aetherealization of the human body, and after the Fall is foreclosed as a question, its sense relegated once again to the terms of a classical condemnation. If Milton raises the possibility of integrating passion, as a violence that assails the conscious subject's grip on his rational judgment, into the economy of erotic love, he never approaches the possibility of such an integration of the body of death.

It is not clear that this integration has ever been achieved. In the final part of this book I turn to the twentieth century to works by Conrad and Lacan in which, despite the closing in of existential shadows, the relation to the body of death continues to be defined in terms derived from the idealist tradition.

The thought, indeed the smell, of the body of death or body of corruption which is for Christianity the heritage of a forbidden knowledge underlies Marlow's entire narrative in *Heart of Darkness*. Yet with this text, written on the threshold of the twentieth century, we find ourselves farther than ever from thinking the question of thanato-erotic anxiety all the way through. Here the hold on human beings of nature and death is assimilated in the most mystified and atavistic fashion to the embrace of a woman, and the desire to be mourned manifests itself with Akhillean exorbitance in what I read as Kurtz's vengeful drive to inflict mourning. "I will wring your heart yet," he shouts at the wilderness on the trip downriver with Marlow, and Marlow concludes the narrative by wringing the heart of Kurtz's Intended, eliciting from her the terrible cry that I read as the *telos* of the entire tale.

The flaw in the libidinal logic of the desire to be mourned lies, of course, in the fact that the dead cannot enjoy the tribute of grief that their death occasions: a serious flaw, but one that may be overcome in several ways. We are, after all, in the realm of the intertwining of fantasy and "reality." Even if one submits to death, it is always possible to drink in anticipation, imaginatively, the pleasure of being-grieved; and once the pleasure is tasted, the actual dying can be postponed into the indefinite future.[15]

Or, as in *Heart of Darkness*, one might have a double who survives one's death and who can then act as witness of mourning.

In this way, one might also veil the motive of vengefulness that is involved in the desire to be mourned, which is necessarily also a desire to inflict mourning. The motives of cruelty and vengefulness might be attributed to a dark double who dies, and the one who survives to enjoy the woman's grief might be, like Marlow, a most moral, sublimating type.

Is vengeful automourning a characteristically *masculine* affect? What is certain is that the tradition of thanatoerotophobic metaphysics has been defined by male writers; that this tradition has always attempted to keep the lid on mourning by keeping libidinal expenditure in check whenever a mortal being is the object; and that the paradigm of the libidinal snare set by mortal beings for our male sages has been the erotic allure of a woman.

I have argued elsewhere that even the great antimetaphysician Nietzsche is not immune to thanato-erotic *ressentiment* and vengefulness; in the final chapter of this book I argue that Lacan, too, presents the libidinal object as a disruption of the self's most authentic self-propriation, its drive to be only and absolutely itself. Freud is equivocal on this point, but Lacan is not. Lacan never, in any text of his that I know, swerves from his adherence to the Christian-Platonic view of this world as a world of shadows and illusions where any actual object of desire is only a "lure" that captures the self in the toils of what he calls the 'Imaginary'.

Lacan is the most powerful of the heirs of Freud, but his work gives us little reason to think that psychoanalysis makes a fundamental break with the idealizing tradition.

Some readers may worry that this book treats texts in isolation from their historical contexts. My own belief is that, in the final analysis, there is nothing but history, that history is what "reality" analyzes into. On the other hand, there are all sorts of ways of nailing down what is to count as the most relevant aspect or slice of history in any particular instance. Much recent historicizing theory has tended toward an atomizing periodization of the diachronic flow, and some of the formulas sanctioning this atomization seem to me to have gained a rather uncritical acceptance. I am thinking in particular of notions of "the emergence of a new subject" at some fairly precise moment, usually in the eighteenth or seventeenth century.

The methodological assumption by which I have been guided in this book is that any given text produced at a given historical moment is constituted at different levels by heterogeneous threads of discourse, each of which has its own complex historical provenance; and insofar as I can think of "the historical subject" it is by analogy with such a structure. Like the so-called realist text that slips here into the mimetic register of the picaresque, there into that of the folk song or the didactic tract or pure comic caricature or gothic, the socially constructed individual is indeed historically constituted, produced not by a present that is self-identically present but that is traversed by ideological remnants and *revenants* from previous moments in the history of the culture. To take an example that brings together fictive and real historical subjects: What would Dorothea Brooke's desire be, and what George Eliot's, what would the entire structure be of the analysis in *Middlemarch* of a society at a specific cultural moment, the reform agitations of 1829 in England, without the model of the desire of St. Theresa that Eliot explicitly invokes at the beginning and end of the novel, and that, as Kathryn Bond Stockton has recently shown, works Eliot's life and art at the deepest level?[16]

Thus investigations that seek to establish the historical specificity of restricted moments in the development of a culture (whether or not they seek to define a "new historical subject") may be complemented (rather than contradicted) by investigations like mine that seek to define a field within which it would be possible to describe the migration of structures that are "grafted" (in Derrida's sense, with everything it implies concerning transformation by context) from the texts of one period to those of another.

PART ONE

TWO ARKHE-TEXTS

CHAPTER TWO

Before Transcendence: The *Iliad*

NOT ONLY PRE-CHRISTIAN BUT PRE-PLATONIC, THE "ILIAD" REP-
resents a relation to death and mourning that is not yet sedimented with
the strategies of idealization and transcendence that we will encounter in
later works. With the figure of Akhilleus the *Iliad* tears away all the cultural palliations of the absoluteness of death in order to expose the limitless agony they veil.[1] Akhilleus's penetration beyond the warrior ethos
unleashes the darkness of illimitable mourning in a way that sums up the
stance toward death that Platonism and Christianity will come to relieve.

Perhaps it is as a consequence of the absence of any ideology of transcendence that the *Iliad* poet(s) can represent in such an unmitigated
fashion the impulse of vengeful automourning. In the *Iliad,* at the very
beginning of the European textual tradition, we already find an extraordinarily sophisticated theorization of an individual's libidinal speculation on
his own being.

There are obviously numerous aspects of the representation of subjectivity in the *Iliad* that need to be historicized—to be understood in terms
of the specific forms of community, ownership, authority, and so forth
that are presumed by the poem and which are so fundamentally different
from those of our own period. I will not ignore these cultural inflections.
And yet, across cultural and historical differences may be discerned a very
precise analysis of certain structures of subjectivity the operation of which
is perhaps not restricted to the historical moment of archaic Greece.[2]

I am not suggesting that these structures are universal: the argument is, rather, that the history of a culture such as ours, one informed by a continuous or semicontinuous textual tradition, cannot always be bitten off in mouth-sized chunks, that the historical horizon against which we must interpret the "constitution of subjectivity" at a given period may be broader and more difficult to construe than is sometimes assumed.

Of course the society or societies represented in the *Iliad* correspond to no actual historical societies, but this makes the representation of Akhilleus even more significant, because, constrained only very loosely by history, it manifests all the better the consciousness of the society out of which the representation springs. Thanks to recent developments in Homeric scholarship, and above all to the monumental studies of Gregory Nagy and Berkley Peabody, we now understand better than ever before the eminently communal process of the composition of these poems, communal not only on the side of generations of singers but also on the side of generations of audiences whose responses contributed in an essential way to the shaping of these poems.[3] We are therefore faced with the apparent paradox of a supremely communal act of formative imagination which for centuries refines the representation of an individual's rejection of group solidarity and of his agonized relation to his own property and his own death.[4]

The "property" involved is women; there is an initial dispute over Agamemnon's "prize" Khryseis, and this then leads to the quarrel over Akhilleus's prize Briseis. Even the close similarity of the names indicates the interchangeability of the two women in the operative system of exchange; but the women are more than purely arbitrary markers of distinction. Agamemnon describes the virtues, physical and mental, of Khryseis and declares his intention to have her in his bed; Akhilleus will later tell us he loved Briseis "from the heart," and Briseis herself will inform us that plans were afoot to make her Akhilleus's wife. Nevertheless, the women also function as conventional, if not purely arbitrary, markers of distinction. Each woman has been assigned to her respective possessor by the Akhaians acting as a collective authority, as his rightful prize from the booty taken by the army.

This is, however, a special category of prize, one that goes beyond the ordinary *moira* 'portion' of the warrior. The term for this special kind of prize is *geras*, which Emile Benveniste defines as an "honorific portion" that is "over and above" the ordinary *moira* (335–36); Jean Lallot in his summary prefacing Benveniste's chapter calls it an "honorific supplementary share."[5] Thus the *geras* is a special, or "supplementary," mark of distinction; this is why Akhilleus takes it as such an injury to his *timē* 'honor' when he is left without this special prize. Akhilleus still possesses a large share of booty from his maraudings, as he admits in book 9 when he says that in addition to the wealth he left at home, "from here there is more gold, and red bronze, / and fair-girdled women, and grey iron I will take back; / all that was allotted to me." Yet all this cannot balance the loss of his "honorific supplementary share": "But my *geras*: he who gave it . . . has taken it back again / outrageously" (365–69).

The women are involved in a structure of "supplementation" in something like Derrida's sense of the word. They are extra, a luster added to the fullness of the warrior's *moira,* and yet they imply an unfillable gap in the plenum from which they turn out to be missing. Khryseis, Agamemnon's *geras,* is held by Agamemnon illegitimately; she is the daughter of the priest of Apollo and therefore cannot be held against her father's will. There is a transcendental boundary that excludes her from the circle of Agamemnon's possessions even while he holds her captive. Thus a structural disequilibrium is built into the situation with which the *Iliad* opens, and the lack that causes this disequilibrium is one that is incapable of being filled. If Agamemnon gives up Khryseis, he, the paramount king, therefore the most to be distinguished by *geras,* would be in the anomalous and intolerable position of being the only one of the Akhaians who would have no *geras* (1.118–19). As Akhilleus points out, all the booty has been distributed, and there exists no common store from which Agamemnon could have his loss made good (1.121–26). From this it follows that Agamemnon must take the *geras* of one of the other heroes, and that this in turn will necessarily leave a new and once again intolerable absence of *geras* for someone else.

Briseis thus becomes the apple of discord, the movable marker of distinction that leaves a yawning absence of distinction in its wake, throwing social relations among the competitors into disequilibrium. If such disequilibrium were not regulated in some way, the resultant violence could rupture the entire social system (this is what threatens when Akhilleus contemplates killing Agamemnon, a crime that would violate the most fundamental and thus divinely sanctioned of rules).

Therefore there exists a system of conventional equivalences according to which compensation or reparation may be made for injury suffered or loss incurred and in this way the vengeful anger of the injured party appeased. This system gives Agamemnon a publicly acknowledged and thus face-saving way of conciliating Akhilleus; when Agamemnon realizes the disastrous nature of his affront to Akhilleus, he offers him *apoina* 'reparation' that is considered by the other Akhaians, though not by Akhilleus himself, more than adequate to make up for Akhilleus's loss of Briseis.

In this system, even the most extreme sort of injury—which could easily be felt as incommensurable with any compensation—the murder of close kin, is reparable by the paying of a material equivalent, *poinē* 'blood money'. Blood money is the last brake on vendetta, the hinge between the functioning of lawful order and the outbreak of murderous violence. Because there are compensatory equivalences, there are limits on violence, which is to say limits on the boundless augmentation of a particular kind of affect: anger, vengeful fury.

There is no clear line between community and noncommunity with respect to the problem of vengeful fury. On one hand, the violence that unleashes vengefulness infects even the innermost core of community, the kinship group (16.573; 13.694–97). On the other hand, even between enemies equivalences are available that make exchange possible, and these exchanges palliate the absoluteness of war, introduce some limit to the irruption of absolute violence (ransoming of prisoners, gift exchange among enemies, ritualized duels, restoration of things stolen). These exchanges function as the medium of a kind of "conversion" of affect, its transformation from one form into another (hostility into friendliness) or its "capturing" in objective social form (hostility captured or contained in a formal relation of friendliness). Ransom, reparation, and blood money are mediations between the subjective order and the political order. The subjective wound finds its symbolic equivalent, and the stream of affect is rechanneled in a way less destructive to culture.

The operation of various sorts of limits in the war between the Trojans and the Akhaians has in fact created up to the moment that the *Iliad* opens a condition of stalemate: for nine years the war has remained undecidable. The gift exchanges between both Aias and Hektor and Glaukos and Diomedes, in the early part of the poem, are reminders of this earlier stage of the war in which the enemies still recognize the option of "conversion" of hostility through symbolic exchange, thus still recognize some symbolic order that encompasses both sides and keeps the enmity of war from being total. We are also repeatedly reminded that taking prisoners in battle and holding them for ransom was formerly a common practice, but, as Robert Redfield points out, in the *Iliad* even though ransom is offered in several instances, it is always refused and not one prisoner is taken for ransom.[6]

The *Iliad* thus marks the breakdown of the condition of stalemate/

equilibrium, and this breakdown takes the form of a breakdown in the circulation of equivalences. Agamemnon will not accept *apoina* 'ransom', 'reparation' for Khryseis, Akhilleus will not accept *apoina* for Agamemnon's insult to him, and later Akhilleus will not accept *apoina* for the body of Hektor. These three refusals are the pivotal points on which the plot of the *Iliad* turns.

What is at issue in the *Iliad* is thus an accelerating crisis of equivalence which is set in motion by Agamemnon's refusal to accept the ransom offered by the priest of Apollo in exchange for his daughter Khryseis.

If Agamemnon had accepted the value of the proffered *apoina* as proportional to his desire for the daughter and his frustration at losing her, he could have fulfilled his obligation to respect Apollo's priest while at least publicly maintaining the honorable stance that he had received a prize that adequately supplied the lack of the one he lost. In that case order would have been maintained and no quarrel with Akhilleus would have ensued. If Akhilleus, in turn, had been willing to accept Agamemnon's reparation as proportional to his pain at losing Briseis and the damage to his *timē* 'honor' at being publicly humiliated, he could honorably have let go his anger and rejoined the Akhaian host.

The crucial point is that *apoina* or *poinē* are only worth the injury they come to make up for if the injured party agrees that they are, and this agreement is not in the *Iliad* easy to secure. It is in the interest of the group that such equivalence should be accepted, as we see from the way the other Akhaians urge Agamemnon and Akhilleus in their respective cases to accept *apoina*. But the injured party finds it more difficult than those not directly involved to feel that the reparation actually does measure up to the loss.

Akhilleus wants vengeance against Agamemnon, and his motivation is strongly colored by erotic passion, by the sexual rage of having another man publicly take his woman. This is of course a form of the underlying motivation for the entire war, as the poem presents it. The Trojans as a collective body have despoiled the Greeks as a collective body of the woman Helen, and the Greeks are out for erotic vengeance. This motive is very concretely pictured in its individual manifestation at the end of book 4, where the poem cinematically jumps from Helen's chamber, where she is reluctantly about to yield sexually to Paris, to the battlefield, where her enraged husband looks to murder the Trojan for the very outrage that Paris is in the act of renewing. The transfer of Menelaos's motive to the collectivity is visible in the aged Nestor's exhortation to the Argives: "Therefore let no man be urgent to take the way homeward /

until after he has lain in bed with the wife of a Trojan / to avenge Helen's longing to escape and her lamentations" (2.354–56).

(Hetero)sexual passion is clearly involved in some fundamental way in the crisis of equivalence at the center of the poem. But exactly in what way? A long tradition, now updated by Thomas McCary, suggests that it is really Patroklos and not Briseis whom Akhilleus loves.[7] Is Briseis only a secondary issue, a pretext for the heroes to carry out their competitions with one another? Does Akhilleus not really love her? As we will see, the form of these questions is too simple, too naively psychologistic.

Briseis occupies a crucial structural role in the *Iliad*. On the one hand, she is a possession, a 'prize,' like a horse or a tripod; on the other hand, she is a woman whom Akhilleus says he loves and calls his 'wife' (*alokhos*), a woman whose loss he grieves. She thus functions as the transitional link between the social and the libidinal orders. The *Iliad* articulates libidinal economy in terms of socioeconomy, in terms of the exchange of symbolic value-equivalences. In order to understand the role of Briseis we must reconstitute the whole of this double articulation, of this sociopsychic economy.

Akhilleus in book 9 (342–43) says of Briseis *ego tēn / ek thumou phileon*, and even across the cultural and temporal differences between us and the Greeks the sense seems unmistakably to be that which the English translation conveys: "I loved her from the heart." The Greek clearly means this; but it means more as well, because *philein* belongs to a semantic network more extensive than that of its English equivalent, 'to love'. Benveniste, who always keeps in sight the embeddedness of Homer's language in a specific social/institutional context, points out that the emotive sense of *philein* is rooted in the institutional sense that has reference to a pact prescribing certain behavior between those who thereby become *philos* (masc.) or *philē* (fem.) 'dear', 'bound in friendship' to one another. Thus *philein* means not only 'to love' but 'to entertain as a guest', behavior that itself entails the entering of host and guest into a formal relation, with reciprocal obligations of "friendship" to each other (281). What emerges from Benveniste's discussion is that the senses of *philein* and *philos* all radiate from the institution of the *oikos* 'household'. The guest, the wife, the blood kin, the domestics—all are called *philos* or *philē* because they belong to the interior of the *oikos* (281–82). The boundary of the *oikos* is the boundary between inside and outside, between the *xenos* 'alien' and, as we could now translate *philos*, the 'proper', what is closest to oneself as one's own. It naturally follows, as Benveniste argues, that *philos* also acquires the sense that is translated into English as a simple possessive, 'his' or 'hers'.

It is clear in what way the notion of *philotēs* can be extended to those with whom one shares mortal peril every day and upon whom one depends for one's own preservation. When Patroklos is called *philos* by Akhilleus, however, the narrower sense is invoked as well as the sense 'comrade', 'friend' because Patroklos grew up in the same household as Akhilleus, like a member of the family (23.89).

Finally, if we have any doubt concerning the concrete sense of the expression *ek thumou phileon*, the same expression is used by Phoinix in his pathetic account of his love for the infant Akhilleus. Here the context leaves no doubt as to the concrete manifestation of the emotion described. "I . . . loved you out of my heart" (*se . . . ek thumou phileon*), he says to Akhilleus,

> . . . for you would not go with another
> out to any feast, nor taste any food in your own halls
> until I had set you on my knees, and cut little pieces
> from the meat. . . .
> And many times you soaked the shirt that was on my body
> with wine you would spit up in the troublesomeness of your
> childhood.   (9.486–91)

This, the most naturalistic description of parental *philotēs* in the *Iliad*, not only gives us an unmistakable sense of what loving "from the heart" means but connects the notion concretely with the life of the *oikos*. It also suggests something like parity between the kind of love a man feels for his (surrogate) son and the love Akhilleus claims to feel for his female captive Briseis.

Once we have in mind the network of definitions, relationships, and their associated emotional cathexes that constitutes the fundamental relation of the individual to the grounds of his identity in the *oikos*, it becomes obvious why Briseis, though very *philē* to Akhilleus, is not so much so as Patroklos, and why her loss is not as painful—even though he loves her "from the heart." She is simply not as deeply integrated into either the *oikos* or the experience of Akhilleus as is Patroklos.

But if Briseis is not first in the hierarchy of *philotēs* for Akhilleus, this is not because a woman cannot in this social system occupy that position. The poem informs us at a crucial point, in the "paradigmatic" story of Meleager that Phoinix narrates in book 9, that an *alokhos* 'wife' may indeed be most *philē* of all. As J. T. Kakridis demonstrated, there is in

Greek literature a motif of an "ascending scale of affection" involving a
"fixed gradation of friends and relatives," with the wife typically named at
the top of the scale, and in the Meleager story, in accord with this
traditional motif, it is Meleager's wife, Kleopatrē, who occupies the place
of honor as more *philē* than even his *hetairoi* 'comrades' who occupy second place.[8] Unlike Briseis, Kleopatrē is a wife in the full sense, dwelling
in the bosom of the *oikos*. The *oikos* is the system of relationships that in
its totality constitutes the inner face of the social identity or being of the
warrior (the outer face being that of his relation to other warriors); and
we cannot investigate the question of love in the *Iliad* except through the
mediation of this system.[9] The assumption that Akhilleus loves Patroklos
more than he loves Briseis simply because homosexual love is here more
powerful than heterosexual ignores the social structure that gives meaning
to the language of affect in the *Iliad*. As Gregory Nagy points out (*Best of
the Achaeans*, 105ff.), the structural analogy between the Akhilleus/Patroklos
nexus and the Meleager/Kleopatrē nexus is directly alluded to in the *Iliad;*
the name Patro-klos inverts the members of the name Kleo-patrē, *kleos*
'glory' and *pateres* 'ancestors'.

It is true that women are brutally "commodified" in this world, treated
as possessions and as objects of exchange.[10] But it is also true that this is a
world in which one can, and indeed in certain circumstances ought to, accept material compensation for the murder of one's brother or son. What
we need to understand is thus a global system of exchange and of symbolic transformations of value the ultimate purpose of which is the per-
petuation of the entire social system the fundamental units of which are
the *oikoi* of which individuals function as representatives.[11]

Akhilleus's complaint against Agamemnon in book 9 wavers between
his claim that Briseis is his *alokhos* 'wife' and his claim that she is his *geras*
'prize'. Insofar as he loves her and wants her to be his wife, Akhilleus sees
Briseis as at least incipiently belonging to the matrix of relationships (that
of the *oikos*) that defines the interior face of his social identity. Insofar as
he sees her as his *geras*, she belongs to the system of exchange, the system
of social relationships that defines the exterior face of his identity.

Akhilleus wants Briseis to be redefined as no longer belonging to the
system of exchange, as coming to rest once and for all in his possession.
Agamemnon puts her back into circulation, first taking her away from
Akhilleus to replace Khryseis, then offering to return her to him; but
Akhilleus will not, at least at first, accept her back. Briseis restored is
somehow not equivalent to Briseis lost; her removal from the interior of

Akhilleus's circle of propriety leaves a gaping wound that no restitution or reparation can stop, a wound to Akhilleus's being.

Does it follow, then, that what Akhilleus "really" cares about is not the loss of Briseis but his disgrace, the wound to his *timē*? If he really loved Briseis, wouldn't he accept Agamemnon's offer to give her back? But it is not a simple matter of *timē* either, because if it were, then Briseis plus the vast *apoina* would restore it (as Phoinix emphasizes in book 9), and if it were his *timē* in any conventional sense of the term that he really cared about, Akhilleus should once again accept Agamemnon's offer.

There is therefore no question of deciding between Akhilleus's concern for Briseis and his concern for his *timē*. It is, rather, a question of a reconception of *timē* that Akhilleus argues as against the culturally sanctioned definition that Phoinix and the other Greeks urge him to accept—a reconception that threatens to shatter the entire system of symbolic equivalences that holds together the Iliadic economy.

We recognize in the motif of the loss and return of Briseis that type of circulation of a symbolic object that functions at a meta-narrative level, here not in the sense of a self-representation of the text but as a representation at a higher level of abstraction than the level of characters and plot. Once we are alerted to the level of abstraction at which the poem represents the circulation of symbolic objects, we see that it articulates a continuous problematic of exchange, loss, and symbolic reparation, a problematic the most prominent articulations of which are five types of refusal of reparation (*apoina* or *poinē*). We may schematize them thus:

1. refuse *apoina* 'ransom', kill male captive (recurring instance)
2. refuse *apoina* 'ransom', keep female captive who is *philē* (Agamemnon and Khryseis)
3. lose female captive who is *philē*, refuse conciliatory *apoina* 'reparation' (Akhilleus and Briseis)
4. lose one's *philos*, refuse conciliatory *poinē* 'reparation' (pictured on Akhilleus's shield)
5. keep body of slain captive, refuse *apoina* 'ransom' for body (Akhilleus and Hektor)

These situations form a transformational series in which the same basic themes are variously intertwined and a single complex problematic is elaborated. The crisis of equivalence that is set in motion by Agamemnon's refusal of *apoina* for Khryseis is finally resolved, at least for the purposes of poetic closure, by Akhilleus's acceptance of *apoina* for Hektor's dead body.[12] We may reconstruct the underlying logic of this series in

terms of an initial situation involving possession of an object, one that is
libidinally cathected (a woman or friend); followed by the loss of this
object, against the will of the possessor and without compensation; after
which reparation is required, either through vengeful aggression against a
substitute object that comes into one's possession (the living or dead body
of the enemy), or through the option that is so hard to come by in the
Iliad, acceptance of *apoina* as conciliating reparation.

The crucial link in the diagetical unfolding of this problematic is
Akhilleus's refusal of Agamemnon's offer of *apoina* and the restoration of
Briseis. Now, whereas love and sexual desire are powerful motives in the
Iliad, Akhilleus's motives remain arguable. He says he loves Briseis, and
appears to do so, but he will not take her back. He dwells on his public
humiliation and his desire for vengeance, and it will develop that Patroklos, not Briseis, is most *philos* to him. It is not surprising that the
authenticity of Akhilleus's love for Briseis has been questioned. But in
terms of the problematic of the poem as a whole, what matters is not the
true nature of Akhilleus's affect, which is in any case indeterminable, but
the structural ambivalence of Briseis's role, the way she functions on the
level of both libidinal and social economy. Because the *Iliad* maps libidinal economy onto the economy of exchange, her rape opens the question
of irreparable loss—that is, the question of mourning. The full force of
mourning will of course befall Akhilleus as a consequence of the loss of
Patroklos, not Briseis, but we shall see that there is no opposition, no
either/or, between Akhilleus's love for Patroklos and his or other men's
love for women, for example Hektor's for Andromakhe. Rather, the
former lays bare a libidinal structure that inhabits the latter as well. The
remainder of this essay will be a demonstration of this thesis.

We must now consider in closer detail the nature of *timē* and the way it
is related to the forms of compensation called *apoina* and *poinē*.

Timē is the regard in which a warrior is held by others, the tribute of
respect he is accorded; and the same word also names the material advan-
tages (women, cuts of meat, booty) that the group allots him as the sign
of that regard. It is really inadequate, however, to call material *timē* the
"sign" of *timē* as respect or honor; it is more like its embodiment or
realization. As Redfield says, "In one sense the *geras* marks the status; in
another sense it confers status, so that the loss of *geras* . . . threatens a loss
of status" (175).[13] *Timē* belongs entirely to the system of conventional
equivalences—so much booty as one's portion, so much honor.

This is why Phoinix tries so hard in book 9 to persuade Akhilleus to give in while gifts are still being offered, and not, like Meleager, hold out too long and lose the gifts:

> . . . No, with gifts promised
> go forth. The Achaians will honor you as they would an immortal.
> But if without gifts you go into the fighting where men perish,
> your *timē* will no longer be as great, though you drive back the
> battle.   (602–5)[14]

The Homeric warriors are supposed to be motivated by the pursuit of greater and greater *timē* in both senses of the term, of prizes as embodying honor. Yet the action of the *Iliad* is set in motion by a yawning insufficiency of booty such that someone, either Agamemnon or one of the other heroes, must necessarily be left at least temporarily without his honorific portion and thus without his proper share of *timē*. This means that the *timē* that is in question at the center of the poem must come belatedly, not as the positivity of the glory that a warrior pursues but as reparation for a loss that he has previously endured. Honor in this narrative is recurrently bound to reparation rather than augmentation, as when the *apoina* 'ransom' offered by the priest Khryses is supposed to make good to Agamemnon the loss of his *geras* Khryseis, or when the *apoina* 'reparation' Agamemnon offers Akhilleus is supposed to restore Akhilleus's *timē*.[15]

There is, further, an analogy between Agamemnon's offer of *apoina* to Akhilleus and the payment of *timē* 'tribute' asked by Agamemnon of the Trojans as reparation for the rape of Helen. Here is how Agamemnon proposes the payment:

> . . . if the fair-haired Menelaos kills Alexandros,
> then let the Trojans give back Helen and all her possessions,
> and pay also a *timē* to the Argives which will be fitting.
> . . . .
> Then if Priam and the sons of Priam are yet unwilling
> after Alexandros has fallen to pay me the *timē*
> I myself shall fight hereafter for the sake of the *poinē*.   (3.284–90)

The situation envisaged here is precisely parallel with the situation in book 9, where Agamemnon offers not only to return Briseis (as the Trojans are to return Helen and the stolen treasure) but offers Akhilleus huge gifts in addition. In book 9 this additional tribute is called *apoina*; the same thing is here called *timē*. If this *apoina* or *timē* is not forthcoming, its place will be supplied by punitive reparation, *poinē*.[16]

Not only do we see once more, in Agamemnon's vow of what he will do if the Trojans refuse to pay, that *poinē* as vengeful retribution or forcefully exacted reparation comes belatedly to make up for a *timē* denied, but the *timē* which he demands and they deny is itself already an *apoina* that should compensate for a yet earlier violation of *timē*.

In one way it seems that to kill one's enemies, and to kill them as brutally as possible, humiliating them in the process, would be the fulfillment of the warrior's vocation, that the warrior would then be most himself. Of course this is also how he gains *timē* 'honor' and subsequently the *kleos* 'glory' of poetic renown; and this form of *timē* seems to be the true warrior honor, beyond the apportionment of tributes and women. And yet the poem also portrays the pursuit of *timē* as vengeful in its essence, since there is always an anterior violation of honor to be repaired.

This principle is made manifest by the example of Akhilleus. He is the best of the Akhaians, and yet not even he can escape the violation of his honor. When he declares the incommensurability between his suffering and any possible material reparation, Akhilleus unleashes the vengefulness that is normally kept in check by the system of symbolic equivalences. Here is the crescendo of hyperbole with which he rejects Agamemnon's *apoina:*

> Not if he gave me ten times as much, and twenty times over
> as he possesses now, not if more should come to him from elsewhere,
> or gave all that is brought in to Orchomenos, all that is brought in
> to Thebes of Egypt, where the greatest possessions lie up in the
> houses,
> Thebes of the hundred gates, where through each of the gates two
> hundred
> fighting men come forth to war with horses and chariots;
> not if he gave me gifts as many as the sand or the dust is,
> not even so would Agamemnon have his way with my spirit
> until he had made good to me all this heartrending insolence.
>
> (379–87)

Akhilleus rejects the "conversion" of his vengefulness by the formal process of reparation; he wants what we could call a raw equivalation, "pain for pain, dishonor for dishonor," as Robert Fitzgerald freely, but I think accurately, translates the last line above.[17]

Animals of course do not seek vengeance; vengeance is not "raw" in the sense that it could exist outside the context of language and culture. The very fact that vengeance is essentially a form of compensation or equivalence means that its conception involves a mental operation of a sophisticated order. Furthermore, the enjoyment of vengeance requires an acute perception of the subjectivity of the other, a sense of the reality and intensity of the suffering he or she experiences at our hands. If nevertheless I call vengeance a raw equivalation it is to mark its tendency to escape and undermine the system of conventional equivalences established by culture. "An eye for an eye" is already an attempt to limit vengefulness by a conventional definition; the *Iliad* suggests that what unconstrained vengefulness seeks as compensation for suffering undergone is not the formal equivalence of objects or body parts but the quantity of suffering that the other experiences within his or her interiority. And there is no way of measuring or setting a limit to this subjective sensation. As long as I am in the throes of suffering over an injury done me, the sensation of grievance is unbounded. If the entire substance of my being is convulsed by pain or grief over an injury or loss, if the loss can never be undone as such, only an equally unbounded and irremediable suffering on the part of the transgressor can count as a compensatory equivalent. Such suffering is what Akhilleus attempts to exact from Agamemnon, and later from the Trojans.

Vengeance here is the attempt to find an equivalent for the incommensurable, reparation for the irreparable. It is, in other words, the last measure for stanching the flow of mourning. Thus Euphorbos says to Menelaos:

> . . . you must now pay the penalty
> for my brother, whom you killed, and boast that you did it,
> and made his wife a widow in the depth of a young bride chamber
> and left to his parents the curse of lamentation and sorrow.
> Yet I might stop the mourning of these unhappy people
> if I could carry back to them your head. . . .   (17.34–39)

This logic of equivalence according to which *mourning inflicted* can compensate for and assuage *mourning suffered* structures the entire *Iliad*, but is most insistently and nakedly visible in a sequence near the end of book 14. Poulydamas, having killed a Greek, Prothoënor, "vaunted terribly over him" and "sorrow (*akhos*) came over the Argives at his vaunting," stirring the vengeful anger of Aias, who kills a Trojan. Aias then shouts at Poulydamas, "Is not this man's death a worthwhile exchange (*anti . . . axios*)?" In response, "sorrow (*akhos*) fastened on the Trojans," and the Trojan Akamas kills Promachos, at which *akhos* once more comes over the Greeks, so that Peneleos kills Ilioneus and then vaunts:

Trojans, tell haughty Ilioneus' beloved father
and mother, from me, that they can weep for him in their halls, since
neither shall the wife of Promachos, Alegenor's
son, take pride of delight at her dear lord's coming.   (501–5)

This logic is carried to its limit in Akhilleus's attempt to assuage his grief
for his losses first by humiliating Agamemnon and then by the holocaust
of vengefulness in which he engages against the Trojans: measureless
reparation for his measureless pain.

The warrior's violence that brings *timē* is represented in the *Iliad* as
essentially vengeful, thus as a substitute satisfaction, a compensatory value
that comes to make up for a loss that is always anterior and irremediable.
Beyond the exploits of the battlefield, beyond the desire for conquest and
honor that seemed to Nietzsche the innocent and healthy expression of
barbarian Greek exuberance, this is what we read in the *Iliad*, and above
all in the exemplary figure of Akhilleus.

We learn from Akhilleus that in the final instance it is life itself for
which *timē* 'honor', 'public regard' comes to compensate. Akhilleus, weeping like a baby beside the sea, says to Thetis:

Since, my mother, you bore me to be a man with a short life,
therefore Zeus of the loud thunder on Olympos should grant me
timē at least. But now he has given me not even a little.
Now the son of Atreus, powerful Agamemnon,
has dishonored me (*etimēsen*), since he has taken away my prize and
     keeps it.   (1.353–56)

That he is "a man with a short life"—that is what grieves Akhilleus so
deeply and for which he feels he is owed compensation. But it is the
definition of men in general that they are born to a short life. Akhilleus's
is very short indeed, but no shorter than that of many other warriors in
the *Iliad*, and the perspective of the immortal gods is always there to
remind the Iliadic warriors that even the longest human life is pathet-
ically short.

And yet even this limited recognition of *timē* as having a value that
might compensate for shortness of life is withdrawn by book 9. If the size
of the reparation is proportionate to the *timē* bestowed, the reparation
Agamemnon offers Akhilleus is an extraordinary *timē* indeed. And yet for
Akhilleus now even an infinite amount of such *apoina* would mean nothing. Akhilleus is no longer thinking or feeling within the system of
cultural equivalences. He feels so aggrieved, he has nursed his resentment

so assiduously, that he touches his own subjectivity in a profound new way. Whereas his *timē* could earlier, so long as it remained intact, still mask his sense of the fleetingness of his own life, the violation of his *timē* by Agamemnon makes him feel the full surge of grief over his own death. And now he becomes conscious of the subjective essence of his own being as *psukhē*, the elusive breath of life that is incommensurable with any *timē* that booty can bring:

> . . . For not
> worth the value (*antaxion*) of my *psukhē* are all the possessions
> they fable were won for Ilion. . . .
>   . . . Of possessions
> cattle and fat sheep are things to be had for the lifting,
> and tripods can be won, and the tawny high heads of horses,
> but a man's *psukhē* cannot come back again, it cannot be lifted
> nor captured again by force once it has crossed the teeth's barrier.
>   (9.400–409)

Akhilleus does not mention *timē* in these lines, but within the structure of distribution of booty that these lines presuppose, the same structure within which Briseis and his other honorific portions have been bestowed, booty must be allotted by the group after it has been taken, and embodies *timē*.

The *psukhē* is here pictured by analogy with precious possessions, objects that may be wrested from the possession of someone else and made one's own, that can circulate from one owner to another, be lost and then regained or at least compensated for. These are the objects in terms of which the conventional system of exchange and equivalence functions. But the *psukhē* does not belong to this system; it is a precious object that will not circulate; once lost it is lost forever.

In the *Iliad*, reparation fails to catch up with the anteriority of loss, which reasserts itself at the end of the series of reparations. Culture declares the commensurability of loss with compensation or reparation, but culture also generates tensions that rupture the equivalences it proclaims, that reveal some final inadequacy in them to balance the loss they come to repair. The logic of this regression is implied in the ironic double sense of the word *moira*, which means, on the one hand, the warrior's rightful portion, and on the other hand fate, and specifically the final and inevitable outcome of death. The economy of *moira* shadows the official ideology of the warrior culture, its oikonomics, voiced by Aias, according to which no loss is uncompensatable and everything finds its equivalent, even the loss of one who is most *philos* or *philē*. This is good sense, good management; the system of exchange and substitution must reach all the way into the interior of the *oikos,* for only then can it properly regulate the retaliatory violence that would otherwise shake the foundations of social order (for instance, in the regicide that Akhilleus almost commits). But Akhilleus, far from accepting a substitute or equivalent for Briseis, refuses to accept Briseis herself as reparation for herself; he reacts as though her loss were absolute, as though she were dead. (This is what Aias senses when he tells Akhilleus that a man accepts *poinē* even for a dead son.)

We now see how it is that Briseis's structural location at the intersection of inside and outside as both prize of honor and beloved wife opens the possibility of Akhilleus's break with the official ideology—a break that also reveals the inner dynamic of that ideology, the resentful urge for vengeance that is the naked form of the demand for reparation, the insatiable maw that all material forms of *timē* attempt to appease. Briseis, who is *philē* to Akhilleus, is at the same time part of Akhilleus's *moira,* the supplementary part, the part that both is and is not part, the part that somehow escapes and leaves an unstanchable wound, unstanchable even by Briseis herself, restored. As such, she breaks open the system of circulating equivalences and hurls Akhilleus into an aggrieved awareness of the ironic meaning of *moira,* of the economy ruled by this meaning, which unfolds within and ruins *oikonomia*: "*Moira* is the same for the man who holds back, the same if he fights hard. / We are all held in a single *timē,* the brave with the weaklings. / A man dies still if he has done nothing, as one who has done much" (9.318–20).[18] This aggrieved awareness will in turn lead to the loss of Patroklos, and only then will Briseis return.

What we see in the *Iliad* is a chain of desires for reparation for the suffering incurred in the foregoing loss of objects of desire, such that each of these desires for reparation substitutes for the preceding and in its turn fails of satisfaction; or more precisely, the very attempt to obtain reparation leads to the next loss that in its turn calls for compensation.[19] The case of Akhilleus shows us that the pursuit of *timē* is involvement in this chain, is in fact a culturally mediated expression of *ressentiment* against the world and other people for the deprivations it and they necessarily inflict upon even the most powerful, and fundamentally for the ultimate deprivation of death. This is the bitter irony in Akhilleus's words to Lykaon in book 21 as he refuses Lykaon's plea that Akhilleus take him for ransom. Once he took the Trojans for ransom "in droves," Akhilleus says, but no more; now that Patroklos has died, Akhilleus sees that he too must die and pursues a different kind of compensation:

> So, friend, you die also. Why all this clamour about it?
> Patroklos also is dead, who was better by far than you are.
> Do you not see what a man I am, how huge, how splendid
> and born of a great father, and the mother who bore me immortal?
> Yet even I have also my death and my strong destiny . . .   (106–10)

> . . . die all an evil death, till all of you
> pay for the death of Patroklos and the slaughter of the Achaians . . .
> (133–34)

Nature itself, in the form of the river Skamandros, revolts against the gruesome extremity of Akhilleus's vengeance that chokes Skamandros's water with corpses.

But there is a most refined delectation of vengeance beyond even that of killing the enemy, one that comes from the imaginative anticipation of the helpless abjection of mourning that one inflicts upon the wife and parents of the slain enemy. To be the cause of mourning, and most specifically of the mourning of women: this is the final resonance of the satisfaction of vengeance, of the reparation vengeance offers for one's own grief. Of course the women are in more obvious ways the final index of triumph over the enemy; as Nestor says, each Achaian must bed a Trojan wife in vengeance for Helen. But here is how at one point Akhilleus describes the vengeance he intends for Patroklos: "Now I must win excellent *kleos* 'glory' / and drive some one of the women of Troy, or some deep-girdled / Dardanian woman, lifting up to her soft cheeks both hands / to wipe away the close bursts of tears in her lamentations" (18.121–24). Similarly, the cruder sensibility of Diomedes expresses itself in the boast that "if one is struck by me only a little . . . that man's wife goes with cheeks torn in lamentation" (11.391–93). Or the women of the enemy may be made to grieve for *one's own*, even while their husbands and brothers are slaughtered. Akhilleus thus makes this promise to the dead Patroklos:

> Before your shining pyre I shall behead twelve glorious
> children of the Trojans, for my anger over your slaying.
> Until then, you shall lie where you are in front of my curved ships
> and beside you women of Troy and deep-girdled Dardanian women
> shall sorrow for you night and day and shed tears for you . . .
> (18.336–40)

Foremost among these captive women is his prize of honor Briseis, who, now at last restored to Akhilleus, leads the mourning for Akhilleus's greatest loss. The theft and rape of women by these two comrades comes in the end to this, that they might have a mourning chorus.

Akhilleus weeps, and makes women weep, for himself and for his loss. To wreak vengeance in the *Iliad* means finally: to be the cause of mourning, to transform the passive affect of grief into the active, compensatory pleasure of inflicting grief upon others and most conclusively upon women.

And yet grief tends to become generalized, for vengefully inflicted grief is no more than the reflection of the avenger's own. In the end victim and avenger weep together, as Priam and Akhilleus will do.

Beyond conventional equivalence, there is vengeance; but a man cannot avenge himself for the loss of his own life. He can, however, avenge the loss of his *philos* 'nearest and dearest', and if the *philos* is a mirror of his own mortality, then vengeance for the *philos's* death would be a sort of vengeance for his own; and mourning for the *philos* would be mourning for himself. Nagy has shown how deeply woven into the language and traditional material of the *Iliad* is the theme of mourning. Even the name "Akhilleus" appears to be derived from the word *akhos* 'grief' (Nagy, *Best of the Achaeans*, 77–83); and Nagy offers a fascinating argument that Akhilleus's epic glory in the *Iliad* is an extension into poetry of the institution of lamentation for him as represented in his hero-cult (174–84).

Nagy builds on Kakridis's demonstration that even though Akhilleus's death and burial are not represented in the *Iliad,* in book 18 where Thetis and the Nereids mourn the living Akhilleus "Homer used as a model an older epic description of the prothesis of Achilles and his funeral" (Kakridis, 72). The existence of this model is known to us from references in the cyclic *Aethiopis* and the second Nekuia of the *Odyssey*. Kakridis points out that in the established form of the mourning ritual as we see it in the cases of Patroklos and Hektor, one woman, the nearest kin to the dead man, leads the lamentation and a chorus wails in response. In Hektor's case, his wife Andromakhe begins the *goos* 'death-lament' (24.723), which is then taken up in turn by his mother and his sister-in-law Helen. In the Greek camp, however, there are no kinswomen; "but custom exacts that [Patroklos] shall be mourned by women, and the place of his kinswoman is taken by Briseis and the other captive women" (Kakridis, 71). Similarly, Thetis begins the *goos* for Akhilleus in 18 while her sister Nereids play the chorus to her lament (50–51). And when Thetis after the death of Patroklos takes the head of grief-stricken Akhilleus in her hands she reproduces what Kakridis identifies as a ritual gesture of mourning (8.71). Kakridis thus demonstrates that although it is Patroklos who has died, at this moment it is Akhilleus who is mourned.

As Nagy argues, however, "the Iliadic tradition requires Achilles to prefigure his dead self by staying alive, and the real ritual of a real funeral is reserved by the narrative for his surrogate Patroklos" (113); "the death of Patroklos is a function of his being the *therapōn* of Achilles: this word *therapōn* is a prehistoric Greek borrowing from the Anatolian languages . . . where it had meant 'ritual substitute'" (33.292–93).

Patroklos is most intimate, most *philos* to Akhilleus; he belongs to the inmost interiority of Akhilleus's circle of propriety. They sleep in the same tent, and Akhilleus had hoped that one day, when Akhilleus was dead, Patroklos would take Akhilleus's son, Pyrrhos, back to Phthia to see the domains of his father. When Akhilleus retires to privacy from the forum where warriors appear for one another in order to win *timē*, he retires in the company of Patroklos. *Timē* 'honor' is the modality of the manifestation of a warrior's selfhood before the group to which he belongs; the reality of *timē* is public appearance, the self invested in its *timē* is a self as seen by the group. It is of the essence of the giving of honorific shares, *moira* and *geras*, that these are public rituals; they are not possessions with an independent value that could be enjoyed in private, like the miser's gold. So too the loss of *geras* is feared as a public humiliation.

When Akhilleus refuses Agamemnon's *apoina* he is attempting to step outside the system of social valuations that makes his *timē* a dependent and relative variable. In the end, of course, Akhilleus is drawn back little by little into the matrix of social valuations, first by the appeals of Phoinix and Aias, then by that of Patroklos; but even then he is not fully reconciled to the sphere of mutuality. If the self is dependent on its reflection in the eyes of others, he wishes at least that he could retreat to the minimal sphere of self-reflection. There is a very strong evocation of the exclusiveness of the dual relation between Akhilleus and Patroklos, their tendency to form a dyad independent of the rest of the Akhaians. Patroklos's ghost recalls that in life the two of them would "sit apart from our other / beloved companions and make our plans" (23.77–78). And in a striking image, Akhilleus expresses to Patroklos as Patroklos goes forth to battle the apocalyptic wish that "not one of all the Trojans could escape destruction, not one / of the Argives, but you and I could emerge from the slaughter / so that we two alone could break Troy's hallowed coronal" (16. 97–100). And Akhilleus intends that he and Patroklos should be buried in the same grave mound (23.126).

There must be at least one other human being who reflects his glory back to him; but ideally there should be *only* one other to perform this function, and this one other should be as close as possible to Akhilleus himself, differing from himself only far enough to provide his reflection. Akhilleus would then be an autonomous totality, or as nearly so as a being can be who must split himself in two in order to feel himself as himself. In the immediate proximity to each other of these two *philoi* who are, in Derrida's language, one self differed there would be no opening for such woundings of the self as even Akhilleus cannot fend off so long as he subjects himself to the system of public valuations. Akhilleus's *timē* would circulate in a closed circuit between himself and the one who remains most proximate to him. But precisely in proportion as Patroklos is *philos* to Akhilleus, Akhilleus is exposed to the possibility of another kind of loss, one more profound than the loss of *geras* or *timē*, but which reveals the hidden essence of what those losses partly express and partly occult.

Mourning in the *Iliad* is represented as a structure of self-reflection in which the death of the other arouses automourning in the onlooker. We have just considered this specular relation in the case of Akhilleus and Patroklos. The mimetic stimulation of mourning culminates in the reconciliation scene between Priam and Akhilleus in book 24. "Take pity upon me / remembering your father" (503–4), says Priam to Akhilleus, and Akhilleus sees in Priam's grief for dead Hektor the grief of his own father, Peleus, for Akhilleus's expected death. Akhilleus imagines his father weeping inconsolable tears for him, then weeps for his poor father weeping for him and in this way affects himself deeply with the pathos of his own disappearance. Akhilleus's grief for his own death thus arises here in a double reflection as he sees Peleus's grief reflected in Priam's and then in the mirror of Peleus's mirrored grief finds the magnified representation of his own grief for himself.

There is an earlier suggestion of the structure of self-reflection involved in Akhilleus's spectation of his father's grief in book 19, when Akhilleus remarks that nothing could be worse suffering for him than the death of Patroklos, not even the death of Peleus, "who now, I think, in Phthia somewhere lets fall a soft tear / for bereavement of such a son, for me" (323–24). Here Akhilleus's evocation of the grief he would feel at his father's death instantly gives way to the more pressing and vivid imagination of his father's grief for him, which he imagines as proportional to the magnitude of his own greatness, the greatness of "such a son."

And now we see that this same movement of automourning shapes the farewell of Hektor to Andromakhe in book 6. After Hektor says that it is her pain to come that troubles him above all, when she will be led away captive and become the servant of some Greek, he continues:

> and some day seeing you shedding tears a man will say of you:
> "This is the wife of Hektor, who was ever the bravest fighter
> of the Trojans, breakers of horses, in the days when they fought
>   about Ilion."
> So will one speak of you; and for you it will be yet a fresh grief
> to *be widowed of such a man* who could fight off the day of your
>   slavery.
> But may I be dead and the piled earth hide me under before I
> hear you crying and know by this that they drag you captive.
>
> (459–65; italics added)

In a moment of profound feeling Hektor projects himself as witness of a widowed Andromakhe who weeps for him dead, with a grief he imagines in the shape most fulfilling to the desire to be mourned—a grief that springs always anew across the passage of time at the reminder of what a man it was whom she has lost ("and for you it will be a fresh grief, / to be widowed of such a man"). Of course this grief of the beloved is unbearable to contemplate, even though it has been contemplated, and in the most vivid detail, and *must* be contemplated, because it would be even more unbearable to think that his death would inflict no indelible wound of loss, that the loss might quickly begin to heal. Hektor imagines the first unbearability and then flees from it: "may I be dead . . . before."

Hektor's words anticipate Akhilleus's fantasy of his father's grief precisely: "To be widowed of such a man": *khētei toioud' andros* (6.463); "bereaved of such a son": *khētei toioud' huios* (19.324). Each imagines a scene from which he is missing, a scene in which the pathos of self-lack is indeterminately (and thus sublimely) great, as proportional to the greatness indeterminately indicated by "such a ——." The sense of this locution is fully unfolded in Hektor's speech: the occasion for renewal of Andromakhe's grief is the speech, apparently imagined as overheard by her, that names Hektor's greatness as bravest or best of the Trojans *(hos aristeueske)* in battle. Hektor imagines, in other words, his *kleos* 'fame', 'report of his glory', and his captive wife as memorial of this fame, a fame parallel to that of Akhilleus, who, as Nagy has shown, is consistently named by the *Iliad* as best (*aristos*) of the Akhaians (26ff.). Again consistent with Nagy's studies, Hektor's *kleos* arouses unforgettable grief in the wife who will have lost him;[20] but Hektor describes his own *kleos* precisely in order to imagine most vividly Andromakhe's grief over the loss of him, her grief as the ultimate resonance of his pathos of self-loss, a resonance that gives full affective value to the thought of this *kleos* which is the sonorous trace of his absent being (*kleos* comes from the root *kluō* 'hear', 'hearken').[21]

The economy of Hektor's self-affection here is thus not far from that of Akhilleus's association of his desire to win "some excellent *kleos*" with the aim of making "some one of the women of Troy . . . to wipe away the close bursts of tears in her lamentations" (18.121–24). Mourning as vengefully inflicted, mourning as unbearable and most necessary tribute from the beloved: there is no absolute boundary between the two. What is necessary is that *I should be mourned,* that the anguish of the other should supplement the self-affection of resentful automourning. Hence the specific form of Akhilleus's anger that is the theme of the whole poem. His wish as he withdraws is that his absence will wring the tribute of grief from the hearts of his *philoi*:

> some day longing for Achilleus will come to the sons of the
>   Achaians,
> all of them. Then although you be stricken with *akhos,* you will be
>   able to do nothing . . .
> And then you will eat out the heart within you
> in sorrow, that you gave no *timē* to the best of the Achaians.
>
> (1.240–45)

The aesthetic representation of someone else's mourning is capable of stimulating the affect of mourning in the audience because mourning "itself" is already spectatorial and specular. This means that the separation between the affect of epic and that of cult is not as clear as Nagy suggests. Nagy writes that the death of Akhilleus "may have been unsuitable for the *kleos* of the Iliadic tradition partly *because the audience itself was involved* in his death," and his death would thus be an *akhos* 'to the community at large, in cult' (*Best of the Achaeans,* 113–14). But everything about the *Iliad* is constructed in such a way that it involves the spectator in the scene of mourning it constitutes, to remind him/her that mourning always flows in an unbroken circuit between other and self. And Nagy himself actually blurs his own distinction between *kleos* and cult when he argues that Akhilleus's epic is an "extension" of the "lamentation sung by the Muses over the hero's death" (184).

Kleos 'glory' is supposed to be the warrior's ultimate consolation or compensation for the *akhos* or *penthos* 'grief' of his mortality. But if

Akhilleus's own song, the *Iliad*, is an extension of the *threnos* of lamentation over his death, then if Akhilleus could hear his own *kleos* sung it would bring him to tears. Something like this actually happens in the *Odyssey*, where Odysseus hears the singer Demodokos singing Odysseus's *kleos* and is overcome with grief; "we see from the evidence of epic itself," Nagy concludes, "that the *kleos* heard by its audience may be *akhos / penthos* for those involved in the actions it describes" (*Meter*, 101). Odysseus's grief is for his sufferings and those of his companions rather than for his own death; by means of the figure of Patroklos, the *Iliad* represents Akhilleus mourning his own death while he yet outlives it.

But in the *Iliad* the mourners are predominantly, overwhelmingly, female. Aged fathers are prominent, too, among the mourners,[22] but when we come to the great concluding ritual scenes of mourning it is the women who take center stage—at least in two of these three scenes. First, Thetis and the Nereids mourn Akhilleus. Last, Andromakhe, Hekabe, and Helen mourn Hektor. In between, Akhilleus mourns Patroklos. The place of the chief mourner is marked in each scene by the same gesture: Thetis holds Akhilleus's head; Andromakhe holds Hektor's head; Akhilleus holds Patroklos's head. As Plato disapprovingly recognized, Akhilleus as mourner occupies a structural slot that is marked as a woman's.[23] Mourning belongs preeminently to women, and a man when he mourns ceases to be a man. This is what Akhilleus says to Patroklos at the beginning of book 16, when Patroklos is overcome by grief at the sufferings of the Akhaians. Akhilleus tells him that he is "crying like some poor little girl" who wants to be comforted by her mother (6–19). But it is Akhilleus who cries out to be comforted by his mother in book 1, when it is himself he mourns, and whose cries bring her pityingly to him once again in book 18 after the death of Patroklos.

Deeply inscribed in the tradition of epic poetry, Nagy shows, is the antithesis between deathless *kleos* 'glory' and unforgettable woe; the former belongs to the triumphant, the latter to the losers. And yet *kleos* and grief turn out in the hands of the *Iliad* poet(s) to be intimately interwoven. How could it be otherwise once Akhilleus must die young in order to gain his *kleos*? *Kleos* is *timē* in the mode of *tēle*, *timē* at a distance, *tēle-timē*; in its essence it implies the absence of the one celebrated. Akhilleus rejoices when he sings the *klea* of the other heroes but would have to weep if he heard his own. *Kleos* is structured according to the ironic logic of *moira*. On the one hand, this is the logic of heroic masculinity as something that secures for itself an ever-expanding share of *timē* and ultimately of *kleos*. But it is also the logic of reparation that is ultimately ineffectual for a loss that is always anterior and that reasserts itself at the end of the series of reparations. Thus it is a logic that will sooner or later feminize the hero, render him powerless and grief stricken as a bereaved mother or wife, and reduce him to tears in the face of his own death through the mirror of the death of those he loves, or of their grief for his.

And yet Akhilleus's desire is only temporarily extinguished by the death of Patroklos. The narcissistic wound is profound—"there will come no second sorrow like this to my heart again" (23.46–47), Akhilleus moans—yet once Patroklos is avenged and buried, Akhilleus returns to the ways of the living. Patroklos is not many days dead when Priam goes to ransom Hektor's body, and that night not only does Akhilleus eat and drink, but he goes to bed with Briseis (24.675–76). (Similarly, on the night of the embassy, when Briseis was still in Agamemnon's possession, Akhilleus's grief and anger did not prevent him from sleeping with another captive, "Phorbas' daughter, Diomede of the fair colouring" [9.665].) Freud's words on the termination of mourning seem appropriate here: "Each single one of the memories and situations of expectancy which demonstrate the libido's attachment to the lost object is met by the verdict of reality that the object no longer exists; and the ego, confronted as it were with the question whether it shall share this fate, is persuaded by the sum of the narcissistic satisfactions it derives from being alive to sever its attachment to the object that has been abolished."[24]

It could be argued that what we find at the conclusion of the *Iliad*, even as we approach the concluding scene of mourning for Hektor, is the termination of Akhilleus's mourning—that green shoots of desire are beginning to sprout in his breast even now, when he knows that he is fated to die soon.

Following Pietro Pucci's remarkable readings of the intertextuality of the *Iliad* with the *Odyssey*, we could term this subdued note of reburgeoning desire the implied victory of *gastēr* over *thumos*.[25] *Thumos* means roughly 'heart', and in the *Iliad* tends to signify courage, manliness, adherence to the heroic code. The *gastēr* 'stomach', which is in the foreground in the *Odyssey* in an ironic critique of the high-mindedness of the *Iliad*, "is portrayed as a lower *thumos*, a vital principle that forces upon men its irresistible needs. . . . It forces upon man forgetfulness of his griefs and makes him mindful only of eating and drinking" (Pucci, 174). Pucci points out that the word *gastēr*, common in the *Odyssey* in this sense, occurs only once in the *Iliad* with the meaning "human 'appetite' or 'hunger',", and then it is put in Odysseus's mouth as he reproaches Akhilleus for carrying too far his grief for Patroklos. An army cannot fight on an empty stomach, Odysseus argues against Akhilleus, who wants to attack immediately and get on with his revenge:

> There is no way the Achaians can mourn a dead man by denying
> the belly (*gasteri*). . . .
> . . . .
> No, but we must harden our hearts and bury the man who
> dies, when we have wept for him on the day. . . .   (19.225–29)

Pucci says that the word *gastēr*, used here "in the context of the somber theme of mourning, sounds snappy, irreverent, vulgar" (168). "In this confrontation between the man of *gastēr* and the man of *thumos* the *Iliad*, with devilish accuracy, depicts Odysseus's character as it is drawn in the *Odyssey*. . . . Odysseus [in the *Odyssey*] grieves only a few hours—even after the loss of all his friends—then eats and faces life again. Achilles knows that because Patroclus is dead, he cannot remain among the living." (169). Pucci concludes that Odysseus and Akhilleus "represent two opposite economies of life" (173).

And yet, when Akhilleus urges Priam to leave off mourning for Hektor and join him in eating (29.601–20), does he not submit to the wisdom of the belly that had been earlier enunciated by Odysseus (though Akhilleus characteristically does not descend to the low diction of *gastēr*)? Pucci notes the incident and its general significance as a "return to the controlled economy of life" (171); but this admission throws into question his judgment that Akhilleus's economy is the *opposite* of Odysseus's and that Akhilleus "cannot remain among the living."

Even in the fresh agony of mourning, Akhilleus had never unconditionally renounced his desire to live. "The spirit within does not drive me / to go on living and be among men," he says to Thetis, but he then adds: "except on condition / that Hektor first be beaten down under my spear, lose his life / and pay the price for stripping Patroklos" (18.90–93). It would be the humiliation of the failure to avenge Patroklos that would deprive Akhilleus of the will to live, not Patroklos's death itself; the clear implication is that vengeance would make life desirable for him once more. It is true that Akhilleus knows he himself is fated to die soon after Hektor, but this is not his desire; it is, rather, something he accepts as the fated consequence of the vengeance he must exact, as his *moira*. Yet to be fated to die "soon" (98) is still to be fated to die at some indeterminate time, which is in any case the fate of mortals; thus Akhilleus philoso-

phizes that "not even the strength of Herakles fled away from destruction, / although he was dearest of all to lord Zeus" (117–18). And in the
space of this indeterminancy, in the play between "now" and "soon,"
Akhilleus continues to speak of his death as not necessarily certain, as an
"if": "So I likewise, if [*ei dē*] such is the *moira* which has been wrought
me, must lie still, when I am dead" (121–22). As intensely as Akhilleus is
attached to Patroklos, his selfhood and his desire—for more life, more
sex, more food and drink—are capable of surviving Patroklos's death.

Thus, if death chooses Akhilleus, it is not at all certain that Akhilleus
chooses death.

Still, as plainly as the beginning of renewal of appetite and desire in
Akhilleus is depicted, the dominant impression with which we are left is
of something like total mourning and desolation, as though the *Iliad*
makes only a coded reference to this *gastronomic* principle that would
unsettle the tragic severity of the economy of *moira,* undermining with its
comic irony the absoluteness of the experience of loss from which the
poem draws its primary effects.

Here we recall that in book 9 there is already an ironic undermining of
Akhilleus's claim of bereavement in the case of Briseis, as he is offered
multiple replacements and he himself says that there are "many Achaian
girls" and "any one that I please I might make my beloved lady" (9.395–97).
The lost object is not absolutely irreplaceable; the force of the species-
urge is, in the final instance, no respecter of individuals. The *Iliad* reminds us of this even as it indicates the opposite, as though its form were
already beginning to rupture internally toward the gastronomic stance of
the *Odyssey*.

CHAPTER THREE

How the Spirit (Almost) Became Flesh: The Gospel of John

ONE OF THE MOST FAMOUS PASSAGES IN THE NEW TESTAMENT, AND possibly the most spiritually desperate, is I Corinthians 15:32, in which Paul declares that "if the dead rise not" all that is left is to "eat and drink, for tomorrow we die." Either there is eternal life, Paul seems to say, or there is no value to exertion that goes beyond the needs of survival and (physical) pleasure. Tennyson, in *In Memoriam*, rephrases Paul's remark and draws out its meaning as follows:

> My own dim life should teach me this,
>   That life shall live for evermore,
>   Else earth is darkness at the core,
> And dust and ashes all that is.   (34, ll. 1–4)

>   . . . If Death were seen
>   At first as Death, Love had not been,
> Or been in narrowest working shut,
>
> Mere fellowship of sluggish moods,
>   Or in his coarsest Satyr-shape
>   Had bruised the herb and crush'd the grape,
> And bask'd and batten'd in the woods.   (35, ll. 18–24)

Without the transcendence of death, Tennyson feels, love would be mere lust or at best accidental psychological concord of a very primitive sort, no more than a reflex of the physiological state of the body ("fellowship of sluggish moods"). This is indeed the nausea that merely natural existence arouses in the Christian spirit, nausea at a life whose essence, or *telos*, is that it will be reduced entirely to the natural elements of which it is compounded and which is therefore meaningless. As Rudolf Bultmann says in his commentary on the Gospel of John, "existence" is "sheerly unintelligible" if it is not enlightened by the transcendent light that "necessarily includes freedom from death."[1]

Christian transcendentalism and the *Iliad* appear to converge in the bleakness of their vision of a life that would at the limit be merely organic. Of course Christianity offers the antidote to this bleakness: human life is not in the end merely that; it has an immortal essence that triumphs over its reduction to nature in death. And yet the horror of natural reduction is not thought through as such; is not confronted and overcome in itself by Christianity—it continues to fester in the darkness to which it is consigned, fascinating the imagination of the man of faith as that which would overpower the ethical consciousness if it could not be negated. Christianity's vision of death in an essential way remains that of the *Iliad*, only with an alternative posited where the *Iliad* sees none. Death as a natural fact remains the essence of pure destructiveness of the form of the human, and the Christian imagination is driven by the loathing of this destructiveness.

Is the reduction of the human to mere nature necessarily the unbearable, purely destructive thought as which orthodox Christianity imagines it? What if, on the contrary, it were possible by means of this thought to descend into the innermost interior of the passion of mourning, palliated by no transcendence that would not itself be through and through the passion of living flesh, and in this way to transfigure mourning into love, not by negating or sublating it but by making it absolute? And what if it were possible to read in one of the foundational texts of Christianity—indeed, in the one styled since antiquity "the most spiritual of the gospels"—this thought of absolute nontranscendence, of the universality and finality of organic death and of love as acceptance of this?

I ask the reader to consider what follows as an experiment in reading. Perhaps it is merely an accident of language, a function of its illimitable capacity for ambiguity, that makes it possible to read or pervert the message of the Gospel of John, as I will do, into a purely naturalistic meaning; but perhaps it is significant that at the depth of John's meditation language should become ambiguous in this way. At any rate, the experiment is to push the possibilities of this ambiguity to the limit, to attempt to read the text in its entirety in terms of a more radical descent to the flesh than that of historical Christianity, whether in its more traditional formulations or in their "demythologized" translation by Bultmann, who recuperates the meaning of the gospel for the modern age by translating it into the terms of Heideggerian existentialism.[2] This essay will thus be as much a debate with the Christian interpreters, and above all Bultmann, as it will be a reading of the text of John "itself."

I focus on Bultmann because he manifests so clearly in a theological mode the duplicity of a modern thought that with one gesture demythologizes and demystifies while with another, simultaneous, gesture it secures the movement of transcendence more firmly than ever against the mere organicity of the body of love.

On the one hand, Bultmann will show how we can understand the miracles of Jesus not as violations of natural process but as symbolic pictures that speak of an eschatological reality that is already present here and now. Bultmann thus attempts to peel away all concern with mere *things* in order to preserve what is most agonizing and authentic in the Christian experience of salvation in Christ.

But, on the other hand, under the pretext of liberating from the text of John its deepest spiritual or existential significance, Bultmann removes not only its materialist miraculism but also the references to the sacrament of the Eucharist, which Bultmann chooses to understand as crudely miraculist. In so doing Bultmann closes the possibility that is given in John of a truly radical descent to the flesh and closes it yet more decisively than had been done by the orthodox interpretations Bultmann revises.

The Logos is said by John to "become flesh," and here in this one phrase, *ho logos sarx egeneto,* is our whole problem in a nutshell, the endless tantalizing oscillation of the concepts of flesh and spirit already set in motion. John's Logos does not take on flesh only as a disguise of his divinity (this is the Gnostic or "docetic" interpretation); rather, the Incarnation is the very essence of the process of cosmic redemption. But the real descent of the divine Logos into the flesh sets off a general deconstruction of all the oppositions that belong to the system of the original distinction between Logos and flesh. After it is asserted that the Logos became flesh, in the very act of assertion, neither Logos nor flesh can any longer mean what it meant before, nor can the transformation be elucidated by means of the other concepts that are themselves placed under erasure by the transformation they would be called on to explain.

The history of Christian doctrine is the history of the containment of this general deconstruction.

The insistence that in Jesus God became fully human in a complete physical sense defines the essence of orthodox Christianity throughout the centuries of doctrinal conflict. Fully god, and fully man: this is the difficult thought that had to be defended, and always was successfully defended, against heretical attempts to separate the divine and human elements.[3] The doctrine of the dual nature preserves the thought of mediation between a transcendent God and finite humanity in a way that the heretical tendencies cannot do, and there is a genius in this doctrine that I do not underestimate. Nevertheless, this doctrine depends on the same discursive rules as do the doctrines to which it is opposed.

That the Logos is divine means for all parties in the dispute that it is transcendent, eternal, and impassible; which is to say that its predicates are negations of the predicates that define the flesh. Conversely, flesh in its doctrinal sense is conceived by its contrast with Logos; it is all the things that Logos is not. The sense of the two concepts is derived from their contrast. And this is the most fundamental of metaphysical oppositions; it opens the space of the language game of metaphysics. How then is it possible to think the thought that would be conveyed by the expression *ho logos sarx egeneto*?

Only, it turns out, by neutralizing the *sarx* 'flesh', or rather its most radical "sarctic" essence.[4]

The meaning of "the Word became flesh" will always, even in the hypothesis of the hypostatic union of divine and human, be dominated without question by the metaphysical hierarchization that preserves the pneumatic element in its purity as the essence of the composite. If the Word becomes flesh, this must not imply any degradation of the Word but only the exaltation of the flesh. And this remains true even despite the insistence in orthodox theology on the humiliation of the Son, on the fact that it is the Divine Person as the unity of the two natures that really does suffer and die on the cross. This suffering is temporary and instrumental; it issues in the overcoming of the condition that renders it necessary. If, as Jaroslav Pelikan says, the "content of the salvation for which he became incarnate" is "freedom from corruption" (272), then "the Word became flesh" means that the Word traversed the *sarx*, sojourned in it, precisely in order to annul its sarctic essence. "What Jesus lays aside," as Edward Schillebeeckx tells us, "is not his humanity, but the transitoriness of the *sarx*."[5]

The orthodox insistence on the actual consubstantiality of the divine and human natures of Christ is a genuinely daring innovation, one that goes hand in hand with the insistence (derived from Judaism) on the resurrection of the body. Both of these doctrines contradict the "pneumaticism" of the Gnostics and of pre-Christian transcendentalism, which can conceive of the realm of the spirit (*pneuma*) only as completely severed from the body. The intellectual and spiritual-emotional consequences of the Christian insistence on packing the body along in the adventures of the *pneuma* and the Logos are immense (its consequences for literary history in particular were chronicled by Erich Auerbach in *Mimesis*). And yet, from another perspective, the conflict between docetism (the doctrine that Christ's humanity is only an appearance) and incarnationism is an intramural dispute that never transgresses a common boundary, "a conflict of dualisms," to appropriate a phrase used by Birger Pearson in his study of I Corinthians 15.[6] In the passages commented on by Pearson, Paul is concerned not with the Incarnation but with the resurrection at the last day; but the play of Paul's terminology makes clear the intramural character of the dispute concerning the Incarnation. As Pearson shows, Paul's opponents in Corinth probably believed in the immortality of the soul but denied the resurrection of the body (17), whereas "for Paul a bodiless existence is unthinkable; for him man's individuality is expressed not in terms of *psukhē* or *pneuma*, but in terms of *sōma*. Man in the old aeon and in the new aeon as well is *sōma*. To the opponents' view that a *pneumatikos* element in man's soul is that which guarantees his continuity after death, Paul must answer that man both in body and soul, as a *psukhikon sōma*, belongs still to the old Adam. . . . Man's full spiritual existence as a *pneumatikon sōma* lies in the future with the resurrection" (25).

This account shows very clearly the nature of the conceptual operation worked by Paul and in his wake by Christianity in general. In place of the simple distinction *pneuma-sōma*, Paul asserts the more subtle distinction between *two kinds of sōma*, based on a distinction between the associated life principles, one mortal and one immortal (*psukhē* and *pneuma*). In the view of Paul's Hellenistic-Jewish opponents, two sets of oppositions are precisely parallel and reinforce each other: *pneuma-sōma* and immortality-mortality. The dualism of Paul's schema is mitigated by a more complex articulation; *sōma* with its two forms now bridges the distinction between mortality and immortality.

Paul's insistence on the resurrection of the body is rooted in his Judaism; as Pearson shows, Paul's views are based on traditions of interpretation associated with Qumran and with rabbinical commentary on Genesis 2:7 (Pearson, 20–24). But the doctrine of bodily resurrection assumes an entirely new importance in a Christian context, since it is of a piece with the question of the precise nature of Christ's mediation. Christ must have *really died* on the cross if there is to be any contact between his appearance on earth and the needs of sinful sarctic humanity. The distinctiveness of the thought of this redeemer is precisely in his actually sharing the flesh of humanity; otherwise the crucifixion is only a symbol or display. Conversely, the believer must be one with his/her body in order to participate in the power of the salvific incarnation, crucifixion, and resurrection (Romans 6:5–11).

Yet in order for the *sōma,* or *sarx,* to play the essential role that it does in Paul's theology, he must ultimately subtract from it its somatic or sarctic character. Paul still insists that flesh and blood, *sarx kai haima,* cannot inherit the kingdom of heaven; the perishable cannot inherit the imperishable (I Corinthians 15:50). "All *sarx* is not the same *sarx*" (15:39); the pneumatic *sarx* is glorious, powerful, and immortal whereas the psychic *sarx* is the opposite (42–44). Thus the pneumatic *sōma* inherits the supernatural powers of the somaless *pneuma.* What is different in Paul's account from that of the pure pneumaticists—and this is, to be sure, a massive difference, but one the effect of which exhausts itself at a certain point—is the itinerary by which the seeker after salvation passes from a lower to a higher state. In the state itself that is arrived at, the presence of the somatic element seems to be little more than the formal residue of the real vehicle that was necessary for the transit.

Is John's *ho logos sarx egeneto* to be understood within the circle of concepts that subserve the Pauline project of pneumatic recuperation of the flesh?

Within the circle of concepts of the metaphysics of spirit and flesh, the alternative to the pneumatic recuperation of the flesh can only be conceived as the capitulation of spirit, the triumph of darkness over light.

Darkness is conceived by Christianity in a double aspect. On the one hand, it is the evil deeds of those who do not live in a spirit of love and unity, obedient to God's commands. On the other hand, it is the darkness of death, of the corruption of flesh that returns to its natural elements. Conversely, to live in and by the light is at once to live in loving harmony and to live forever.

Does not John confirm this linkage in the most categorical fashion? John's Jesus says little more than "love one another" (*agapate allēlous*) and "everybody who believes [in me] has eternal life." And as soon as we speak of resurrection and eternal life, we have passed over into transcendence of the *sarx,* whether by a pure or a qualified, pseudosomatic pneumaticism.

And yet it is none too clear what "eternal life" means in the Gospel of John: this is one of the central difficulties of its exegesis. It is clear that John shifts the focus of the thought of eternal life from the future to the present. Whether there remains, in addition to the eternal life that is here now, *another* eternity associated with the resurrection at the last day: this is less clear.[7]

The question of literal and metaphoric expression that runs all through John's gospel and is the quicksand under all exegesis of John becomes most urgent with respect to the meaning of "eternal life." Does it refer, let us say, "metaphorically" to the life a believer lives here and now after undergoing the transformation of faith or does it refer to a "literally" eternal life that the believer resumes after "literal" death and "literal" resurrection?

The terms *literal* and *metaphoric* are strained to the breaking point here; I am applying them only in the absence of any better way of marking the necessary distinctions, at least initially. What can it mean to speak of a "literal" reference to eternity? Furthermore, what I am here calling the "literal" reference to resurrection belongs to what orthodox interpretation knows as the "spiritual" meaning of John, according to which the believer is indeed called upon to believe in the "literal" resurrection of Jesus and of all the faithful. This spiritual literality is to be distinguished from the "fleshly" literality of those who do not apprehend the divinity of Christ and the salvific efficacy of belief in him. Yet Bultmann when he pares away the last residues of "fleshliness" from Christian spirituality identifies this life that is here and now as the proper referent of the term *eternal life,* relegating the "literal" resurrection to the realm of symbol.

I will thus not take the distinction between literal and metaphoric too seriously; the differences it marks are relative and mobile, and I use these terms only in a provisional fashion in attempting to map the system of these relations and this mobility.

John addresses the question of the literal and the figurative primarily in relation to Jesus' *semeia* 'signs'. The *semeia* are mostly miracles, "literal" disruptions of natural process, which must, however, be understood not as mere literal events but as vehicles of a transcendent significance. It is well established that John incorporated into his text a tradition "which held that the miraculous acts of Jesus evoked faith on the part of those witnessing them," but that John himself undertook to criticize that view.[8] But the interpreters disagree concerning the radicality of John's critique.

Does he reject signs altogether as a factor contributing to faith, or does he merely assign them a restricted role (Kysar, 69–73)?

Bultmann seems to adopt a moderate view: John opposes the demand for miracles as a prerequisite for faith, yet "the miracle to which man has no right, since he may not require the Revealer to give proof of his authority, is nevertheless on occasions granted to man in his weakness"; "for where it is granted it can lead man on beyond the faith that is based on miracles" (209). But, on the other hand, with respect to precisely the most crucial miracle of all, the one by comparison with which all the others are ordinary thaumaturgy and window dressing—the raising of Lazarus—Bultmann will express a more difficult conception.

The raising of Lazarus takes us into the realm of the essential, the innermost mystery of the Christian religion. Jesus' other miracles may be considered "rhetorical" in nature, "speaking pictures" that illustrate (but also obscure) Jesus' message: images of miraculous bread and divine water, of restored vision and health. These are metaphors or allegorical images of the power to bestow the new life that belongs to Jesus.[9] They are also manifestations of that power, but indirect or mediated manifestations: they do not concern the bestowal of life directly but rather the preservation and repair of a life already in existence.

In the raising of Lazarus, on the other hand, the power manifested and the medium of its manifestation appear to coincide; the image seems to be minimally if at all allegorical. Jesus here demonstrates the very originative power of life itself that is his, or is he, as the object of belief; the resurrection of Lazarus is not one miracle among others but the culmination of the series and its raising to a higher level. Indeed, the resurrection of Lazarus mirrors in small the major resurrection that is the *telos* of the entire gospel, the resurrection of Jesus. The raising of Lazarus is thus also central to the structure of the gospel, as we see from its location in the narrative sequence: it is Jesus' final miracle, and after that John's narrative moves inexorably toward the Passion.

But the resurrections of Lazarus and Jesus point toward yet another resurrection, that of all believers, a resurrection that according to the orthodox view will take place on the Last Day, when there will be an absolute rupture of historical time and what presently appears in glimpses as miraculous will be revealed as the true and eternal reality. Thus the stakes increase exponentially as we move along the series from the miraculous to the eschatological, and everything rests on the character of the Absolute that manifests itself in Jesus' life and death, which determines the spiritual significance of the miraculous. According to the orthodox view, there is a confluence of the spiritual and the literal at the limit of the miraculous, where the miraculous passes into the eschatological: the believer is called upon to believe not only in the transcendent power that shows forth in Jesus' resurrection but in the "literal" reality of that resurrection itself—not as a preliminary to faith (as in the case of the lesser miracles), but as the essential element of that faith. And if eternal life means that the believer "literally" rises again on the Last Day, as Jesus once did, then all the supernatural events of the gospel can be read as "literal" demonstrations of Jesus' power to overrule natural process, and this miraculous power is as such a manifestation of the nature of godhead.

But if one holds consistently to the notion that belief in miracles is a preliminary form of faith that must be outgrown, one is led to Bultmann's conclusion that the three resurrections are also only symbolic, an allegory of the true eternal life that does not involve literal resurrections of any kind, whether in this aeon or the next. This would arguably be the most consistently "spiritual" reading in the sense that it would leave behind "literal" belief in miracles in the most thoroughgoing fashion.

Here is the crucial exchange between Jesus and Martha, sister of Lazarus, when Jesus arrives at Bethany to find Lazarus four days dead:

> "Your brother," said Jesus to her, "will rise again." Martha said, "I know he will rise again at the resurrection on the last day." Jesus said:
> "I am the resurrection.
> If anyone believes in me, even though he dies he will live,
> And whoever lives and believes in me
> will never die.
> Do you believe this?"
> "Yes, Lord," she said, "I believe that you are the Christ, the Son of God, the one who was to come into this world." (11:23–27)[10]

Bultmann reads the exchange between Martha and Jesus as corresponding to the "Johannine technique of misunderstanding" as we have seen it in connection with earlier events (e.g., the woman at the well who cannot understand what sort of water Jesus speaks of). In Bultmann's account, Martha misinterprets Jesus' remark that her brother will rise again when she understands it as referring to the resurrection at the Last Day, for "the future resurrection of Martha's belief becomes irrelevant in the face of the present resurrection that faith grasps. The raising of Lazarus is only a symbol of this" (402). The "present resurrection" of the *living* believer is simply the passage from darkness to light, from an inauthentic life that is the spiritual equivalent of death to an authentic life that is already, here and now in this life, an "eschatological reality" (404) for which *both* life and death "in the human sense" cease to be real (403).[11]

For Bultmann, thus, the miraculous and the eschatological never converge; the irruption of the Absolute into this world takes place purely and simply in the becoming-flesh of Christ and in his proclamation of the Father in his words and deeds, and the miraculous can be nothing more than an expressive element, "neither more nor less than words, *verba visibilia*" (*Theology*, 2:60), even in the case of Jesus' resurrection itself.

Bultmann's entire reading of John is centered on his conception of the authentic or eschatological *zōē* 'life' as at once the most intimate reality of the living human being and as the transcendent source of the life of the individual. This conception is established straightaway by reference to the opening lines of the Hymn to the Logos with which the gospel begins:

> In the beginning was the Logos
> the Logos was with God
> and the Logos was God
> He was with God in the beginning.
> Through him all things came to be (*egeneto*),
> not one thing came into being (*egeneto*) without him,
> All that came to be had life (*zōē*) in him,
> and that life was the light (*phōs*) of men,
> a light that shines in the dark,
> a light that darkness could not overpower.

These lines say that the Logos = *zōē* = *phōs*. That the Logos is the *zōē* of all things means that it is the origin of their vitality, "the power . . . that creates life," not the vitality itself that belongs to what is created (Bultmann, *Commentary*, 39). For, in the first place, the Logos was already there *en arkhē*, before the creation of the world, and, in the second place, it remains the unseen *phōs* of a vitality that though still living has fallen into darkness.

Organic vitality and its cessation are, thus, according to Bultmann, only figures for the genuine life and genuine death that have to do with alienation from or recognition of God's *alētheia* as the transcendent life of what lives. To refuse this recognition is to be dead even while one has one's natural vitality; to attain to authentic self-understanding in relation to the Creator is to have a *zōē* so far transcending the sphere of natural vitality that "literal" resurrection can only be a figure for it, a figure still overly bound to the sarctic concern with mere natural life and natural death.

The experience of the eternal *zōē* must not be understood as a mystic rapture; it is a moment *in* the "this-worldly life" (258n) and its significance is in the resoluteness of the believer with respect to the future death that he/she now overcomes. Each believer must endure the hour of anguish in the face of death in which the decision for God is made, a decision that is only possible because Jesus made this decision once and for all as the Revealer of the way (427–29). When Jesus announces his forthcoming death he says:

> Now my soul is troubled.
> What shall I say:
> Father, save me from this hour?
> But it was for this very reason that I have come to this hour.
> Father, glorify your name!   (12:27–28)

This hour of Jesus' decision "is at the same time the hour of decision for the man to whom the Revealer directs his word." Jesus' teaching receives its "seal" in his death, is "completed in death as radical surrender to the glory of God" (430).

Thus Bultmann reformulates for a new age the classical Christian teaching in its most profound and paradoxical moment, the moment at which it is proclaimed that what is most loathed and feared must be endured to the utmost in order that it may be annulled.

Bultmann shows that it is at least possible to read John as focusing his teaching on this life as the only candidate for the true *zōē*. Thus far I go with Bultmann. But why must the true or "eternal" *zōē* be interpreted in terms of a radical split from the natural vitality of which it is nevertheless the principle? Obviously, in the context of Christian orthodoxy this is the proper way to interpret it. But is it certain that this is what "John" means?

What interests me in Bultmann's recasting of Christian dualism is the way in which he repeats with the aid of a contemporary ("existentialist") idiom Paul's gesture of denying that the pneumatic *zōē* is a life of flesh and blood, *sarx kai haima,* and denies it in a more conscious and thoroughgoing fashion, with an "idealizing" fervor that Bultmann shares in a crucial respect with commentators on Christianity from whom he is otherwise far removed: Hegel and Feuerbach. What these writers share is contempt for certain, let us say, primitive, literal-minded, or materialist tendencies in traditional Christianity. Of course Bultmann proclaims the historicity of Jesus in the strongest sense, as the unique manifestation within creation of the supreme Creator. Yet there is a curious affinity with

Hegel and Feuerbach in Bultmann's subtle depreciation of the sacrament of the Eucharist, the references to which in the gospel cannot for Bultmann belong to the authentic profundity of John's meditation.

In fact, orthodox Christianity comes up against this enigma in a way that Bultmann does not—and does so precisely in proportion as the orthodox doctrine of the Eucharist leaves open the possibility that the eating of the flesh and blood of Jesus will be interpreted in a magical-materialist fashion. It doesn't matter in this respect whether one is a Catholic or a Protestant, says Feuerbach; in both cases the mystified mind of the believer holds that the bread and wine are "transmuted into flesh and blood."[12] There is no telling to what extremes the materialism of the Christian doctrine might lead; Feuerbach notes with apparent glee that "at Anspach there arose a controversy on the question—'whether the body of Christ enters the stomach, and is digested like other food'" (244).

Bultmann for his part does not reject the sacrament as such, but why does he find it so important to assert that the references to it cannot belong to the authentic intention of the "original" text of John?[13] Here is the crucial passage that Bultmann declares must be a redacter's interpolation:

"I am the living bread which has come down from heaven.
Anyone who eats this bread will live forever;
and the bread that I shall give
is my flesh, for the life of the world."

Then the Jews started arguing with one another: "How can this man give us his flesh to eat?" they said. Jesus replied:

"I tell you most solemnly,
if you do not eat the flesh of the Son of Man
and drink his blood,
you will not have life in you.
Anyone who does eat my flesh and drink my blood
has eternal life,
and I shall raise him up on the last day.
For my flesh is real food
and my blood is real drink."   (6:51–58)

Equally curious is Bultmann's rejection of 19:34b, which declares that after the soldier's lance-thrust in the side of the dead Jesus "there poured out water and blood" from Jesus' flesh—a verse that other interpreters from antiquity to the present have read as evidence of the physical reality of Jesus' death. Bultmann is convinced that the event, which he takes to have been added as an allusion to the sacraments of baptism and the Lord's Supper (678), is intended to be miraculous. That the reference to the piercing of Jesus' side could be both intended naturalistically *and* also as an allusion to the sacraments is an obvious possibility that Bultmann does not even consider.[14]

With the excision of the allusions to the Eucharist, Bultmann removes the most shockingly sarctic language in the entire gospel. Even though Bultmann lays so much stress on the fact that *ho logos sarx egeneto*, he recoils when the flesh of Jesus is opened and the visible form of the speaking, acting man begins to dissolve into an undifferentiated mass of flesh and liquid. We have seen that for Bultmann all Jesus' actions in the world are to be understood as proclaimed word; but his ability or willingness to recuperate the *sarx* as Logos in this way flags when he approaches the limit of the revelation of the *sarx* in the rending and eating of Jesus.[15]

Death as the cessation of vitality and the falling apart of the flesh has only an auxiliary significance; as in Heidegger, it is really a certain experience of *Dasein* and not physical "demise" that is the thing itself.

Of course Bultmann and Heidegger are right; mere physical demise can have a variety of meanings or no meaning at all. One can die in one's sleep and one might have been asleep all one's life. Nevertheless, if death as a biological occurrence is not in itself and as such the death proper that the human being dies, this does not mean that the merely biological aspect can be bracketed off as a natural event that has no essential relation to authentic Being-toward-death.

Is the horror at the dissolution of the integrity of the living form of the human body a merely inauthentic reaction, one that has no claim to being thought through in an authentic meditation on death? What if, on the contrary, this were the very thing that most needs to be thought through, and what if the fundamental ontology of *Dasein* along with all the Christian and non-Christian pneumatologies, anthropologies, and existentialisms were motivated at an essential level by the need to evade or contain the nausea aroused by the reduction of the living soma to the generic and putrefying *sarx*?

This thought is the irreducible kernel of the thought of "nature" and of the body as belonging to nature, the sarctic body. More primordial than the thought of the body of pleasure or of the "body in pain" is that of the body of dissolution.

Why should the thought of this body be so abominable? Why should it require redemption from a transcendent source in order not to shatter the meaning and coherence of human life? What Christianity calls the cor-

ruption of the flesh is nothing but an effervescence of new life at a
nonhuman level, and when the individual life ruptures it does so because
organic life has passed through it as its momentary instrument on its way
to new configurations. Is this not what Jesus says?

> Unless a grain of wheat falls into the earth and dies,
> it remains alone (*monos menei*)
> but if it dies,
> it brings forth much fruit.   (12:24)

This seems a grotesque misreading of Jesus' words, the worst sort of
nonspiritual interpretation of words meant in a spiritual sense. If it is a
fixed and unshakable presupposition that no natural life can be the true
life, then the reading I am proposing or imposing is the most "fleshly"
imaginable, in the sense of the flesh that appears to be explicitly condemned in the gospel.

> It is the spirit that gives life,
> the sarx has nothing to offer.   (6:63)

But, as Bultmann notes, "the sarx is ambiguous" (446), since the Logos
became *sarx* and the *sarx* of Christ is the essential medium of salvation.
The *sarx* that has nothing to offer is a *sarx* that is not properly illumined
by the *phōs* 'light' of understanding; spiritual blindness is the inability to
see the *sarx* in terms of its source in the eternal *zōē*, in the life that exceeds
the life of the individual and to which the life of the individual belongs.

But why should not the eternal *zōē* be conceived as life itself, universal
life that all living things share in common?

Here an account in terms derived from Hegel offers itself. That the
Word becomes *sarx* means that universal life is restricted or constricted
into the bounds of finitude; death is the limit of constriction, the point at
which the truth of the individual as determination of the universal is fully
manifest in the cessation of the individual's existence, the cessation that
belongs to the finite individual as the "proper" of its finitude and individuality. But at this limit the individual passes back once more into the
element of universality. Self-understanding life is illuminated by the insight into the unity of essence between itself and the universal life into
which it dissolves.

This formulation is, however, even more allergic to the sarctic element
than is Christianity, which insists in a way Hegel deplores on mourning
the dead and decaying body of Jesus and then on affixing the "mundane
reality" of a "real human form" to the resurrected god (*The Spirit of*

Christianity, 293–94).[16] Nevertheless, it articulates with great clarity a certain aspect of the matter of death. We need only to fill in the abstraction in Hegel's account of the passage-through-the-limit of individuality with the thought of the body of dissolution, the thought the lineaments of which I am tracing in John's gospel.

The language that speaks of the natural reduction of living form and of the flow of vitality across the process of dissolution and into new forms is "subliteral" or "hyperliteral." It is the language of absolute humiliation, of the lowest descent of the principle of the eternal *zōē*, language the ultimate reference of which is to the generation, birth, growth, repair, and— as *telos* of all these—the death and dissolution of the body, together with all the flows and functions belonging to each moment of this circulation.

What if John were struggling however darkly with the exigency of this lowest descent, attempting to make it imaginable as such as glorious with divinity? For him the thought of the infinite constriction of death can only be transformed into a meditation on the *phōs* of the eternal *zōē* if there is imagined a being that leads the way into death, a light-filled body whose light can shine all the brighter in and by means of the passage through the *angustiae* in which it is extinguished. And only in this way can he think the otherwise intolerable thought of the dissolution of individuated being as a consecration, as a willed act, and, above all, as an act of love.

If it were not for love, then the meditation on the body of dissolution would be an exercise of pure theoretical or scientific neutrality. And such neutrality could then easily subserve a project of detachment or decathexis of a Stoic or Lucretian type: "Yes, we die and decompose and little worms grow in our decomposing flesh: no need to get hysterical about this. 'Nature has need of matter,'" as Lucretius says.

For such a project there would be no need to read John. But we read in John that Jesus dies for love of the *philoi* 'friends'. Jesus gives the commandment of love, *agapate allēlous*, and then he says:

A man can have no greater love
than to lay down his *psukhē* for his *philoi*.   (15:13)

If this only meant the heroic death of the martyr it would be an oddly restricted formula. Insofar as it refers to the martyr's death, must it not name it as manifesting the essence of love in its connection with death such as anyone can and should experience it, martyr or not? This would mean then that death is precisely not one's "ownmost" but the explosion of all self-appertaining.[17]

We are pursuing the thought of this explosion in terms not of the
Christian or Hegelian *Aufhebung* of flesh into spirit but of the uttermost
agony of flesh. The question is whether we can think a purely natural
death and dissolution as an act of consecration, while thinking it purely *as*
natural.

Let us return to Jesus' words in 12:24, "Unless a grain of wheat falls into
the earth and dies. . . ." The spiritual reading is obvious: as applied to
Jesus, death here refers to his coming martyrdom; in its application to the
believer, it means dying to the world that does not know the Savior; and
in both cases bringing forth fruit means doing the works of God and thus
bringing others to salvation.

And yet the words themselves have a complex and disturbing resonance that one must suppress in order to arrive at the simplicity of the
spiritual reading. Since the tenor of the metaphor bears on the death of
human beings, the vehicle suggests the image, grotesque from the spiritual perspective, of an interred human body that putrefies and out of
which new life springs. Or at least this is what it suggests to an imagination
that responds to it hyperliterally, as for example the imagination of a child
who hears these words and doesn't know any better. Is it merely a mistake
to hear them in this way? Can we know for certain that it is merely a
mistake? We cannot exclude the possibility that the image was constructed
intentionally in such a way as to give this meaning to be read, for it is
without parallel elsewhere in the Synoptic gospels or in the Old Testament,
this notion that "only through death is the fruit borne" (Brown, 472).

Let us pursue the ramifications of the hyperliteral understanding of the
grain of wheat. Out of the fruit of this grain is made—bread; and now we
are back in the circuit of food and drink, back on the question of literal
food and spiritual food and on the question of the Eucharist. But is it not
evident that the food Jesus brings is not made out of grain, that it is spirit
food, the food of his word? This is what Bultmann maintains; but he feels
that the purity of this meaning must be insulated from the disturbing
carnality of the Eucharist. That is why he deletes these words:

For my flesh is real food (*alēthēs estin brōsis*)
and my blood is real drink (*alēthēs estin posis*).   (6:55)

Orthodoxy keeps the words, but it makes their meaning spiritual; thus
the orthodox reading, like Bultmann's, keeps firm the contrast between
the food of Jesus' flesh and the food that feeds the stomach (although not
entirely firm, as we have seen in the case of the poor theologians of
Anspach).

But if eternal life is this very life that we live, only under a different aspect, then why should not spiritual food be this very food that we eat, only grasped in the *phōs* of the eternal *zōē*—the sacramental meal understood as the communion of universal mortality, of an infinity of lives each of which must undergo a dissolution that is unbearable and that yet must be endured, an absolute humiliation of substance and an expenditure of self that is absolutely without return: but not without issue. And why should the thought of this issue of merely natural vitality not be enough to sustain human life as human—provided that human beings bind themselves together in their mortality by means of love?

"Binding themselves together in their mortality" does not mean only, or mainly, that human beings must huddle together in the face of the great darkness—and certainly not in defense against or defiance of it. What we are reading in John is that it is *in* the passage into death itself that the binding is effected, and not as merely affective phenomenon but as ontological or eschatological consummation. The empire of universal death is precisely coextensive with that of universal life, and the *philoi* are to know that *after the first death there is no other*, there is only one (universal) death, and the sharing in this single essence of universal death binds all life together beyond all boundary of individuation. This is perhaps the humbling that Anaximander thought, in a very different modality, long before Jesus, when he declared that all things in passing away must make restitution to one another for their injustice, in accordance with the ordinance of time; but Anaximander did not speak of love. Jesus, as he goes toward death, says this:

> There are many rooms in my Father's house;
> if there were not, I should have told you.
> I am going now to prepare a place for you,
> and after I have gone and prepared you a place,
> I shall return to take you with me;
> so that where I am
> you may be too.
> You know the way to the place where I am going.   (14:2–4)

Jesus will die, and when he dies he will enter once again the round Zion of the water bead and the synagogue of the ear of corn, where the *philoi* too must follow; only they will come knowing that he has gone before, that to die is to enter the embrace of the eternal *zōē* for which the ordinary distinction of life and death is unreal—for which the distinction is, rather, between the universal movement of lifedeath and the constriction of this

universality that constitutes the necessary condition of its movement.[18] The
(eternal) universality exists only as its (mortal) constriction: God manifests
himself only as Jesus.[19] Jesus is sent by God, he is subordinate to the Father
("the Father is greater than I"—14:28), and yet he is identical with the
Father ("I am in the Father and the Father is in me"—14:11); or, again,
everything the Father has is *his* (16:14–15). And the *philoi* are consubstantial
with Jesus even as Jesus is consubstantial with God, in this asymmetrical
identity of the living being and the life the being lives.

> I have given them the glory you gave to me,
> that they may be one as we are one.   (17:22)

But this complete identity of substance requires the step beyond; Jesus
must die in order to return to the Father and to prepare a place in the
Father's house for the disciples:

> because unless I go,
> the Paraclete will not come to you.   (16:7)

Jesus' final "going" is the completion of a movement that is represented
as an ascent *(anabasis)*, yet as an ascent that is at the same time a descent
or that takes the form of a descent *(katabasis)*. This descent is not merely
the descent from heaven to earth emphasized by Schillebeeckx (*Christ*,
366–67); it is precisely coextensive with the ascent to the glorification on
the cross that is the *telos* of the entire movement. The *katabasis* 'descent'
is, at the limit, a *ptōma*, 'fall'—that is what Jesus says in 12:24—the last
descent of the fruitful flesh into the ground from which it will fructify,
pesōn eis tēn gēn.

Jesus tells the disciples that he must be "lifted up" (*hypsothenai*) in
order that they may have eternal life, and the orthodox commentators
agree that he is alluding here to the crucifixion. But for them being lifted
up on the cross is only a transitional moment in Jesus' ascension back up
to heaven in "the upward swing of the great pendulum of the Incarnation" (Brown, 146). The "being lifted up" (*hypsothenai*) of 8:28 must,
however, be understood with reference to the *sklēros logos* 'hard speech',
'language difficult to bear' of 6:51–58, where "the Jews" are scandalized by
Jesus' declaration that they must eat his flesh and drink his blood. When
Jesus says "the bread that I shall give is my flesh, for the life of the world"
(6:51), he is alluding to the crucifixion just as he is in 8:28 when he speaks
of being lifted up by the Jews; and 6:59–60 make it clear that the crux of
the difficulty in understanding Jesus' references is his identification of the
most spiritual and elevated with the most humiliating and fleshly. After

Jesus declares that believers must eat his flesh and drink his blood, he asserts that his words have nothing to do with the *sarx*.

> The words I have spoken to you are spirit
> and they are life.   (6:63)

But, as Bultmann points out, the words he has spoken are "precisely the *skandalon*," the intentionally paradoxical and repellant utterance that "the Jews" cannot grasp. And in that case, the further remarks concerning the spirit cannot be "an alleviation that helps to remove the offence, as if it invited to a spiritualizing reinterpretation" (446).

Rather, Jesus must be proposing a difficult new thought, one that minds accustomed to the distinction between flesh and spirit cannot grasp so long as they cling to this distinction in its old form.[20] What if it were the thought that *pneuma is* flesh and blood, *sarx kai haima*, only seen with new eyes and consecrated by the passage into death that is an act of love? Jesus' words will bear this meaning quite easily; what is difficult is the mental act that could overcome the repugnance of such a meaning and think this most intolerable thought. Consider, in this context, the hyperliteral sense of the miracle by which Jesus symbolizes the passage from spiritual blindness to spiritual vision: he mixes his saliva with earth, and it is by bringing blind eyes in contact with this mud that they attain to *spiritual* vision (9:1–7). (The commentators do not generally mention Jesus' saliva when they list the liquid flows of this gospel.)[21]

Let us continue to reread on the basis of the hypothesis that Jesus' *anabasis* 'ascent' is through and through and along its entire length a *katabasis* 'descent'. This *katabasis* is also a journey toward a *telos* 'goal'. Jesus early in his ministry declares the following:

> My food (*brōma*)
> is to do the will of the one who sent me,
> and to complete his work (*teleiōsō . . . to ergon*).   (4:34)

Strange intertwining of linguistic registers: the bringing of an *ergon* to its *telos* described as food.[22] And the hyperliteral eye notices that the initial image slides associatively into more talk that mixes work and nutrition:

> Have you not got a saying:
> Four months and then the harvest?
> Well, I tell you:
> Look around you, look at the fields;
> already they are white, ready for harvest!
> Already the reaper is being paid his wages,

already he is bringing in the grain for eternal life,
and thus sower and reaper rejoice together.
For here the proverb holds good:
one sows, another reaps;
I sent you to reap
a harvest you had not worked for.
Others worked for it;
and you have come into the rewards of their trouble.   (4:35–38)

I do not question that these words function in the ways elucidated by the
orthodox commentators; but I want to call attention to the strangeness of
another function, of the circulation of words across the boundaries of the
message that is spoken. For Jesus will say that *he* is the food of eternal life,
that *he* is the grain that is sowed in the earth. He is thus at once the sower,
the grain that is sowed, and the food that is to be eaten; and his accom-
plishment of this cycle constitutes the *telos* of the *ergon* entrusted to him
and the food that nourishes his being.

The most spiritual gospel is the gospel of eating and drinking and of
that which is eaten and drunk.[23] Wine and water at the wedding in Cana,
loaves and fishes to feed the multitude, water at the well in Samaria,
fountains of living water flowing from the breast of Jesus (7:38), the vine
that bears fruit (15:1–8), in addition to all the other references I have
mentioned—this gospel can scarcely proceed without touching on some
facet of ingestion.

What is figurative and what is proper in all this? Bultmann is partly
right when he says that the essence of nourishment is not that it is
chewed with the teeth, but he is right in the wrong direction: passing
food or drink through the mouth does not express the essence because it
does not get at the full *materiality* of the process of nourishment; it is too
paltry a synecdoche for this process. And when the food is bread, rather
than meat, it is easy to forget that life subsists on death, that ingestion and
digestion are the exchange point at which life dissolves back into life at
the cost of life.

In the Gospel of John the characteristic movement of annulment/
fulfillment of Jewish belief involves an initial raising of a "literal" Jewish
belief to a spiritual level and then a return to a more "literal" or "material"
level than that which had been initially surpassed. Thus:

1. Martha expresses her belief in "the resurrection at the last day."
2. Jesus replies that *he* is the Resurrection, and that death does not exist
   for the believer in him.

3. He then proceeds to a miraculous immediate raising of the dead body of Lazarus.

Similarly, in the Bread of Life discourse:

1. Jesus evokes the manna called down from heaven by Moses, in order to
2. Declare that *he* is the true bread, and that belief in him is equivalent to eternal life.
3. He then proceeds to translate the image of bread into that of flesh and the action of belief into that of eating his flesh and blood.

The third moment in each of these crucial discourses makes the logic of the entire sequence strangely tortuous. If Jesus merely "spiritualizes" the understanding of "the Jews," then why the reintroduction in heightened form of the material element that has been surpassed in the second moment of each discourse?[24]

The materialism of the crowd that asks Jesus for heavenly bread is a materialism that exists within the division of body and spirit. Jesus does not merely spiritualize their understanding; Bultmann is at his most resourceful and eloquent in demonstrating this. But, driven by the demands of his own hyperpneumatism, Bultmann must excise the return to the flesh of 16:5iff. from the authentic text of John. The herbivorous spirituality of the metaphorical eating of grain is digestible for Bultmann's understanding; with unerring instinct he rejects the transition to the eating of flesh.[25] But if we read the entire discourse on the Bread of Life as one movement, it appears that Jesus moves precisely from the "literality" or "materialism" of the crowd, first toward a figurative or spiritual account in "I am the bread of life," and then toward the revelation of the hyperliteral or sarco-pneumatic essence of the sacramental eating of the bread of life.[26]

Bultmann in one way and orthodox Christianity in another spiritualize the sacramental eating; and death itself, however anguishing, is easily spiritualized so long as it is not brought into contact with this most meaningless and inhuman of processes, so long as it is not conceived as a *becoming-food* and passing once more into the organic cycle.

Death is the ultimate agony of individuation, and it is being eaten, and it is falling into the ground and bringing forth fruit. Bread is meat, water is wine, and wine is blood, and there is no horror in all this if it is understood as the fleshly passion of the Logos and the agapetic action of spirit.

Perhaps John learned something of all this from the Dionysian mysteries. Bultmann and Barrett suggest that there is a link between the miracle at Cana and the mysteries. Brown rejects this possibility, but the possible links are suggestive indeed. Not only is Dionysus "the cause of miraculous transformations of water into wine," but Philo had spoken of the Logos in "pseudo-Dionysiac terminology" (Barrett, *Gospel*, 188). Bultmann notes that the early church dated the marriage at Cana to January 6, date of the Dionysus feast, and celebrated it as part of the Feast of Epiphany (119). When we consider also that this is the only one of Jesus' miracles that "has no parallel in the Synoptic tradition" (Brown, 101), and that John makes it the first of Jesus' miracles, as Lazarus will be the last, the Dionysian associations are especially striking.[27]

If the *ergon* of Jesus is the manifestation of the divinity of flesh, of universal lifedeath, then we can take him at his word when he declares at the moment of his death on the cross the single word *tetelestai*, 'it is consummated', 'the telos has been achieved and is now present'. If the pendulum would have to pass through this moment on its way upward in order for Jesus' *ergon* to come fully into its own, then the *telos* would not now have been achieved; it would still be in the process of unfolding.

And in order that we should remember the sarctic nature of this death, Jesus' last act, just before he dies, is to ask for a drink.[28]

> Knowing that everything was now completed (*tetelestai*), in order to bring the scripture (*graphē*), to its fulfillment (*teleiōthēi*), Jesus said "I thirst" (*dipsō*). (19:28)

Bultmann resists to the end. "It is hardly likely that we are to understand that Jesus, who himself offers the water of life that stills all thirst (4:10ff.), here reaches the deepest point of fleshly existence" (674 n. 2). It is, for Bultmann, simply the fulfillment of Scripture that "determines the narrative" here; everything is on the level of a Logos that in its essence does not pass through the stomach.

But there need be no contradiction between bringing the Scripture to its *telos* and the *katabasis* to "the deepest point of fleshly existence." Christianity itself has always held that the fulfillment of the Hebrew Scripture is a radical revision, that its fulfillment contradicts what the Jews themselves believed to be the sense of their Scripture: a matter of the opposition of the letter and the spirit, according to Paul. Only, what is spirit?

When Jesus says "I thirst" he brings to manifestation the *telos* of Scripture *as* the descent or fall of spirit to the deepest point of fleshly existence which is also the *telos* of Jesus' love for the "friends."[29] And as soon as we start to think of drinking as an act too banal to be the fulfillment of anything, we are immediately hurled back into the ineluctable circulation of life on its way down to its elements, and into the act of consecration by means of which Jesus transforms its visage: Jesus says *tetelestai*, his head droops in death, the soldier pierces his side, water and blood pour forth, and we are back once more to the hyperliterality of what the gospel both declares and enacts. There is nothing left over to see or know beyond what is made visible in the *ergon* of Jesus; even though the Father exceeds the Son, is greater than the Son, there is nothing more to know of the Father than what Jesus is:

> To have seen me is to have seen the Father
> so how can you say, "Let us see the Father?"
> Do you not believe
> that I am in the Father and the Father is in me?   (14:9–10)

> In a short time the world will no longer see me;
> but you will see me,
> because I live and you will live.
> On that day
> you will understand that I am in my Father
> and you in me and I in you.   (14:19–20)

How could the community of *philoi* united in the love of Jesus not be, as commentators from Hegel to Rensberger have complained, a restricted community, with a love "directed . . . strongly inward toward the group's own members" (Rensberger, 131) but divided from the world? The limit of constriction is absolute uniqueness, the individuated being as apocalyptically distinct and separate. Even within the original group of *philoi*, there must be *one* who is singled out as "the disciple Jesus loved" (13:23; 19:26). An abstract, universal love of others would dissipate the force of mourning that is involved in the passage through the limit of individuation, a passage the affect of which is initially constituted in a minimal, irreducible relation of duality; I must love another as myself in order to affect myself with the force of my self-relation (which is to say, to love myself as another).

Hence at the origin, the *arkhē*, there is a strange duplicity in unity. God and the Word are both one and not one, they are bound together by love, and one of them must die.

This death is the corollary of the love that binds everything together in the infinite *zōē*.

For God so loved the world
that he gave his *monogenēs* Son.   (3:16)

Monogenēs does not mean 'only begotten'; it means 'precious', 'unique'
(Brown, 13–14). There is only one Son because there is only one death,
this unique death that is the seal of individuated being or *telos* of individuation; God's love and God's sacrifice must equal the force of my love for
my own only, precious life and the autoaffection set off by the thought of
giving up this life.

We must think the *Iliad* and John's gospel together. The *Iliad* depicts
the intertwining of hetero- and automourning, the very intertwining that
is implied by the Johannine account of Jesus' sacrifice for the *philoi*. But
the only response to the ultimate humiliation of death that the *Iliad* can
imagine is vengeful *ressentiment;* thus nothing could bring out more forcefully the radicality of the thought John thinks than the contrast with the
Iliad.

The body of dissolution *as* the body of love: we have through John
approached the possibility of such an identification. But we have so far
only grasped the problem of this approach in its most generalized aspect,
in relation to love in general. We are still within that moment in the dialectic of mourning at which the religious-philosophical tradition grasps
the question of mortal eros in the generalized terms of libidinal, but not
sexual-erotic, investment in a finite and mortal being. In the next section
I will pursue the question of mortal love in what is perhaps, at least for
the Western tradition, its most problematic form—in the sexual, and
specifically the heterosexual, relation.

PART TWO

THE TROUBADOURS AND THEIR AFTERMATH

CHAPTER FOUR

Cruel Lady, or The Decline of the "Gay Science" from the Troubadours to Dante

𝒲E SAW IN CHAPTER I THAT FOR PLATO PHILOSOPHY AIMS AT DE-
liverance from mourning; whereas poetry endlessly elaborates the pathways of mourning, of attachment-and-its-consequences, like a labyrinth
the exit from which it would be constitutionally incapable of showing.[1]
And yet Platonism as antimourning would invade the generative system
of Western poetry at a fundamental level, by the perversely brilliant
doctrine of eros that holds its true nature to be not attachment to but
transcendence of the object, and in fact of all objects. As Gregory Vlastos
puts it, according to Plato's doctrine "the individual, in the uniqueness
and integrity of his or her individuality, will never be the object of our
love," will never be, in the phrase Vlastos borrows from the *Lysis,* the
prōton philon. Only "the 'image' of the Idea" in the mortal individual can
be the *prōton philon,* the true, ultimate object of love.[2] The true unmixed
beauty that is the object of desire is such that when individual "beautiful
things . . . are born and perish *it* becomes neither less nor more and
nothing at all happens to it" (*Symposium* 211b).[3] Allied with Christianity
by Augustine and, in more problematic form, by Italian Neoplatonism (to
say nothing of its pervasive seepage into Christian textuality by means of
indirect sources), this doctrine exercised for centuries a tremendous attraction on the European poetic imagination.

Refracted through various medieval sources, with what Joseph Mazzeo
calls their "unconsistent blend of Neoplatonism with Aristotelianism,"[4]
and mixed with the influence of the troubadours, the Platonic conception

of love as that which, drawn by beauty, raises the soul to the divine, finds its fullest poetic efflorescence in Dante's *Commedia*.[5]

Despite the similarity in outline of the Dantean and Platonic ascents, however, there are significant, possibly fundamental differences between the two doctrines of love. The doctrine of erotic ascent in the *Symposium* and the science of measurement in the *Republic* are devoted to making the lover more rational and less perturbable, thus loosening his attachment to the particular libidinal object that had filled his field of vision by teaching him to see it as unimportant. Loving beautiful bodies in general, the lover may "relax the intense passion for one, thinking lightly of it and believing it to be a small thing" (*Symposium* 210b). Dante, too, aims at transcendence of sensuality; but thinking Beatrice's body to be unimportant does not involve thinking *Beatrice* to be unimportant. Both Plato and Dante "ascend" from the physical to the spiritual, but Dante preserves right to the threshold of the beatific vision the relation to the individual that is Beatrice.

Of course Dante's valuation of the individuality of Beatrice is fundamentally Christian. For Christian doctrine each soul has absolute individuality, rooted in the individuality of the physical body, which is preserved eternally; and each Christian is enjoined to be united in love to all the others.[6] Yet in orthodox Christianity there remains a powerful tension between the love of the creature and the love of the creator, and, despite the theological subtleties by which they are reconciled, the latter has a tendency to obliterate the former—especially during the soul's sojourn in this life.[7] Following Guido Guinizelli and Guido Cavalcanti, however, Dante strengthened the love-relation to the individual by mixing the *fin'amors* of the troubadours (loosely, 'courtly love') into his Christianity. Dante thus creates an intriguing new form of erotic ascent, one that in some ways revises Christianity as much as it does Platonism, since, as Roger Valency remarks, "None of the doctors of the church had any idea of involving the female form in the ladder which led to heaven."[8]

Now, no courtly love poet of any persuasion, and certainly not Dante, could countenance the first step in the Platonic ladder of ascent, that by which the lover "rises" from the exclusive admiration of the body of the beloved to the admiration of beautiful bodies in general. This turn toward beautiful bodies in general is not ideal enough for the idealizing tendencies of courtly love. It is of course an idealizing move in the technical sense, in that it moves toward abstraction and universality; for this sense of idealization it does not matter what kinds of bodies are in question. But because we are in fact speaking of human bodies that arouse an erotic interest, the movement toward universality violates both Christian sexual pudency and the pieties of courtly idealization.[9]

It is true that in the *Phaedrus* Plato valorizes the lasting attachment to an individual, and this doctrine, heterosexualized, is not so far from that of Dante. But even here there remains a fundamental difference, because for Dante it is the *death* of Beatrice that furnishes the ineluctable pressure that forces the mind to spiritualize its libidinal relation to her, whereas death plays no such role in Plato.[10] The Dantean ascent is a form of the work of mourning, whereas the Platonic ascent, even in its *Phaedrus* form, circumvents mourning altogether.

And yet, granted all the differences between Dante's doctrine and Plato's, the fact remains that Beatrice is preserved as object of love only by being annulled in her earthly existence and raised to the level of spirit.[11] And even as spirit, neither Beatrice nor any other created being can be the *prōton philon;* at the limit of the Christian's spiritual ascent, love must find its way *beyond* the creature and back to its transcendent source and goal. Thus, even in Dante there remains the injunction "Troppo fiso!" against the absorption of the soul in a beloved creature:

> Tranced by the holy smile that drew me there
>   into the old nets, I forgot all else—
>   my eyes wore blinders and I could not care.
> When suddenly my gaze was wrenched away
> and forced to turn left to those goddesses:
> "He stares too fixedly" [*Troppo fiso!*], I heard them say.
>   (*Purgatorio* 32.4–9)[12]

Even if individuals persist in the presence of God, and are to be loved qua individuals precisely because and insofar as they come from God, it is the turn away from these beloved individuals toward their source that marks the moment of transcendence. "The good that you love is from Him," says Augustine, "but its goodness and sweetness is only because you are looking *toward Him.*" "If bodies please you, praise God for them and *turn your love* back from them to their maker" (*Confessions* 4, 12; italics added). Thus as Dante approaches the vision of God he exchanges looks for the last time with Beatrice, and then she turns away from him to look to God:

> quella, sì lontana
> Come parea, sorrise e riguardommi
> poi si tornò all'etterna fontana.   (*Paradiso* 31.92–93)

"She smiled and looked at me, then turned toward the eternal fountain."

Unlike Platonism, Christianity traverses mourning en route to transcendence; but this transcendence baffles mourning, by cheating death of its ultimate and unbearable sting. Whether or not there is in the *Vita Nuova*, as Charles Singleton claims, "what the Middle Ages would have recognized as an *analogy of proportion*" (*Essay*, 114; italics in original) between the death of Beatrice and that of Jesus, the process of mourning and idealization by which Beatrice is preserved on the other side of death is quite clearly that which Christianity institutes through the mourning for Jesus Christ.[13] Christians are the masters of mourning, both in the sense that they are the mourners par excellence and that they know how to master mourning for all individual deaths by the triumphant mourning for the god who dies and rises once more. Thus Dante knows how to meditate on the figure of a unique individual all the way up to and beyond death, and by this means, apparently, to bring peace at last to the turbulent yearnings of troubadour love.[14]

The path toward transcendent love had been pursued, more or less uncertainly, by some of the troubadours. In the poems of Jaufré Rudel, for example, there is a quite sophisticated strategy of idealization and interiorization, the famous *amor de lonh* 'distant love' that does not involve the death of the *domna* but something that comes close, her permanent separation from the lover, so that she continues to exist for him only in his mind.[15] But Dante does not jump as quickly to idealization as had Jaufré; much less does he merely give up *fin'amors* for the love of God as Peire d'Alvernhe had done. Rather, Dante's heart clings to his lady "with its nails," as Arnaut Daniel says in his famous sestina, "like the bark on the branch" (C'aissi s'enpren e s'enongla / mos cors el sieu cum l'escorssa en la verga).[16] Dante thus goes simultaneously in two apparently antithetical directions (directions that had been severally pursued by various troubadours) in a movement that is genuinely dialectical: his transcendence of courtly love comes only through its heightening. Even at the top of the mountain of purgatory, having already passed through the fire that purifies love of all sin (a fire that indeed he enters only at the mention that Beatrice is on the other side), when Dante sees Beatrice he tells us that he "felt the great power of ancient love" (d'antico amor senti la gran potenza) and turns to Virgil to say: "Not a drop of blood is left in me that does not tremble; I know the marks of the ancient flame" (*Pugatorio* 30.37–48). Here, on the verge of the transition to heaven, Dante invokes once more the conventions of courtly poetry in the image of the trembling lover awestruck at the sight of his beloved. It is thus only by clinging to the image of his *donna* as resolutely as any troubadour, all the way beyond this world to the very threshold of the beatific vision, that Dante achieves the final letting-go.

The Beatrice of the *Divine Comedy* is the image of woman pushed to the absolute limit of idealization, just short of a complete transparency to the divine in which she would cease to be a gendered individual. We have seen what is gained for a project of transcendence by the construction of such a figure. Now I want to trace some aspects of the prehistory of the ideal Beatrice. First, I will reconsider the erotics of troubadour poetry, which is in certain essential ways not what the standard accounts suggest that it is. Then, against the background of this reconsideration, I will return to Dante to consider some early poems of his in which the figure of Beatrice first begins to emerge out of the troubadour matrix. What will emerge from this reconsideration is that the relation between Dante and the troubadours is more complex and problematic than is generally realized.

Despite the impression that is given by generalizing treatments of "the troubadours" as a totality, troubadour poetry does not speak with one voice. In order to avoid the inaccuracies of summarizing generalization, then, I will focus primarily on the single poet who is most frequently recognized as the paradigm of the "courtly" *fin'amors* troubadour, Bernart de Ventadorn, and I will measure other troubadours by their closeness to or distance from Bernart.

The central problem that I will be concerned with is the place of sexual desire in Bernart's erotics. There is a persistent tendency in English-language troubadour scholarship, a tendency that has grown stronger in recent work, to treat physical sexual desire as a dissociated element in troubadour poetry—an element that is inimical to or that satirizes with a "bawdy wink" the "courtliness" that divinizes the figure of the woman.[17]

The most elaborate indictment of courtly *fin'amors* as the dissimulation of coarser motives is probably Laura Kendrick's in her remarkable *The Game of Love: Troubadour Wordplay.*[18] Kendrick's complex thesis is that underneath the courtly game of love there is a "facetious" or "burlesque" reference to sexuality in its most physical and unvarnished forms; picking up a suggestion made by Stephen Nichols, she suggests that the troubadour *canso* 'love song' is really a *con-so* 'cunt song' (122). The element of sexual burlesque functions in tandem with a kind of deconstructive wordplay in which each individual troubadour tries to "assert personal prowess" (184). "The early troubadours' language of desire," according to Kendrick, "is really a desire of language" (185); but their language games have genuine social effects, for by this means not only do the troubadours advance their status as individuals, but they participate in the stabilization of the new forms of authority that are beginning to develop at the time by helping to "dissipate social tensions in laughter" (186–87).

I am not entirely persuaded by Kendrick's attempt to make out the pure physicality of the sex urge, the "desire of language," and the pursuit of status as interlocking elements of a single thesis. Nevertheless, Kendrick's work and that of other recent demystifiers of troubadour love is of the highest interest; no doubt there operates in troubadour poetry, as everywhere in literature, a complex economy of forces that ultimately involves the entire social and political milieu. The thesis I argue in this entire book is, however, that ideologies of erotic relation are one crucial determinant of the constitution of the desiring subject, and that we blind ourselves to one of our own most fundamental structures of motivation if we treat these ideologies as mere epiphenomena of more "real" forces. Hence, I am going to argue, against the prevailing critical tendency, for a certain irreducibility of the doctrine of love in Bernart de Ventadorn and those other poets whose work, or a significant portion of whose work, is akin to his (e.g., Giraut de Bornelh, Peire Vidal, Raimbaut d'Aurenga, Bertran de Born).

My view of Bernart's erotics is not far from that of L. T. Topsfield, who perceives the centrality for Bernart of *foudatz* 'erotic rapture' or 'folly'— the "willingness to be carried along by desire, feeling and love of *Jois*, like the leaf following the wind."[19] But Topsfield touches rather too delicately the question of physical desire, and he does not address the question of just how the "'natural' desire of the senses" (120) in which Bernart's *Amors* is rooted is to be reconciled with his courtliness—that very courtliness that other critics see as antithetical to "natural desire."

We must hear the precise tonality of Bernart's voice in order not to think that his poetry is dissociable into sincerity and burlesque, ideality and carnality. It is the tone of erotic gaiety or rapture, the tone of what the troubadours themselves insistently call *joi*.[20] In order to know how to hear Bernart's tone, however, it is necessary to break through the stereotypical picture of him as abject lover, condemned to grovel in his sincerity before a cruel mistress who scorns him, as well as the apparently contradictory interpretation that sees his sincerity as a surface lampooned by underlying references to sex.

Physical sexual desire is everywhere in the forefront of Bernart's discourse on love; it is his explicit theme—as it is in much of troubadour poetry—not in the background or underground, as the theorists of the "bawdy wink" would have us believe.[21] Admittedly, Bernart does not always explicitly mention the physical *telos* of courtship; but he does so enough times that it seems obtuse not to recognize the nature of the *joi* he proposes to himself:

> Ara cuit qu'e·n morrai
> del dezirer que·m ve
> si·lh bela lai on jai
> no m'aizis pres de se,
> qu'eu la manei e bai
> et estrenha vas me
> so cors blanc, gras, e le.   (36.30–36)

I think now I shall die of the desire I have if the beautiful one does not bring me close to her, where she lies, so that I may caress and kiss her and take to me her white body, round and smooth.

Or, slightly more circumspectly:

> del melhs es sos cors establitz,
> los flancs grailes et escafitz,
> sa fatz frescha com roza par
> don me pot leu mort revivar.
> Dirai com? No sui tan arditz.   (40.28–32)

Her body is formed of the best; her hips are slim and slender while her face appears fresh as a rose. With these she would rouse me from death. Shall I say how? I am not so bold.

And again, in the mode of a more exotic sensuality:

> Mal o fara si no·m manda
> venir lai on se despolha,
> qu'eu sia per sa comanda
> pres del leih, josta l'esponda,
> e·lh traga·ls sotlars be chaussans,
> a genolhs et umilians,
> si·lh platz que sos pes me tenda.   (26.29–35)

She will do ill if she does not bid me come to her boudoir [literally, "there where she undresses"], where, at her command, I may be near her bed, or at the edge of it, so that, humbly kneeling, I may remove her well-fitted shoes, if she pleases to offer me her foot.

Such utterances are common in Bernart's poems and completely integral to their eroticism (cf. 8.33–40; 28.33–40; 39.19–24). There is no gap between praise of the lady and the mortification to which the lover subjects himself, on the one hand, and the desire for consummation, on the other.[22] The goal of consummation is the whetstone on which desire is sharpened; thus it must be simultaneously what the lover desires with all his being and also what he willingly defers for as long as possible, so that it may set every moment of the approach to the lady aglow with erotic fire. That is why a kiss, a smile, even a glance from her can acquire a supreme value: "What shall I do then with her fair covert glances? Just let them go? Sooner would I let the whole world go!" (Que farai doncs dels bels semblans privatz? / Falhirai lor? Mais volh que·l mons me falha) (35.35–36).[23]

The "lubricity" of the troubadour love song is not, in the hands of a master like Bernart, *something apart;* it is not the detachable "physical" or "lustful" component that ironically counterpoints, undermines, or burlesques the courtly surface. It is, rather, the erotic lifeblood, the gaiety or rapture of the song, and it is so precisely because it is submitted to the refining pressure of courtliness.

We need make only a subtle, yet fundamental, adjustment in the erotic theory of Plato's *Phaedrus* to apply it to Bernart's practice. In the *Phaedrus* we find a discipline of love that involves lifelong devotion to one partner, "service" to the beloved in almost a courtly sense, and erotic intimacy that stops short of consummation (a practice reminiscent of the *asag,* especially if we supplement the remarks of the *Phaedrus* with Alcibiades' account in the *Symposium* of his chaste night with Socrates).[24] Plato thus here comes to the very verge of acceptance of the physical sex urge, not as the raw expression of divine Eros at the level of the animal (as in the *Symposium*), but as a force that inhabits the movement toward all "higher" goals while retaining its essence as sensual drive.[25] Yet even in his closest approach to such a view, Plato retains the condemnation of sexuality as the "bad horse" that must be harshly treated and ultimately overcome.

To conclude that the physical sexual urge cannot permeate the entire process of refinement of spirit while *remaining physical* is to submit to the Platonic-Augustinian judgment of physicality. The inability of many troubadour scholars to grasp the precise erotic tone of the *canso* 'love song' in the hands of Bernart is a direct result of the ideology of transcendence by which the troubadour erotics is prejudged. This ideology is implicit in the love/lust antithesis with all its metaphysical baggage; but occasionally a critic explicitly develops the presuppositions of this antithesis. Thus

Goldin assures us, on what authority I do not know, that "no one in this world can really love [Bernart's] way," because "no one can appoint his beloved as his judge. No human being can so spiritualize his daily desires and transform them into service; and no human object of desire can survive such exaltation" (118).

From Bernart's perspective, however, it is not that one appoints the beloved as judge but that one is judged or judges oneself by how one comports oneself with respect to the beloved, and there is no higher judgment. An artificial difficulty is created by the ascription to the troubadours of an "exaltation" that lifts the lady above the mere flesh; it is only on this assumption that the perpetual presence of the sexual element in troubadour poetry becomes a comic or disruptive element. The "exaltation" of the beloved for Bernart excludes nothing that belongs to a physical love for a physical woman, and the discipline of love for the poet is precisely his struggle to accept the reality of the situation and to deem it good, whatever it might be.

I am not arguing that Bernart or any other troubadour is "sincere." His art, like that of troubadour poetry in general, has a strongly formalist bent. Not only are the poems of the troubadours full of witty and ingenious allusions to and revisions of the poems of their predecessors and contemporaries, but, as scholars like Jörn Gruber have brilliantly demonstrated, the intertextuality of troubadour poetry is driven at the level of form by a dialectic of near-mathematical precision.[26]

We need not, however, conclude from the pervasiveness of this formal imperative that, as Amelia van Vleck says, "ultimately, eros is subsumed into language" in troubadour poetry (27). In making this judgment van Vleck deploys a sophisticated new version of the old convention/sincerity antithesis, as do other recent demystifiers of troubadour love. But this is a very undialectical antithesis, one closely related to the equally undialectical form/content antithesis.

Everything in this debate turns on how we define "eros." I am taking it as the *voluptas* that is the ultimate motive force of all movement of psyche. In the Platonic-Augustinian-Freudian terms I am both criticizing and extending here, language itself can do nothing other than trace pathways for libidinal flow, whether toward the object of desire or away from it in strategic movements of rejection, containment, or sublimation. Linguistic pathways always have structure, even in the most everyday uses of language; but the level of complexity of the structure involved corresponds to the sophistication of the libidinal strategy manifested. Thus the primitivity of form of the formula "the grapes are probably sour anyway" is the primitivity of the libidinal pathway that it structures; this "ordinary language" structure may then be developed and complicated by literary art (as in Stephen Dedalus's, "Madam, I do not eat muscatel grapes"). In poetry, the possibilities of form are exploited to the limit at the level of both sound and sense, to the degree that the pursuit of form might begin to look like an end in itself; van Vleck shows how deeply the reflection on the shape and shaping of the poem is woven into the language of the troubadours (see especially her fascinating chapter "Nature Enclosed," 133–63). But, from the perspective adopted here, it can never be the case that eros is "subsumed" by a formal project, that the poet somehow manages to transcend the problematic of libidinal economics or *desire*. The troubadour is enmeshed in this problematic not only because he is a mortal, embodied being but also because the textuality of his culture, the textuality out of which his poetry is rewoven, is through and through a discourse on desire. Thus, as Sarah Spence has argued, we must understand the rhetoric of the troubadours in relation to Augustinian rhetoric, which in turn is activated by a transcendent desire that must itself be reconfigured by the troubadours as they make the transition to the love of a mortal object.[27]

Eros is a sea that will float, and eventually capsize, any number of formal projects. Under the formalist microscope, the *canso* decomposes into threads of pure linguisticity; but then we lose our sense of the vast historical agitation of the "ethical substance" of Western humanity that is the question of eros, and the significance of the troubadours in this agitation.

What I want to argue, as against Kendrick, Sarah Kay, van Vleck, and others—but in agreement with commentators from C. S. Lewis to Jacques Lacan—is that the formal linguistic game of the troubadours is not the mill for which love is merely the grist, but the means by which love as a symbolic system (or aspect of "the Symbolic," in Lacanian terms) is elaborated and the libidinal being of Western humanity is drawn out in ways that are historically new.

The crucial point is that there is no conflict between the formal imperative in troubadour poetry and the *askesis* of libidinal being that this poetry constitutes. To think that there is is to misunderstand the nature of an *askesis*, which is by its very nature a formalism, and which thus always has a variable relation to the putative authenticity of the subject who engages in it. In the case of a "generative" formalism, one that by its nature calls for inventiveness and makes it possible, the relation between form and subjectivity is even more undecidable than it is in the case of a relatively static *askesis* such as, say the *Spiritual Exercises* of St. Ignatius.

I am thus by no means reluctant to interpret Bernart as a formalist. If we read Bernart's forty-plus extant songs from a formal perspective, it is apparent that at the level of theme they constitute a series of explorations of the "grammar" of erotic moods and situations. Bernart lays out a number of possibilities generated by this grammar: the lover hopes, despairs, wins through; or the lover gives up and goes away with bitter remonstrances toward the lady; and so forth. It is important to realize, as against the prevailing stereotype, that in more than one-third of Bernart's poems the lover attains some measure of the joy he seeks, and occasionally all of it (1, 8, 13, 15, 18, 20, 21, 24, 27, 32, 36, 37, 41, 42). In "Lancan folhon bosc e jarric" (24), for instance, the poet is, at least momentarily, completely happy in his love: "I love and am loved by the most beautiful woman whom God ever made," a woman who "never showed a fickle and glittering appearance or any deceit" (17–32). In "Pois preyatz me, senhor" (36), his lady loves him, and the difficulty is merely geographical, for he is "here, not there" (14). In "Can vei la flor, l'erba vert e la folha" (42), he has received "mercy" from one lady and has played the cad, chasing off after another one who won't look at him; a move he now bitterly repents. And in one remarkable poem, "Era·m cosselhatz, senhor" (6), which we will consider in detail a little later, the lover consents to sharing his lady's love with another man. At one point Bernart even rejects the fundamental condition for the existence of the courtly *canso*:

> . . . lonja paraula d'amar
> es gran enois e par d'enjan
> c'amar pot om e far semblan alhor   (39.51–53)

Talking a long time about love is a great annoyance and seems a trick, for one can go ahead and love and yet elsewhere put on a deceitful front.

On the reading I am proposing, Bernart is neither sincere nor insincere. He is carrying out a poetic-erotic *project,* on the basis of a formalism that generates new—at times, radically new—articulations of erotic desire. Criticism of the troubadours is intensely conscious today of the limitations of their view of love. The *canso* addresses only the relation between one man and one woman, and only on the level of furtive and evanescent extramarital passion in a very restricted social context. Yet such love consists of precisely the aspects of mortal eros that have been most indigestible for the transcendentalizing tradition, and we might take it as an initial thrust in the direction of a general transvaluation of erotic values. Can the erotic discipline that makes a mortal beloved the untranscendable condition of joy be elaborated in such a way as to encompass married love or its equivalents?[28] (As we will see, this is almost the question at which Milton arrives; it involves a meditation on death that goes far beyond anything attempted by the troubadours, who do not push their project to the point of confrontation between organic death and the swooning death of desire.)[29]

I stress that I am asserting here only the extraordinary character of a textual inscription, which is to say, of certain pathways traced in the cultural Symbolic by the troubadours. What the relation of these pathways in the Symbolic might be to the subjectivity of the living historical beings who traced them is something that can only be guessed at. It is, nevertheless, inescapably the case, and must be acknowledged, that the society in which troubadour poetry flourished did not recognize women in general, even women of the nobility, as full "subjects" in the post-Hegelian and poststructuralist sense. Whether things were better for women in the twelfth century than later, as Joan Ferrante says, does not make much difference by our standards.[30] There is a corpus, small but significant, of poetry by women from this period, the *trobairitz;*[31] but these poems suggest that the experience of love for the women was less exalting than it was for the men—in Kay's words, "their subjectivity, when it is not annexed, is silenced or oppressed" (III).[32]

It is true that Bernart, as well as Guiraut de Bornelh, articulates an ideal, remarkable for the period, of *voluntatz egaus* 'equal will' between a woman and a man.[33] But even in Bernart and Guiraut the *domna* is never realized as anything more than source and goal of the troubadour's erotic passion, and the various ladies of the various troubadours seem to merge into a generic object of desire. Hence the frequently voiced complaint among critics that the troubadours make "all the ladies the same"; the *domna* is almost always beautiful, sweet, fine, gentle, filled with worth, wisdom, courtesy, humility, "she has beautiful eyes, white breasts, etc." (Ferrante, 68–69).

Thus, despite the ideal of *voluntatz egaus,* it is not in the direction of the mutual recognition of two ethical subjects that we must look to validate Bernart's erotics in the face of the historical indictment with which we are confronted. It is necessary, rather, to interrogate more closely this fact of homogenization of the erotic object as well as the critical response to it.

What in fact is it that critics are complaining about when they charge that the *domna* is not granted full individual agency? On the one hand, they are condemning history itself, the society of the Middle Ages in which the subjectivity of women is silenced or oppressed. Such condemnation is a coherent and valid ethicopolitical speech act that has, or can have, real effects on the discursive formations within which it circulates. On the other hand, this ethicopolitical condemnation runs together with a literary-critical judgment the status of which is more questionable, for from this perspective it appears that the troubadours are being criticized for not inventing a mode of "realistic" representation of character that literary history had not yet brought to fruition and that in any case only develops in genres other than the lyric—above all, in the novel.

Yet no concept of literary history has been more thoroughly undermined in this century than has that of the "real" fictional character. We now know how to analyze realism as itself a formalism, a form of "motivation" of the "literary motif," as Boris Tomashevsky says.[34] Even a character like Jane Eyre, who is designed to bring the literary heroine down to earth, is located at a precisely definable intersection of conventions which she partly subverts, and, in becoming the romantic heroine she initially does not resemble, partly confirms.[35] The formal nucleus of the subversion that she represents (replacement of the marker "beautiful" with the marker "not beautiful") is already present in "My mistress' eyes are nothing like the sun."[36]

But things are more complicated still. Even if we do not reduce realism to a formalism but take it on its own terms, there is an irreducibly generic quality that remains at the core of the novelistic representation of women as erotic objects, whether the authors are male or female. How much difference, qua erotic objects, is there between Eliot's Dorothea Brooke, Hardy's Tess Durbeyville, and Woolf's Mrs. Ramsay? Across the differences in age, class, marital status, and personality, does there not remain the persistent obsession with their beauty, gentleness, worth, etc.—the very qualities that characterize the schematized object of the troubadours' desire? Conversely, characters like Mr. Rochester in *Jane Eyre* and Will Ladislaw in *Middlemarch* are equally schematic representations of the male as erotic object.

The entire textual tradition of the West attests to the fact that the individuality of the autonomous ethical individual, both as desiring subject and as object of desire, is in some profound way effaced by the movement of the wave of eros. And this comedy in which the boundary of individuation is overwhelmed by the triumphant species-urge is precisely what sets off the erotic hysteria of the religious-philosophical-political tradition that identifies women as the source of the madness of sexual desire. Kendrick, Kay, and others simply reverse the accusation: it is men, not women, who are the culpable and duplicitous vessels of seduction. Whether there is some other eros somewhere, a higher and purer one not attained by the troubadours, they do not say; but the overall effect of their arguments is that the classical denigration of sexual desire as a "fallen," corrupt, and guilty thing remains in place, by way of a *tu quoque.*

The task of speaking on behalf of the individuality and ethical-political agency of medieval women is essential: feminist projects of this and similar types are, I believe, with the discourse on postcolonialism, the most radical and important critical movements of our time. Yet sometimes the general indictment of phallocratic class culture by demystifying critics cooperates with that very metaphysics condemnatory of eros that underwrites the oppression of women in the first place. There are many threads tangled together in the skein of the problematic of eros; the question of the individuality of the *domna* is one such thread, and requires a most delicate action of disentanglement.

Equally as problematic as the question of the specification of individual qualities in the beloved is the question of the lover's ambivalence toward her. The lover of the *canso* is sometimes prey to doubt concerning the 'worth' of the lady he exalts. But there is a more fundamental, structural uncertainty built into the courtly love situation: uncertainty as to whether the lady, having aroused desire, will satisfy it. Bernart uses the notion of 'betrayal' primarily in this rather specialized sense of 'betrayal of expectation': "How I am betrayed (*traïtz*) if she does not wish to grant me her love" (40.13–14). Bernart's use of the notion of betrayal is consistent with the hyperbolic tendency of his rhetoric, and should be read in relation to the erotic gaiety of his entire project. Nevertheless, in troubadour poetry in general the uncertainty of the lover continually threatens to become genuine ambivalence and even to tip over into resentful denigration of women in general, and the *domna* in particular.

In the case of Bernart's contemporary Peire d'Alvernhe, the pursuit of love gives way to a complete skepticism concerning the constancy of the world of the senses that is related to that of Plato or Descartes. Peire's skepticism, however, focuses on the possible unfaithfulness of an erotic object:

Perque qui del ioy munda
s'apropch'e s'aferma

si: 'era·l terras', non l'a,
que, quan creys mais, merma;
quar, s'amors fon bona ia,
qui no·m pliu ni·m ferma,
que no m'o menta dema,
don l'amars s'azerma
fors cum volva a descordier?   (6.37–45)

Therefore if a man approaches worldly joy and measures himself with
the words: "Now you shall possess it," he has it not, for when it in-
creases most, it decreases. For, if love was once kind, if no one can
pledge me or assure me that it will not lie in what it says to me tomorrow, then to what end does loving lead except to change into discord? (Topsfield, 172–73)

Indeed, he so fears mortal love that in "En estiu" the certainty he craves is
the certainty of the woman's faithlessness:

Amor mi lais Dieus trobar
on ia no·m posc afiar,
e qant ieu la tenrai car,
ill pens de mi enganar;
c'adoncs mi tenc per garitz,
qan mi ment tot cant mi ditz.   (9.37–42)

May God let me find a love in which I can never place my trust, and
when I hold this love dear may she be thinking about deceiving me;
for I shall consider myself cured at the moment when everything she
says to me is a lie. (Topsfield, 171)

Peire in the end declares his despair of finding a faithful woman and his
conviction that a man who is "warder of such love" (or "guided by such
love," as Topsfield translates) will "always be sad":

Totz temps deu esser marritz
qui d'aital amor es guitz.[37]

We see defined here one of the central strategies for mastering uncer-
tainity, a strategy that is at the root of at least some forms of misogyny:
anticipatory ejection of the object, accomplished by means of resentful
denigration. The object is lost or losable; therefore I declare it perfidious
and valueless—valueless because perfidious in its essence. Thus, having
already ejected it before it has a chance to betray me, I need not mourn.

This is, for example, what Hamlet does to Ophelia when he becomes obsessed with the faithlessness of women. Such denigration is a constant possibility in troubadour poetry, where the pain caused the poet by the *domna* often threatens to shatter his love of her; it is something like a test of his devotion, of the fineness of his *fin'amors*.

Even Bernart de Ventadorn and Arnaut Daniel are not immune to the mood of misogynistic resentment:

> For I don't find two women in a thousand
> Without false, off-putting words
> Who don't jab you straight through
> And make their preciousness turn vile.   (Arnaut, 4.13–16)

Of course the very idea of the ideal *domna* is that she is the one in a thousand who is not false; but this is a strangely self-corrosive idealization because it rests on a condemnation of women *as a group*. Consequently the doubt is left open as to whether the idealized woman may not in the end turn out, as is statistically likely, to be just like all the others; "I know very well that they are all alike," says Bernart in "Can vei la lauzeta mover" (43.2), one of his most thoroughly bitter poems.

But to pass over entirely into this denigration, as Peire does, is to collapse the uncertainty that keeps troubadour desire aflame. It is crucial to realize that the moments of despair and bitterness in Bernart, Arnaut, and their kin are only moments in a larger movement.

The joy Bernart seeks is maintained by struggle against the resentment and erotic anxiety aroused by the speaker's precarious situation with respect to the lady. "Fear gives me bad advice, and thus the world withers and dies" (Bernart, 7.61). In the lyrics where the conquest of anxiety is achieved, the moment of accusation against the lady plays the role of crisis in the drama of the poem, and the sovereignty of love is reaffirmed by the overcoming of the crisis. Thus Bernart, calling his lady "a false, coarse, treacherous woman of bad blood" (23.25–26), turns about and exclaims that "they are all liars who have made me speak madness of her": "e tuih cilh son mesonger / que·m n'an faih dire folatge" (55–56). "Since all her acts are perfect (*enter*)," he concludes, "one cannot speak madness of her" (59–60).

It is at best an exaggeration to say of the troubadours in general that their lady was, as Lacan writes in Seminar 7, a "terrifying, inhuman partner," "cruel as the tigers of Ircania."[38] One does sometimes run into an account of the *domna* that comes close to Lacan's characterization, as in Peire Vidal's exquisite "Ajostar e lassar":

mas cor a de drago
qu'a me di mal e ri
als autres deviro
e·m fai huelhs de leo   (35–38)

But she has the heart of a dragon,
because to me she says cruel things and smiles
to the others around,
and smiling makes lion's eyes to me.

But the impression made by these lines alone is quite misleading, because
here again the movement of the poem as a whole is toward the conquest
by the speaker of the temptation to think ill of the lady.

Abrazar e cremar
mi fai cum fuecs carbo.
Quan l'esgar, tan vei clar
sos huelhs e sa faisso,
che non sai guerizo,
Si·m cambi ni·m desvi
d'amar liei.   (46–52)

. . . ie·us afi
quan n'aug dir bon resso,
gaugz entiers mi somo
qu'en deia far chanso,
E doncs pus tan l'am e la cre,
ja no·i dei trobar mala fe.   (70–75)

She kindles me and sets me
aflame like fire on coal
When I gaze on her I see such light
in her eyes and her face,
I cannot be restored
if I change or turn away
from loving her.

. . . I swear to you,
when I hear her good fame spread
one simple joy summons me
to make a song of it.
Well then, since I love her so and

follow her command,
I should not find bad faith (*mala fe*) in her.[39]

Of course, insofar as the troubadour lyric remains haunted by the fear of women's treachery it continues to be bound by one of the most deepseated of ideological structures. And yet, in proportion as love of the type celebrated by Bernart and company is frankly directed at a mortal being as its absolute terminus, in proportion as the erotic relation to a woman is envisaged as sufficient condition of earthly joy and the faithful pursuit of this joy as sufficient condition for the ennoblement of the self, this love already represents a radical movement away from the tradition of transcendence. Hence, Bernart writes, "Let the whole world weigh on one side / and I would choose instead the joy by which I am deceived" (qui·m mezes tot lo mon ad un latz / eu preira·l joi per cui sui enjanatz) (22.47–48).

At the limit, in Bernart's "Era·m cosselhatz, senhor," a poem I alluded to earlier, the poet consents to remain faithful to a woman who, having accepted the poet as her lover, takes a second lover:

Pois voutz sui en la folor,
be serai fols s'eu no pren
d'aquestz dos mals lo menor.
Que mais val mon essien
qu'eu ay' en leis la meitat
que·l tot perda per foldat,
car anc a nul drut felo
d'amor no vi far son pro.

Pois vol autre amador
ma domn', eu no lo·lh defen.
E lais m'en mais per paor
que per autre chauzimen.
E s'anc om dec aver grat
de nul servizi forsat,
be dei aver guizerdo
eu que tan gran tort perdo.   (6.25–40)

De l'aiga que dels olhs plor
escriu salutz mais de cen
que tramet a la gensor
et a la plus avinen.   (49–52)

Since I have been driven to madness, I shall really be mad if I do not take the lesser of these two evils; in my opinion, it is better to have

at least half of her than to lose her entirely through folly. For I have
never seen any wicked lover advance his cause in love.

Then since my lady wants another lover, I will not forbid him to her,
though I permit it more because of fear than anything else. If any
man should ever receive thanks for an enforced service, I should certainly have a reward for pardoning such a great wrong.

With the water that I weep from my eyes, I inscribe more than a
hundred greetings which I send to the most gracious and to the most
beautiful lady.

Not only is the *canso* performed before a "live audience," but the
question Bernart here propounds is explicitly posed for public discussion:
"Now, my Lords, give me your advice" (1). Did Bernart mean to scandal-
ize his audience? Did he give a "bawdy wink" as he spoke? This is far
from a "typical" poem, either for Bernart or for the troubadours in
general, but it is generated by the same erotic grammar that generates the
other transformations of troubadour conventions that we considered earlier. The poet justifies his acquiescence by appeal to the very same ethic of
faithfulness to love and endurance in the suffering of love service that he
elsewhere uses as part of the rhetoric of seduction; he would be, he says, a
bad or villainous lover, *drut felo* (31), if he lost her by refusing the arrange-
ment. He hopes things will not turn out quite so badly ("Lady, love
another in public, and me in secret" [57–58]), but there is no escaping the
fact that the *domna* is here guilty of that very crime that the mores of the
courtly lover generally condemn above all others—the crime that more
than any other defines the line between what Kay calls the "feminine,"
disvalued gender, and the "mixed" gender of the *domna*. When Bernart
consents to continue to love her even when he knows she is unfaithful
he articulates, and thus makes thinkable at the level of the Symbolic, a
possibility, the radicality of which is difficult to overstate.

When we pass from the *cansos* of Bernart de Ventadorn, Giraut de
Bornelh, or Arnaut Daniel to the early lyrics of Dante we find ourselves
in an entirely different world. Dante's themes of suffering and death-by-
deprivation are nominally those of these troubadours, but now the enrap-
tured *joi* of love service is almost completely absent, as is the intoxication
of slow approach to the goal of consummation. The distance between
lover and lady is now metaphysical rather than social; the waning of the

lover's vitality is no longer part of a campaign of persuasion but a sign that she is beyond his aspiration:

> . . . cui saluta fa tremar lo core,
>
> sì che, bassando il viso, tutto smore,
> e d'ogni suo difetto allor sospira   (35.4–6)

when she greets someone she makes his heart tremble, so that, lowering his eyes, he turns all pale and sighs over all his faults.

Already in the early lyrics we see prefigured the guilt over his erotic nature that the bearded man will experience under Beatrice's scolding near the end of the *Purgatorio;* the desire the lady inspires is ashamed of itself and is "extinguished" by the light of her eyes that gives rise to it in the first place:

> De gli occhi de la mia donna si move
> un lume sì gentil, che dove appare
> si veggion cose ch'uom non può ritrare
> per loro altezza e per lor esser nove:
>
> e de' suoi razzi sovra 'l meo cor piove
> tanta paura, che mi fa tremare,
> e dicer: 'Qui non voglio mai tornare';
> ma poscia perdo tutte le mie prove,
>
> e tornomi colà dov'io son vinto,
> riconfortando gli occhi päurusi,
> che sentier prima questo gran valore.
>
> Quando son giunto, lasso, ed e' son chiusi;
> lo disio che li mena quivi è stinto:
> però proveggia a lo mio stato Amore.   (30)

From my lady's eyes there comes a light so noble that where it appears things are seen that no one can describe, so sublime and wonderful they are. And from its rays such a fear rains down on my heart as makes me tremble and say: "Never will I return here." But then, losing all power to resist, I return to the place where I am overcome, comforting my frightened eyes which were the first to feel that great power. When I reach that place, alas, see, they are forced to close; the desire which brought them is extinguished there. Let Love then look to my state!

There is no room in the relation to such a lady for Bernart's or Peire Vidal's drama of ambivalence, in which the lover momentarily denigrates the lady but then is brought back to his praise of her by the inextinguishable force of the desire that refines his being. Dante thus must split off from the figure of his angelic lady another woman, a lady of stone in relation to whom he can express the sensuality smothered by the goodness of Beatrice or proto-Beatrice.

In the lyrics of Dante known as the *Rime petrose* 'Stony verses', we encounter the inhumanly cruel lady whom Lacan in book 7 of the Seminar mistakenly describes as the norm in troubadour poetry. In these verses Dante distills out from courtly love the essence of vengeful sexuality that shadows its idealizations, in order then to proceed to the purification of his (poetic) relation to Beatrice.[40]

Dante achieves extraordinary sexual intensity through the single-minded focus on the "stoniness" of the woman; we might surmise that in the *Rime petrose,* as in the closely related "Mountain Song" ("Amor da che convien"), it is precisely her coldness that makes her so unbearably desirable:

> for if she understood what I hear within myself,
> pity would make her lovely face less beautiful.

> (pietà faria men bello il suo bel volto)   (89.14–15)

The *Rime petrose* themselves culminate in a fantasy of sexual/aggressive fulfillment so remarkable that it deserves to be quoted at length:

> Omè, perché non latra
> per me, com'io per lei, nel caldo borro?
> ché tosto griderei: "Io vi socorro";
> e fare' l volentier, sì come quelli
> che ne' biondi capelli
> ch'Amor per consumarmi increspa e dora
> metterei mano, e piacere'le allora.

> S'io avessi le belle trecce prese,
> che fatte son per me scudiscio e ferza,
> pigliandole anzi terza,
> con esse passerei vespero e squille:
> e non sarei pietoso né cortese,
> anzi farei com'orso quando scherza;
> e se Amor me ne sferza,
> io mi vendicherei di più di mille.

> Ancor ne li occhi, ond'escon le faville
> che m'infiammano il cor, ch'io porto anciso,
> guarderei presso e fiso,
> per vendicar lo fuggir che mi face;
> e poi le renderei con amor pace.   (80.59–78)

Alas, why does she not howl for me in the hot gorge, as I do for
her? For at once I'd cry: "I'll help you"; and gladly would I do so, for
in the yellow hair that Love curls and gilds for my destruction I'd
put my hand, and then she would begin to love me.

Once I'd taken in my hand the fair locks which have become my
whip and lash, seizing them before terce I'd pass through vespers
with them and the evening bell: and I'd not show pity or courtesy, O
no, I'd be like a bear at play. And though Love whips me with them
now, I would take my revenge more than a thousandfold. Still more,
I'd gaze into those eyes whence come the sparks that inflame my
heart which is dead within me; I'd gaze into them close and fixedly,
to revenge myself on her for fleeing from me as she does: and then
with love I would make our peace [literally: "I would give her
peace"].

Even more striking than the sadomasochistic overtones (whips, vengeance) of this scene is the description of a heart that is "dead" and yet
"inflamed." The dissociation of sensuality from affect seems complete in
this image. The references to love seem at best ironic, linked as they are to
a "howling" sexual urge that is the sudden inversion of the lady's extraordinary coldness and cruelty that Dante has elaborated across four poems:

> d'ogne crudelità si fece donna;
>   sì che non par ch'ell'abbia cor di donna
> ma di qual fiera l'ha d'amor più freddo;
>
>   ("Amor, tu vedi ben," 79.6–8)

She became lady of all cruelty, so that she seems to have a heart, not
of a lady, but of whatever wild beast has its heart most cold to love.

Dante's persona mourns that he is dying, a woman is killing him by her
lack of response to his desire; yet the "Mountain Song" suggests that if
she felt anything for his suffering her response would mar the perfect
beauty that whets his desire to the limit. What he dreams of is not her
spontaneous sympathetic response, her *pietà*, but the opportunity to penetrate her coldness by an act of sexual mastery that verges on brutality

(*com'orso quando scherza*). We are here very far from *fin'amors* of the type practiced by Bernart, yet Dante is pushing to its limit one consequence of the erotic logic out of which *fin'amors* draws its effects.[41]

The most fascinating thing about the Cruel Lady of the *Rime petrose* is not her difference, but her partial indistinction, from Beatrice. There are elements of both Beatrice and the *petra* 'woman of stone' in the lady of the early *canzone*, "E' mi incresce" (32), where we also see in particularly stark relief the fundamental situation of automourning aggravated by the woman's lack of pity: "I pity myself so intensely that the pity brings no less pain than my suffering," the speaker laments. His soul is parting tearfully from this life; the lady, more beautiful now than ever, is not only not sorry for the suffering she sees, but she seems to laugh and scorn his weeping soul on its way:

> e non le pesa del mal ch'ella vede,
> anzi, vie più bella ora
> che mai e vie più lieta par che rida;
>   e alza li occhi micidiale, e grida
> sopra colei che piange il suo partire;
> 'Vanne, misera, fuor, vattene omai!'   (32.46–51)

According to Foster and Boyde, "There has long been fairly general agreement" that this *canzone* was written "'for Beatrice,'"[42] but the characterization is clearly closer to the *petra* than it is to the Beatrice that we know from the *Vita Nuova* and *Commedia*. The later Beatrice and the *petra* are products of the separation of a single erotic complex, and we begin to feel how much Dante had to exclude or suppress in his *Aufhebung* of troubadour love.

Robert Durling and Ronald Martinez have recently argued that the *Rime petrose* are "the major turning point in Dante's development after "'Donne ch'avete',"" because in these verses Dante worked out the "microcosmic poetics" that structures the *Commedia*.[43] The dense and fascinating argument made by Durling and Martinez reminds us that the Cruel Lady motif is a nodal point in a vast formalism; it is a poetic *topos* the generativity of which cannot be understood by a direct correlation with some presumed psychosexual reality, without an account of the mediations by which the aggressive erotic fantasy that culminates the *Rime petrose* becomes a switch-point in a complex symbolic machinery. Thus, to take only one example, Durling and Martinez find pervasive reminiscences of the *petrose* in the famous episode of Ugolino and Ruggieri in the *Inferno* (221–22).

Yet, as Durling and Martinez recognize, after all the symbolic apparatus has been analyzed, there remains something unresolved in the grand development of Dante's art from the *Rime petrose* to the *Commedia*; perhaps, they suggest, the *Commedia* merely displaces rather than resolves the "dilemma posed by the sexuality of the idealized *donna*" (197). There is to my mind no doubt that this is the case. If so, it is not only justifiable but necessary to pursue the question of the "Cruel Lady effect" as a symbolic and psychosexual problem with a considerable degree of autonomy—indeed, as a problem that is highly resistant to being resolved by the techniques of symbolic manipulation that are made available to Dante by the idealizing tradition within which he works.

It might be argued that Dante in the *Petrose* conducts a scientific investigation of a sinful state of sensual obsession, rather than revealing his own erotic economy. But Dante's erotic economy is not the issue here; the issue is precisely the symbolic system that he works out of and develops further. The scientificity of his investigation operates within the paradigm provided by the tradition of transcendence, and it does not overstep its bounds. In the realm of erotics, there is gay science and there is melancholy science.

Dante's art is the triumph of Christian erotic melancholia over the gay science of the troubadours. This erotic melancholia carries with it an inculpation of the woman of flesh and blood, a woman who is always either too cold or too forward: the *petra*'s counterpart is the Siren of Dante's dream in Purgatory, the temptress who must be ripped open to show the foulness her fair outside conceals (*Purgatorio* 19).

If the flame of eros ignited by a woman of flesh and blood cannot be nurtured, eros becomes mourning: either resentful automourning toward the woman who lives and mocks or ignores him or, as in the *canzone* "Donna Pietosa" in the *Vita Nuova,* the deep mourning in which all vitality pales away and both man and *donna* must die:

> Mentr'io pensava la mia frale vita,
> e vedea'l suo durar com'è leggiero,
> piansemi Amor nel core, ove dimora;
> > per che l'anima mia fu sì smarrita,
> che sospirando dicea nel pensero:
> "Ben converrà che la mia donna mora."   (40.29–34)

While I was thinking of the frailty of my life, and seeing how slight is its power to endure, Love wept in my heart, where he dwells; at which my soul became so dismayed that with sighs I said in my thoughts: "It's time, my lady will have to die."

Do we not see here the last wan echo of the vengefulness of the speaker of the *petrose,* in the conclusion that, if the speaker is waning, then it is the Lady who (regretfully) must die? In that case, it would be his own anger that he projects onto the faces of the angry women who condemn him to death:

> e poscia imaginando,
> di caunoscenza e di verità fora,
> visi di donne m'apparver crucciati
> che mi dicean pur: "morra'ti, morra'ti."   (40.39–42)

Then in my fantasy, all lost to knowledge and truth, women's faces loomed angrily at me, repeating these words: "You will die! You will die!"

The Cruel Lady is she who refuses to mourn me mourning myself for my inability to possess her, my inability to feel all of her being vibrating in responsive resonance with the autoaffecting, automourning movement of my own being. So long as the flame of eros burns bright and clear, it might just possibly be able to contain the force of *ressentiment* that always threatens to break loose in the lover of *fin'amors* or the *stil nuovo;* if the candle begins to gutter and smoke, the lover's idealizing and denigrating tendencies separate into pure, antagonistic forces and the object of erotic desire becomes, rather than the source of life, its opposite, *l'contrario de la vita* ("Chi guardera già," 66.13).

There is no simple choice to be made between Dante and Bernart. Dante *sees* a great deal more than does Bernart, and we need to know what he sees. On the other hand, the folly—"imaginary captivation," in Lacan's terminology—that Bernart embraces is a rarer attainment at the level of the most culturally saturated text (though evidently not at the level of "real life") than is Dante's vision.

Erotic rapture, *foudatz,* is not everything. As elaborated by the troubadours, it will not yield an entire account of sexual relation, much less an ethics or a philosophy of life. But there is a standpoint from which there is no life without *foudatz,* and any ethics or philosophy must begin from its necessity. This is obviously not the only possible standpoint; but it is the one from which this book is written.

To begin from erotic rapture is, however, like any other beginning, to embark on a dialectical process that will flex in unforeseeable ways—a few of which are laid out in the next two chapters.

Infidelity and Death in *Hamlet* and *La Princesse de Clèves*

*T*HIS BRIEF CHAPTER IS DEVOTED TO TWO SEVENTEENTH-CENTURY works, Shakespeare's *Hamlet* and Madame de Lafayette's *La Princesse de Clèves*, that I read as extremely self-conscious critiques of courtly love. I do not have elaborate new readings of these works to offer; rather, I want in this chapter schematically to outline the structure of their respective analyses of the dialectic of eros and mourning. As we will see, the structures of motivation elucidated by Shakespeare and Madame de Lafayette will recur, in a more symptomatic and less critically distanced fashion, in the works of Conrad and Lacan that I treat in the third part of this book.

In *Hamlet* we find both of the major "courtly" complaints against a woman, that her heart is a stone and that she is unfaithful; but Hamlet directs them primarily against his mother rather than his lady. Only the charge of faithlessness (and only by association, according to the "they are all alike" principle) is directed at Ophelia, yet Ophelia becomes the primary target (at least on the level of Hamlet's explicit declarations) of the vengeful lust that is intermixed with Hamlet's aggrieved sense of the brevity of women's mourning. His bantering with her around the performance of "The Mouse Trap" consequently alternates between lewd suggestions and outcries against female inconstancy.[1] Thus:

Hamlet: Do you think I meant country matters?
Ophelia: I think nothing my lord.
Hamlet: That's a fair thought to lie between maid's legs. (3.2.116–19)

Followed by:

> *Hamlet:* What should a man do but be merry, for look you how
> cheerfully my mother looks, and my father died within's two
> hours.   (125–27)

And again:

> *Ophelia:* You are keen, my lord, you are keen.
> *Hamlet:* It would cost you a groaning to take off mine edge.
> *Ophelia:* Still better, and worse.

Leading to:

> *Hamlet:* So you mistake your husbands. [That is, "in these words, 'for
> better or worse,' you falsely vow when you marry."]   (248–51)

Hamlet shows better than any other work I know the hysterical linkage between a man's loathing of women's inconstancy and his hyperliteral awareness of the dissolution of the body by the forces of natural reduction. The relation between these two forms of revulsion is mediated by Hamlet's sense that the processes of putrefaction and sexual generation are one and that in this unity all other differences are homogenized. This is the bottom of the abyss of his nausea, the abomination from which he cannot wrench his mind's eye.[2] The knot of his revulsion is tied most compactly in one passage, when he says to Polonius:

> If the sun breed maggots in a dead dog, being a good kissing
> carrion—
> Have you a daughter?
> . . . .
> Let her not walk i' the sun. Conception is a blessing, but as your
> daughter may conceive, friend, look to't.   (2.2.181–86)

The sense of Hamlet's elliptical remark here is developed in 3.2, where he assaults Ophelia directly on the question of procreation. "Why wouldst thou be a breeder of sinners?" he asks her, then describes himself as one better not born, "crawling between earth and heaven" (120–29). A woman breeds sinners as a carcass breeds maggots, and it is the kiss of the (maggotlike) sun/son that makes it happen. The image of the sun is freighted with meaning, for Hamlet twice idealizes his father by comparing him to the solar deity Hyperion—both times by way of drawing in the most decisive fashion the boundary between the ideal manhood represented by his father and the contamination of fallen sexuality represented by Claudius:

So excellent a king, that was to this
Hyperion to a satyr.   (1.2.140)

And in the bedroom scene, to Gertrude:

Look here upon this picture and on this,
The counterfeit presentment of two brothers.
See what a grace was seated on this brow:
Hyperion's curls, the front of Jove himself. . . .   (3.4.53–56)

According to the hierarchical schema in terms of which Hamlet has been accustomed to think (but which Shakespeare's plays consistently call into question), the order of society nests in and is guaranteed by the order of nature, which itself reflects the order of the heavenly hierarchy. The place of the king with respect to his subjects may thus be thought by analogy with the centrality and elevation of the sun—and this seems to be more than a metaphor, because it reflects the ontological structure of the cosmos.[3] When Hamlet refers to his father as Hyperion, this one word links the principle of legitimate kingship to both the natural and the divine hierarchies. But the integrity of Hamlet's meaning-intention is betrayed by the very image that he uses to guarantee its ontological ground, for in the natural order of things the sun itself descends to an act of generation of abominable foulness.

The process of obsessional sliding from the culturally most elevated to the culturally most debased meaning, from the sublime or sublimated to the hyperliteral, is the dominant characteristic of Hamlet's mental functioning in the play as a whole; and it links him to the obsessionals studied by Freud.[4]

As in the case of Freud's neurotics, Hamlet's obsessiveness is motivated by sexual repression; but in *Hamlet* sexual repression is not the last word. What is at issue is the ultimate reality of organic being, the horror of the identity of the body of dissolution with the body of love, whether that body is male or female. This horror is thought through by Hamlet, all the way along the "progress through the guts of a beggar" that he knows a king may (and in some sense must) make (4.3.20). "A king": some king, any king, *the* king; which is to say Claudius, who is king, Hamlet, who should be, and above all his father, who is the true king, the sun-king of sublime imagination whose touch Hamlet wishes to believe never defiled his mother's flesh but which he also thinks as maggot breeding and maggot eaten. As he says to Claudius after killing Polonius:

> Your worm is your only emperor for diet: we fat all creatures else to
> fat us, and we fat ourselves for maggots; your fat king and your lean
> beggar is but variable service, two dishes, but to one table—that's
> the end.   (4.3.21–25)

We must be attentive to the difference in tonality of two linguistic
registers within which what seems like "the same" truth is uttered by
Hamlet. There is, on the one hand, a classical Christian meditation on
the transitoriness of earthly glory and on the corruptibility of the flesh, a
meditation that looks much like hyperliterality but the purpose of which
is precisely to stimulate the pursuit of purity as an asylum from natural
reduction. This is the register Hamlet uses when he declares, apparently
against Picoesque humanism,

> What a piece of work is a man, how noble in reason, how infinite in
> faculties, in form and moving, how express and admirable in action,
> how like an angel in apprehension, how like a god! . . . and yet to
> me what is this quintessence of dust?   (2.2.303–8)

His slightly earlier comment that "our monarchs and outstretch'd heroes
are beggars' shadows" belongs to this same register (2.2.263–64). These
two remarks in one sense say the same as the remarks I discussed earlier.
Man who is "like a god" descends to dust, just as the sun kisses carrion; a
king is only a beggar's shadow and may go a progress through his guts.
But "dust" and "shadow" communicate only the bringing low of the high
or the insubstantiality of earthly glory, the most conventional *topoi* of
literary reflection on the vanity of human life. These reflections thus
actually function as a prophylactic against the contamination of the thought
that obsesses Hamlet and from which he is in flight—the thought of the
nauseating, defiling character of the organicity through which glory must
make its transit on the way to dust.

It is this that sullies the purity of mourning beyond any philosophical
or religious prophylaxis. The lost object could be internalized, preserved
in its ideality by memory, but then what of this remnant that must be
dealt with, this thing of foulness that no concept of ideality or gambit of
dialectical reason can recuperate? It must be simply and totally excluded—
marked off by an absolutely impermeable boundary from the realm of
love. The rites of mourning, properly executed by the family, as Hegel
explains—and with the deceased properly mourned by a woman, as Hegel
perhaps disingenuously does not explain—are necessary to preserve the
substance of the dead from reduction by worms and water, the "uncon-

scious appetites and abstract entities" of nature.[5] But everything comes unhinged because Gertrude fails in her duty of mourning memorialization of the other Hamlet.

It is essential to the story that Gertrude not only bed down with Claudius but that she do so precipitously, defiling the sacred time during which she ought still to belong to her dead husband. The breach that is opened in Hamlet's consciousness is opened by the double blow of violated mourning and sexual betrayal; the temporal coincidence of these two unveils the deep relation that holds between them and opens the field of thanato-erotic anxiety to our inspection in an unprecedented way (cf. the discussion of *La Princesse de Clèves*, below).

So long as the thought of sexuality does not enter the picture, it is possible to contain the corrosiveness of the thought of the body of dissolution; sexuality is the advance agent of the "unconscious appetites" of nature, gnawing away at the substance of cultural ideals while the body is still alive. Venereal disease, which is one of Shakespeare's most pervasive images, functions as the material representation of the link between the body of dissolution and the body of love; thus the grave digger observes that he buries many "pocky corses" that are already rotten before they die (5.1.166–67).[6] Conversely, what Marilyn French has called "the principle of chaste constancy" in women holds in check the power of victorious corruption that is imaged by venereal rot.

When a man dies, thus, the feminine imperative of chaste constancy converges or becomes identical with that of mourning; and when Gertrude violates this double or single imperative, the barrier in Hamlet's imagination against the hyperliteral awareness of the body is violently opened in a way against which nothing can defend. For it is not just that the son is himself defiled/defiling, "crawling between earth and heaven," not just that he is the "sun" that could make Ophelia conceive. If that were the case—if the indwelling of the body of dissolution in the body of love were simply a matter of the unleashing of sexual lust—then Hamlet could purify himself by the practice of that reason-guided restraint that in the bedroom scene he enjoins on his mother. But "nature cannot choose his origin," as Hamlet has said (1.3.26), and no act of self-purification by Hamlet can undo the fact that it is from the impure loins of Gertrude, from the "rank sweat" of her "enseamed bed" (3.4.92), that he has issued. The corruption of sexuality belongs to Hamlet from his origin, from the dark and vicious place (as he believes) where he was gotten. Life itself belongs to the forces that must be marked off from life; this is the thought that torments Hamlet, the thought that he cannot stop elaborating and yet cannot assimilate to an economy of ongoing life. Hamlet may leap into Ophelia's grave as he declares himself the Dane or he may invoke Providence in resignation to his fate (5.2.219–24), but his philosophical or religious resignation is of a piece with his inability to affirm an ongoing life that is propagated as are maggots from a dead dog.

Hamlet thus anatomizes in a most economical fashion the structural or logical limit of this book, the question of the essential connection between the sexual body and the body of corruption.

If we consider eros in terms of the generic division comedy/tragedy, the account given by Andreas Capellanus in the first two books of *De Amore* is certainly comic. That very jealousy that in a tragic context—in *Othello*, for example—is the cause of tragedy is considered by Andreas Capelanus to be "the mother and the nurse of love" between courtly lovers; without jealousy, indeed, "true love may not exist."[7] Capellanus is closer to the satirical spirit of Ovid than he is to Bernart de Ventadorn or Arnaut Daniel; thus Capellanus has a section titled "How Love May Come to an End" in which he blandly lists the ways, including this one: "An old love also ends when a new one begins" (156).

Something approaching the sort of libidinal mobility projected by Capellanus's view of love is described by Madame de Lafayette as the courtly setting of *La Princesse de Clèves*, in which practically everyone is busy looking for a new lover, shedding an old lover, or deceiving the current one; but death repeatedly intrudes into the permutations of this combinatorium.[8] As a consequence, for Madame de Clèves the game of love is never worth the candle; erotic investment is for her from the outset too serious and painful to take any chances with. Jealousy (Capellanus's "mother and nurse of love") is for this young woman the ultimate anguish, the "worst of evils," and her first real taste of it seals her conviction that she will not submit herself to the possibility of its ultimate sting.[9]

This ultimate sting is represented to her imagination and to ours in the story that her husband tells her about two other lovers, Monsieur Sancerre and Madame de Tournon. This story contains a stunning exposé of the bad faith of the courtly lover and will be the focus of my discussion of the novel.

Madame de Clèves's erotic being is shaped by the courtly ideology that draws a sharp boundary between the role of wife and that of mistress. Thus, as wife to Monsieur de Clèves, she can have, within limits, a relation of genuine friendship and mutual regard with him;[10] as mistress or *domna* to her pursuer, Nemours, she can be the object of an irresistible and undying erotic passion. Given the character of Madame de Clèves, there is no possibility of a physical consummation of her role as mistress, but such consummation would be admissible within the rules of the erotics accepted at the court; as in Capellanus or courtly *fin'amors*, consummation is compatible with continued passion so long as it remains furtive, difficult, and uncertain. This is the case with Sancerre and Madame de Tournon; she has granted him her bed but keeps fending off his desire for permanent possession of her in marriage. Thus the ideological/psychological split between woman-as-mistress and woman-as-wife makes possible a sexual relationship of great intensity that can nevertheless be kept within carefully controlled boundaries, because the man's idealization of the woman is not subjected to the test of genuine conjugal proximity. The erotic expenditure of self is kept within bounds by the mental division of the beloved into a part (woman as erotic object) that is touched and a part (woman as full subject) that is not touched.

It is this division that is subjected to the most severe and ironic scrutiny in the interpolated story of the death of Madame de Tournon and the grief of her lover; Madame de Lafayette here exposes the interlocking mechanisms of idealization and denigration in courtly love within the context of their horizon in the problematic of mourning.

We could say that with this narrative Madame de Lafayette maps the alternate route away from the troubadours to that which Dante took; she represents the death of the beloved in a context of absolute nontranscendence, as the ironic undoing of the mechanisms of idealization. In particular, Madame de Lafayette perceives with unparalleled clarity the structure of retaliatory ejection, and she wires its circuit so ingeniously to that of idealizing bereavement that the pain of deceit flows endlessly with that of mourning, each intensifying the other and creating something like the perfect hell for the idealizing-denigrating lover. "I experience at once the pain of death and that of infidelity," says Sancerre; "they are two evils which have often been compared but which have never been felt at the same time by the same person" (185).

Idealization of the love object is, like its denigration, an attempt to introduce absolute assurance into libidinal relation. Madame de Tournon is thus for Sancerre "the most perfect thing that has ever been" (183). This idealization not only safeguards her image from the taint of possible deceitfulness, it in some measure enables this image to withstand the corrosive force of death. Because her image remains absolutely pure and perfect in Sancerre's mind, he experiences her death as absolute loss: eternal separation from the most perfect object.[11] But even though absolute loss in one sense heightens his pain to the limit, this pain has the character of *perfect mourning*—mourning that is absolutely unsullied, its object so idealized as to be beyond the touch of corruption of any type (whether physical or moral: anxiety treats them as though they were identical).

Into this scene of perfect mourning there intrudes the discovery that Madame de Tournon was in fact unfaithful—and unfaithful in the most thoroughgoing and calculating manner. But the interiorized image of the lost object is now sealed off beyond the touch of disfiguration, transcendentalized by death; she exists now as a mental object, defined as perfect in the most rigorous and unrevisable fashion by the idealizing trends of mourning. And yet the knowledge of her unfaithfulness is also ineluctable. "If I had learned of her alteration before her death, jealousy, anger, rage would have filled me and would have in some way hardened me against the pain of her loss," Sancerre declares (183); that is, he could have put in play the strategies of preemptive ejection. This did not happen; at the moment of her death he was not yet hardened and her loss therefore opened an unclosable wound, through which all of his being pours out toward her without reserve. But this very same object, which opens all his being by virtue of its perfection and its perfect faithfulness, is at the same time the most treacherous and deceitful of objects, so that the pain of loss is carried to its limit by the pain of deceit.

Sancerre is subject to the absolute conflict between deceit and loss because he had idealized to such a degree the image of Madame de Tournon. "Most perfect," "most faithful"—these are ideal predicates that will not bear application to mortal beings. This is not to say that the pain would be tolerable for a more realistic lover who made a similar discovery; it might not be very different. However, there would not be the absolutely clean split between the "good" object that dies and the "bad" object that is unfaithful.

But the two are split by Madame de Lafayette only so that she can suture them back together, so that the two types of painful affect ("pain of death," "pain of infidelity") can be experienced together. The strategy of denigration and preemptive ejection is explicitly evoked as a defense against mourning ("Jealousy, anger, rage . . . would in some way have hardened me"); but the idealization of the dead object, which appears to be the opposite of denigration, is a defensive strategy as well. Perfect mourning is triumphant because even if the suffering it unleashes is *almost* unbearable, it is insulated against the moral dissolution that emanates from infidelity. The dissociation of the pain of death from the pain of infidelity is thus motivated on the level of the figural consciousness by an impulse of bad faith; it is the ultimate form of idealization by which the threat of erotic relation is contained. The entire novel is an acid critique of courtly love as love that is kept alive by distance and deferral, and of the ambivalence by which denigration of the woman is the obverse of her idealization;[12] but it is in the Sancerre–de Tournon narrative that the libidinal structures involved are most perspicuously and profoundly probed.

The dubiousness of the impulse that divides between the pain of death and that of infidelity, and the force of the irony by which in this novel the two come back together, suggest that Madame de Lafayette considers the connection between them to be more intimate, more difficult to break, than a logical analysis of their distinctness would suggest. It is likely that this connection is relative to the context of a specific ethos—an ethos within which infidelity has an intense emotional significance—and that this is not the case in every cultural setting. But wherever infidelity does in fact acquire this affective charge, as in European literature at least since the troubadours, it becomes part of the problematic of mourning.

Of course "infidelity" (the word is anachronistic) is already an issue in Greek literature, famously in the case of Helen. The Greeks appear to have taken infidelity less lightly than Paul Veyne tells us was the case with the Romans;[13] nevertheless, the question does not appear to be intensively "psychologized" by either the Romans or the Greeks.

What is at issue since the troubadours is not the mere physical enjoyment of the woman's body by another man (a situation that is indeed presupposed in those famous exemplars of troubadour poetry in which the lady is married), or even the social humiliation involved, but the interplay of these factors with the question of the interior motions of the woman's spirit.[14] Fidelity in this strong sense is a matter of the directedness of the being of the beloved toward that of the lover, and, at the limit, of the unreserved pouring-out-toward-him of her being. In this sense Madame de Clèves is in fact unfaithful to her husband, since she gives the image of Nemours the place in her mind that should belong to him: a mental relation that is rendered visible in the famous scene in which she passionately admires the portrait of Nemours while he, unseen, watches her from his hiding place.

The possessiveness of the modern lover appears to be more probing and discriminating than that of the ancient lover; it is an endless and inconclusive speculation on the interiority of the beloved, seeking some absolute assurance of fidelity in the depth of her subjectivity.[15] Or of his; but it is primarily the male point of view that we find represented. "But yet, be true!": the reiteration of this injunction by Shakespeare's Troilus to Cressida stands as the ground bass of the libidinal being of an era that encompasses our own time.

CHAPTER SIX

Adam's Choice: *Paradise Lost*

*I*N "PARADISE LOST" MILTON STANDS ON BOTH SIDES OF THE QUES-
tion of eros. He is uncompromisingly committed to the Christian metaphysics and axiology that subordinate to the love of God the erotic bond
with a mortal individual; yet at the same time he is compelled by a conception of conjugal love that cannot ultimately be harmonized with the claims
of Christianity as these claims are reiterated within *Paradise Lost* itself.

We take our orientation initially from a single line, a line that represents the furthest limit of Milton's descent into the riddle of sexed being.
The line is spoken to Eve by Adam when, having learned of her disobedience, he declares his resolve to fall with her:

> if Death
> Consort with Thee, Death is to mee as Life. (9.953–54)

This line reprises the constitutive theme of the tradition of thanatoerotophobic misogyny, according to which it is the male's susceptibility to the
erotic allure of the female that drags him down to death. If Adam here
flies in the face of that tradition, embracing what it rejects, reinterpreting
death as life, no doubt we are meant by Milton to look on with horror, to
see in this acceptance of death only the sinful blindness of a being in the
grip of mortal eros. And yet the very same words, if they could be properly *meant*—and Adam must mean them with every iota of his being if
he is to choose as he does—would cut the knot of revulsion from organic
being that fuels the drive to transcendence.

Platonic and Christian transcendentalism treats death as a contingency, as something that afflicts life from without but does not touch its essence—an essence that is in principle always capable of being extricated from its involvement with death. But the idealizing tradition is simultaneously tormented by the sense that death burrows its way into the innermost sanctum of life, that death is not something that begins where life ceases but rather something that inhabits life in every moment, that it is the self-consumption of the flame of life itself. Platonizing Christianity thus defines organic life as death; yet if, according to this conception, life is death, this does not mean that death is life but that life is not truly life. What we mistakenly call life, organic life, is only a dark figure for a transcendent reality the essence of which repels death absolutely. This is the conception that Adam's words to Eve threaten to shatter.

According to James Grantham Turner, Milton is the only writer in the Christian tradition up to his time to ascribe sexual activity to unfallen Eve and Adam.[1] Augustine and others held prelapsarian sex to have been theoretically possible, but unrealized, probably because the Fall occurred so soon after the Creation. But in "hatching" the possibility that was given in the tradition, Turner remarks, Milton brings to light the "inherent contradictions" that could be left in unnoticed obscurity in the earlier accounts; Milton is left with the task of persuading us that Eve and Adam are "both sexual and innocent, . . . both perfect and ready to fall" (287). Turner thus brings us to the threshold of the problem in which we are interested.

But even the vast literary-theological context that Turner supplies does not quite suffice to tease out the threads of heterogeneous textuality that are entangled in the crucial passages that articulate the nature of Adam's erotic bond to Eve. Nor does it define fully the erotic project in which Milton is engaged. These passages are influenced by the language of erotic idealization that Milton inherits directly from Dante and Petrarch and more generally from the tradition we know loosely as "courtly love," the roots of which reach back to Ovid.[2] This is the tradition of erotic idealization that Milton himself names in the *Apology for Smectymnuus* as the framework of his poetic-erotic project. Beginning with an enthusiasm for the "elegiac poets," and supremely for Dante and Petrarch, Milton says in the *Apology* that he went on to courtly romance, then to Plato, and finally to the doctrine of Christian chastity.

We know from his Latin elegies and Italian sonnets how thoroughly Milton internalized the forms and language of the "elegiac poets"; he learned his craft from them at the most concrete level. Because the tropes of classical poetry that he learned to manipulate as a student are so frequently tropes of libidinal exuberance, this poetic apprenticeship initiated him from the outset into the problem of the purification of sexuality as a linguistic-poetic problem.

Even though in the *Apology for Smectymnuus* Milton gives a sanitized picture of the chaste idealizations of Dante and Petrarch, it is demonstrable that he was aware of the ambivalent complexity of love in Petrarch's *Rime*. As F. T. Prince pointed out, the form of Milton's *canzone* "Upon the Circumcision" is modeled very precisely on Petrarch's Poem 366;[3] and Poem 366, the last poem of the *Rime*, permanently problematizes the love that is celebrated in many of the earlier poems. Because, as Prince points out, Milton never before or after attempted such a complex formal scheme, it could be that Milton's poem marks the zone of a particularly laden confrontation.

Poem 366 is addressed to the Virgin Mary and constitutes a palinode, or recantation, of the speaker's earthly love, which is now referred to as the "blind ardor that flames here among foolish mortals" (20–21).[4] "Mortal beauty, acts, and words have burdened all my soul," the persona complains; "my days . . . have gone away amid wretchedness and sin" (79–91). The speaker asks for the mediation of the Virgin in his quest for salvation ("recommend me to your Son" [135]), but the image of Christ's wounds actually mediates between the Virgin's compassion and the speaker: "Virgin, turn those beautiful eyes that sorrowing saw the pitiless wounds in your dear Son's sweet limbs, to my perilous state" (22–25), "Lady of that King . . . in whose holy wounds I pray you to quiet my heart" (47–52).

Milton takes the cue for his entire poem from the moment in Petrarch's *canzone* at which Christ's "pitiless" wounds become the focus of the lover's prayer. But, as though impatient with the mystifications of Petrarch's rhetoric, Milton goes directly to what is only implied by Petrarch when he throws back the question of Christ's wounds from the crucifixion to its anticipation in the circumcision. Milton thus draws tighter the suggestion in Petrarch's poem that the rending of Christ's flesh is a figure for the erotic torment of the speaker; the circumcision localizes in a very precise way the specific sinfulness of the flesh from which Petrarch suffers.[5] We may thus read Milton as brushing aside the courtly trappings of Petrarch's mourning for his erotic waywardness: "On the Circumcision" goes straight to the most profound and pathetic reality that remains in the background of Petrarch's poem, the image of the infant phallus dripping innocent blood in atonement for the guilty sexuality of (primarily male) humanity.[6]

It should be apparent how complex the problematic of courtly idealization quickly becomes as soon as we get past the clichés about Petrarchan conventions.[7] The two *canzoni* by Petrarch and Milton remind us that, in the hands of a poet who takes Christianity seriously, the language of courtly love, because it is so disturbingly intertwined with that of Christian devotion, opens the question of human erotism in a most consequential fashion.[8]

We thus cannot dismiss as a superficial phenomenon, a matter of literary ornamentation, the courtly Petrarchan element in Milton's representation of Eve in *Paradise Lost*. Eve is the origin and essence of femininity in all the ambivalence of the signification that femininity has for Christianity in general and the Petrarchan tradition in particular. We could say that she splits the difference between Petrarch's Laura and the Virgin Mary, and thus presses to the limit the fundamental tensions of the courtly love complex.

We can trace Milton's development of the erotic idealization of his forebears in a direct line from his Italian sonnets 2, 4, 5, and 6 through *Comus* into *Paradise Lost*.[9] In sonnets 2 and 5 Milton mixes an element that is, I think, new and original into the idealization of his otherwise conventional *donna leggiadra*: he makes her into an Orphic singer ("so that even the tough mountain trees might respond"). The hypertrophy of the virtue of chastity in *Comus* obscures to a considerable degree the continuity of the Lady here with the *donna* of the sonnets, but it is evident that in *Comus* Milton is exploring a contiguous area in the territory of erotic awe. This Lady, too, is an Orphic singer: she breathes "Divine enchanting ravishment" (1.245), and her "sacred vehemence" is such "that dumb things would be moved to sympathize" (1.796). Her power over Comus, whom she declares unworthy to hear her Orphic eloquence, is a development of *topoi* initially explored in Sonnet 2, where the lady's *alta virtu* 'high virtue' and her Orphic song have such power that the *indegno* 'unworthy' is warned to guard the portals of his eyes and ears. And the Lady's invisible cordon of angels, drawn by her chastity to protect her from all evil, is the antecedent of Eve's "greatness of mind and nobleness," which "create an awe / about her, as a guard Angelic plac't" (*PL* 8.557–59).

The decisive moment in which Adam articulates his love for Eve in the courtly or elegiac language of love occurs in lines 529–33 of book 8. Here is the conceit Milton had used concerning the lover's heart in Sonnet 6:

> Sol troverete in tal parte men duro
> Ove Amor mise l'insanabil ago.

Only at a single point will you find it less unyielding: the point
where Love's dart has pierced incurably.

Now here is Adam's variant in *Paradise Lost:*

> here passion first I felt,
> Commotion strange, in all enjoyments else
> Superior and unmov'd, here only weak
> Against the charms of Beauty's powerful glance.

Adam's erotic idealization of Eve is the crux of the entire poem, for when
he tells Raphael that he is "here only weak" he identifies the chink in his
will through which, by the choice that this weakness motivates, sin and
death will pour into the world. Milton chooses or has no choice but to
avail himself of the language of courtly idealization at the moment in the
text when he represents this weakness the consequence of which will be
the Fall itself.

The angel Raphael immediately recognizes as culpable the weakness
that Adam confesses to him, and it might be argued that Raphael's
judgment indicates Milton's rejection of courtly love. But Adam has
earlier said something to God that God has not blamed and yet that
indicates, in terms resonating with Petrarch, the same erotic state as that
which the angel criticizes, which is in fact its antecedent condition. Here
is how Adam describes how he felt when he awoke from his dream of as
yet uncreated Eve:

> what seemed fair in all the world, seemed now
> Mean, or in her summed up, in her contained
> And in her looks, which from the time infused
> Sweetness into my heart, unfelt before,
> And into all things from her air inspired
> The spirit of love and amorous delight.
> She disappeared, and left me dark, I waked
> To find her, or forever to deplore
> Her loss, and other pleasures all abjure.   (8.472–80)

Adam is in Paradise, in the presence of God, and yet his erotic longing is
already so strong that he can in one moment of Eve's absence (an Eve
whom, moreover, he has so far seen only in a dream) plunge into the type
of erotic despair that gives rise to the *Rime sparse*.[10]

On the one hand, the ideal woman of courtly love appeals to the
noblest part of her lover's nature and refines it further. On the other hand,
she stimulates his libidinous urges and whips him into an uncontrollable

passion, a passion that in turn may become a resentment that leads to her denigration. In Dante's hands, the purity of the Lady is such that the latter element is utterly purged away and she is able to lead him to the threshold of the beatific vision. But Dante's achievement is unique in this respect, and with Petrarch we come back in touch with the ambivalence of the mainstream of the tradition. As Turner and Diane McColley[11] have shown in great detail, even unfallen Eve was in Milton's time assimilated in art and literature to the category of temptress or flawed vessel. But they also show that Milton systematically lifts unfallen Eve free of a multitude of taints traditionally ascribed to her; as McColley puts it, Milton "detoxifies numerous motifs associated with Eve" (*A Gust of Paradise,* 158). Any taint on Eve before the Fall would introduce into Milton's representation precisely those elements that reflect ambivalence in the courtly love tradition. Eve before the Fall must be as pure as Mary ("second Eve"), yet she also has the capacity to arouse desire and to satisfy it that Mary cannot have. Milton thus imagines a woman impossible for Dante or Petrarch to imagine: a perfectly pure woman who may be imagined making love and perhaps deriving pleasure from it.

We may thus imagine Milton as attempting to reconcile the spirituality of Dante with the sensuality of the troubadours, thus as reopening the problematic of *fin'amors* that Dante had in one way resolved but in another way merely foreclosed. In the process, Milton goes far beyond anything that precedes him in the courtly tradition; but we cannot grasp the precise nature of this step except in relation to that tradition.[12]

Everything else in the poem is there as a frame for the fall of Adam. If Eve had fallen but not Adam, then, according to the logic of the myth, humanity would not have fallen. Therefore everything in the poem leads back to Eve's hold on Adam's emotions and imagination. Milton's task is to conceive the nature of the bond that ties Adam to Eve in a way that will make comprehensible his choice to die with her. This bond is the crux of the entire poem; the Fall and thus the entire story depend on it. Milton must imagine the unfallen eroticism of Adam and Eve in a way that will preserve its innocence by living up to the highest standards of erotic idealization, while at the same time demonstrating the force of their erotic bond as something that will prove sufficient for Adam to choose Eve over obedience to God.[13]

Milton is thus confronted with the problem of motivation in a peculiarly profound sense of the term—or rather, in a profound double sense of the term. On the one hand, there is "psychological" motivation (why did Adam make this choice?); and on the other hand (but inseparably), there is the question of how this choice is to be represented in such a way that it follows from, is motivated (in Boris Tomaschevsky's sense of motivation) by, the linguistic texture of the preceding narrative. Milton's language is under enormous pressure here, and this pressure pushes it to a new, quasinovelistic mode of verisimilitude that at times passes into the sort of textuality we associate with Freud, Lawrence, and Bataille.

In the crucial exchange between Adam and Raphael in book 8, Milton records a moment of genuine and profound perplexity in relation to eros. We could call it indifferently a linguistic or psychosexual perplexity; the two are indistinguishable here because we are in a realm in which pieces of language of varying provenance (philosophical, theological, literary) are jostling against one another, only partly under Milton's control as he attempts radically to redefine human subjectivity in its relation to eros. To the degree that Milton attains or approaches a new kind of textuality or "motivation," the language of his poem evades ordering according to the classical theological, philosophical, and psychological categories that no longer determine its generation.[14]

My argument is not that the erotic element in *Paradise Lost* undermines or contradicts or deconstructs Milton's doctrine, but rather that the doctrinal architecture at a certain point leaves open a wide space within which other forces can play themselves out.[15] Paradise before the Fall is not a place without tensions, conflicts, and dangers; Adam and Eve bicker a bit and hurt each other's feelings; their sexual rapport seems imperfect.[16] But Stanley Fish, McColley, and others have shown that none of this necessarily means that they are already fallen, nor that God is to blame. Milton's theological machinery, resourcefully redeployed by the critic, can be adapted to explain most of the details of Adam and Eve's speech and behavior consistently with the hypothesis of free will. Since such a procedure sorts best with the apparent intention of the poem, critical rigor requires that we push it as far as it will go before we turn to alternative ways of reading. But after we have granted all the theological cunning to Milton's construction that conservative interpreters have seen, there remain other textual forces at work. It is these forces that I am going to track.

We must now reread the crucial debate between Raphael and Adam, patiently and microscopically disentangling the threads of heterogeneous textuality that are the inherited materials Milton must reweave in his attempt to conceive a full-fledged eros that could be justified in the very sight of his god.

After describing to Raphael his nuptial night with Eve, Adam continues as follows:

Thus I have told thee all my State, and brought
My Story to the sum of earthly bliss
Which I enjoy, and must confess to find
In all things else delight indeed, but such
As us'd or not, works in the mind no change,
Nor vehement desire, these delicacies
I mean of Taste, Sight, Smell, Herbs, Fruits, and Flow'rs,
Walks, and the melody of Birds; but here
Far otherwise, transported I behold,
Transported touch; here passion first I felt,
Commotion strange, in all enjoyments else
Superior and unmov'd, here only weak
Against the charm of Beauty's powerful glance.
Or Nature fail'd in mee, and left some part
Not proof enough such Object to sustain,
Or from my side subducting, took perhaps
More than enough; at least on her bestow'd
Too much of Ornament, in outward show
Elaborate, of inward less exact.
For well I understand in the prime end
Of Nature her th' inferior, in the mind
And inward Faculties, which most excel,
In outward also her resembling less
His Image who made both, and less expressing
The character of that Dominion giv'n
O'er other Creatures; yet when I approach
Her loveliness, so absolute she seems
And in herself complete, so well to know
Her own, that what she wills to do or say,
Seems wisest, virtuousest, discreetest, best;
All higher knowledge in her presence falls
Degraded, Wisdom in discourse with her
Loses discount'nanc't, and like folly shows;
Authority and Reason on her wait,
As one intended first, not after made
Occasionally, and to consummate all,
Greatness of mind and nobleness thir seat

Build in her loveliest, and create an awe
About her, as a guard Angelic plac't.   (8.521–59)

Adam here presents himself as worshipful lover of a woman who is far
above him—in direct contradiction to the authoritative view voiced by
Raphael according to which he is supposed to be Eve's superior.

It is now widely recognized that Raphael's rebuke of Adam is oddly off
the mark, an "angelic" view that fails to recognize the complexities of
human love.[17] From the present perspective, however, what is significant
is not Raphael's perspective but the character of his language—the fact
that, just as much as Adam's, it is derived from the Neoplatonic Renaissance discourse on love. The angel reminds Adam that he has incompletely Platonized his account of his love for Eve, for

> Love refines
> The thoughts, and heart enlarges, hath his seat
> In Reason, and is judicious, is the scale
> By which to heav'nly Love thou mays't ascend.   (589–92)

Yet Raphael completely leaves out the mediating factor of beauty, which,
although it is an ultimately ideal object of intellectual contemplation, is
initially encountered in physical bodies. Beauty is, thus, according to
Plato and to courtly Neoplatonism, rightly to be loved in this initial
encounter. It is true that this is a first stage, which is to be left behind, but
Raphael does not recognize it even as a stage. The notion of love as a
"scale" is thus oddly abstracted from the actual steps that constitute the
ascent. In his oration on love in *The Book of the Courtier*, Pietro Bembo
declares that

> beauty is the supreme adornment of everything; and it can be said
> that in some manner the good and the beautiful are identical, espe-
> cially in the human body. And the proximate cause of physical beauty
> is . . . the beauty of the soul which since it shares in true super-
> natural beauty makes whatever it touches resplendent and lovely, es-
> pecially if the body it inhabits is not of such base material that the
> soul cannot impress on it its own quality.[18]

It is true that Bembo will go on to say that "the body is something
altogether distinct from beauty" (338); but this insight at which the lover
ultimately arrives does not invalidate the doctrine of an earlier stage at
which "outward beauty" is recognized as "a true sign of inner goodness"
(330). Even if the essence of physicality is "altogether distinct" from that
of beauty, there is such a thing as the transfigured body: the body raised

above its mere physicality, annulled-yet-preserved (as a sign) by the power of beauty.

Raphael is thus not, as Barbara Lewalski claims, "a strict Neoplatonist . . . like Bembo in *The Courtier*";[19] it is, rather, to the "strict Neoplatonism," distinctly not of a courtly variety, of Marsilio Ficino that Raphael's view should be compared. Ficino in his commentary on the *Symposium*, known to the Renaissance as *De Amore*, does mention the beauty of the body as a reflection of the beauty of God. But he does so only, like Raphael, to denigrate the body and physical desire as something to be *immediately* seen through and left behind:

> If nature had given you the eyes of a lynx, my Socrates, [Ficino has Diotima say] so that you could penetrate with your vision whatever confronted you, that outwardly handsome body of your Alcibiades would seem very ugly to you. How valuable is that which you love, my friend? It is only a surface, or rather a color, that captivates you, or rather it is only a certain reflection of lights, and an insubstantial shadow. (speech 6. ch. 18)[20]

Thus there are even within what is called Renaissance Neoplatonism at least two doctrines on the nature of the erotic ascent; but these doctrines and what is at issue in the difference between them are not explicitly articulated in the poem. As a consequence of this lack of articulation, the confusion in the debate between man and angel will proliferate.

When Adam describes Eve's charm, he appears to describe it in just the ideal terms that Platonized eros requires at the first level of ascent; yet Raphael, who is working with a truncated notion of the ladder of love, accuses Adam of being drawn by mere animal physicality:

> But if the sense of touch whereby mankind
> Is propagated seem such dear delight
> Beyond all other, think the same voutsaf't
> To Cattle and each Beast   (8.579–82)

The angel has ignored the last part of Adam's speech (545–59) and has responded only to Adam's confession in the earlier part: in relation to Eve, but to no other pleasure, "transported I behold, / transported touch; here passion first I felt, / commotion strange, in all enjoyments else / Superior and unmoved, here only weak" (529–32). Adam then suggests that God "bestow'd / too much of Ornament" on Eve; thus Adam himself in these lines suggests that it is Eve's "outside" that overcomes him. But from line 546 on he gives a quite different account, in which Eve appears as "wisest, virtuousest, discreetest, best" (550). The contrast is between "For well I understand" in line 540 and "yet when I approach / Her loveliness" in 546–47. Adam here draws a clear and explicit distinction between an official doctrine to which he obediently assents—at least, as long as he isn't looking at Eve—and what he actually feels in Eve's presence. He "understands" that her charm is primarily exterior, yet when he is actually in her presence he feels her inward power. Is this only an illusion? If so, is it an illusion that arises simply from the charm of her "outside"? And can the charm of Eve's beauty really be reduced in the end, as the angel reduces it, to the "dear delight / Beyond all other" of "the sense of touch"?

Things are muddled here in the most thoroughgoing fashion. Even if it were indeed only the beauty of Eve's "outside" that is in question, this is not essentially a matter of touch. Adam's words had been: "transported I behold, / transported touch." His linkage of sight and touch, with sight preceding touch and giving to the pleasure of touch its highly specific character, is correct on any analysis of human sexual response. The courtly love tradition in particular always treats sight as the essential entryway for love; the sense of sight is the most "ideal" of the senses, the only one that "has beauty for its true object" (Castiglione, 334). When he ignores Adam's transport of vision, Raphael severs the pleasure of sexual touch from any ideal and even any ideational component; but it is precisely the role of ideation and idealization that is the crucial issue in Adam's speech, in the courtly love tradition, and in general in Christian thought concerning desire. The role of ideation is vividly illustrated by the episode of the dream of the siren, canto 19 of Dante's *Purgatorio*; likewise, Petrarch's Laura poems are almost entirely devoted to exploring the way in which the image of the beloved is mentally elaborated. For Raphael to ignore the issue of ideation and idealization is to miss precisely what needs to be addressed.

The ultimate source of the disturbance in Raphael's language is apparently the highly circumspect account by Adam in 8.510–20 of his love-making with Eve.

> To the Nuptial Bow'r
> I led her blushing like the Morn: all Heav'n,
> And happy Constellations on that hour
> Shed thir selectest influence; the Earth
> Gave sign of gratulation, and each Hill;
> Joyous the Birds; fresh Gales and gentle Airs

Whisper'd it to the Woods, and from thir wings
Flung Rose, flung Odors from the spicy Shrub,
Disporting, till the amorous Bird of Night
Sung Spousal, and bid haste the Ev'ning Star
On his Hill top, to light the bridal Lamp.

The angel appears to refer all of Adam's further remarks back to the raw
fact of copulation that is the referent of Adam's flowery language in those
lines. Nothing in Adam's speech suggests that the sexual act is *in and of
itself* the source of Adam's fascination with Eve; nevertheless, the conver-
sation with the angel calls attention to the very central place of sex in the
enjoyments of Eden.[21]

In Adam's earlier remarks Milton's text opens out in a way that creates
effects Milton then cannot quite control, and necessarily so, given the
conflicting imperatives that govern the writing of *Paradise Lost*. Adam
must be, as Turner says, "'unlibidinous' and 'enamored' at the same time"
(271), so that when he falls, the Fall should be persuasively motivated by
his erotic bond with Eve, yet not in such a way that would suggest that
this bond was already contaminated with fallenness before the Fall.

But Milton cannot by mere fiat translate into actuality what was held
by others to have been a possibility, because as soon as the abstract
"possibility" begins to be specified in detail as a lived reality it begins to
deform its relation to the doctrinal milieu that was capable of containing
it so long as it remained unrealized. But it only *begins* to do so; and my
entire reading will remain within the moment of this incipience. We
know how carefully Milton wraps layer on layer of theological rectifica-
tion over the opening that shows itself in the crucial passages. Something
concerning eros is incompletely articulated in *Paradise Lost,* and in the
space of this vagueness the gears of theology can spin freely until they find
their point of reengagement. I will close this space as I articulate more
fully what Milton partly utters, but the space that closes in my commentary remains forever open in Milton's text.

Now, Platonic and Neoplatonic eros ennobles desire by making it
transcendent, a force that in its essence goes beyond the individual physical being that arouses it to find its true goal in something higher. The
errancy to which eros is always by its nature exposed is that of becoming
attached to a particular created being and hence not finding its way to its
true goal. There is thus a structural instability in erotic idealization.
Insofar as the individual object of desire is *not* left behind on the road
upward, it infects the idealization with a very unideal component. This is

the tendency that Raphael detects in Adam's initial account of his love for Eve.

On the other hand, the erotic ascent correctly carried out repeats in a more refined or sublime fashion the dualism of body and spirit that it overcomes; and Adam's "corrected" reply to Raphael, though less crude than the angel's rebuke, reinscribes its terms. Raphael drove too deep a wedge between the sexual urge and the spirituality of love; Adam insists on reintegrating the two as eros. But the eros on which they agree is aetherealized; Milton's monism qualifies but does not undo the denigration of physical love implied in the angel's contemptuous contrast between angelic merging and the "restrained conveyance" of humans.[22] The lovemaking of Adam and Eve is justified as pure in the last instance by virtue of what it tends toward, its *telos*. Someday, if they stay on the ladder of spiritual ascent, they will be able to make angelic love; and the implication is that in some way this upward tendency is already at work in their lovemaking. If we do not look too closely into the matter, it all seems to make some sort of overall sense as an adaptation of Platonic eros. The concept of angelic sex as *telos* of Adam and Eve's lovemaking lifts some lingering onus attaching to the physical act of sex; it eradicates the element that, however sublimed or sublated by its transformation into one element in a total moral-spiritual phenomenon, the physical act of sex still shares with the animals. But the very fact that it lifts this onus implies that it is there to be lifted. Which means that Adam and Eve's lovemaking is not entirely pure, or, more precisely, that Milton has been unable to work out the terms in which such a purity could be conceived. Milton replaces the absolute dualism of body and spirit with a permeable dualism of dense substance and rarified substance; but dense substance inherits the embarrassment that attaches to body in the old dualism. If Adam is "half-abash't" by the angel's reproach, it is because there remains a demi-shamefulness in the conception of sex by "restrained conveyance"; hence also, apparently, the necessity for Eve's sexual modesty.[23]

What Milton appears to aim at is the notion that physical lovemaking, in its unfallen state, would be the *equivalent* of a perfect interpenetration of the angelic sort. But he cannot quite get around the difficulty that the tradition has always conceived of the passionate body as an impurity that stands in the way of such interpenetration. Thus Adam's exchange with Raphael leaves us with an ambiguous defense of physical sex. The impulse that drives it is held to be pure in its ultimate tendency, but Raphael's criticism of the impurity of the physical component is never controverted.[24]

The focus on the question of dense versus aethereal bodies in the debate between Raphael and Adam only distracts attention from a more fundamental question, which is that of the focus of the being of the creature on the creator. It is a question, for the tradition and for *Paradise Lost*, of never forgetting, never allowing out of one's consciousness, the relation of dependence or indebtedness to the source and maintainer of one's existence.[25] By the lights of the Christian cultural constellation that enforces the sense of sexual guilt, Adam's "passion" and "transport" in his lovemaking with Eve violate the essential boundary between love and concupiscence. It is precisely the transport of sexual passion that classical Christian thought was concerned to proscribe, those motions within the self that arise from another center than that of the conscious volition and then carry the conscious self away into the darkness. Here is how Augustine, who knew about sex from intense personal experience, describes this motion:

> [Sexual *libido*] assumes power not only over the whole body and not only from the outside, but also internally; it disturbs the whole man, when the mental emotion combines and mingles with the physical craving, resulting in a pleasure surpassing all physical delights. So intense is the pleasure that when it reaches its climax there is an almost total extinction of mental alertness; the intellectual sentries, as it were, are overwhelmed. (14.16)[26]

The question of the sinfulness of the flesh thus resolves itself into the question of measure. Aquinas and Luther will agree that there could have been sex in Paradise, and even that it would have been very pleasurable sex, indeed; but they will insist nevertheless that it would have had to be controlled, measured.[27] Luther tells us it would have been "a noble delight, such as there was at the time in eating and drinking";[28] and Aquinas paradoxically suggests that Paradisal sex would have been *more intense* than sex as we know it, yet that there would have been nothing in it that was *ratione non moderaretur* 'not tempered by reason'.[29]

Raphael calls Adam to account for crossing the boundary of measure ("In loving thou dost well, in passion not" [8.588]), and Adam never directly addresses the criticism. He says that he is delighted more by Eve's "graceful acts" than her sexual allure, and that he remains a reasonable being, capable of judging the objects he perceives (8.595–611); he says nothing more about the point at issue, his mental state during his sexual transports. Yet he then appears to turn the tables on the angel by asking about angelic sex, which leads to Raphael's description—but in aethereal terms—of a total interpenetration of lovers such as the transports of human sexuality can only approximate.

Milton is trying in Adam's discourse to define as allowable what the tradition tells him is not allowed: unbound erotic pleasure in ultimate union with a mortal beloved. He tries to define a form of such pleasure that will still count as obedience to God, and he does so in terms adapted from the language of courtly idealization. Erotic transport can then be justified in courtly Neoplatonic terms, but only so long as the precise terms of the justification are not questioned. When he rearticulates the nature of his love for Eve, Adam justifies his erotic passion by translating it into a longing for spiritual-aethereal merging. This is persuasive, for Milton and for us, because physical love does indeed contain something like this urge to "enter in and be wholly absorbed, body in body," as Lucretius says. But this account, true as far as it goes, represses what is stirring in the depths of Adam's *first* account of his passion, the sense of the deathly essence of eros. Milton is in this first account beginning to mobilize the force that will carry Adam to his choice of death. Nevertheless, already in the first account he overlays this force with the idealization of Eve that opens the way to the competing, Platonized version of eros. This is not just an overlay, of course, because it really is Eve's beauty and moral-intellectual qualities that fan the flame of Adam's love; but the courtly extravagance of Adam's idealization of Eve throws a veil over the question of the physical aspect of Adam's erotic pleasure in her.[30]

Whether or not Adam is still fully in command of his unstained free will at the time of his exchange with Raphael, as the conservative interpreters hold, the point at which he might break down has been identified with great precision: his weakness is for the "too much" of Eve's beauty and erotic charm (8.538). And it is clear where this too much originated: it was given to her by God. The question is: Why? Why would God make Eve so attractive that Adam would be in danger of forgetting God for her sake? Raphael's explanation is simple and to the point: she was "made so adorn for thy delight the more" (576).[31]

This explanation seems to me endlessly fascinating. God made Eve so delightful to Adam that when he is in her presence she clouds his unfallen reason. God did this to heighten Adam's pleasure—to heighten it, apparently, to the limit. Eve is the Paradise of Paradise (remember that "Eden" means "delight"; this is clearly always in Milton's mind), "the sum of earthly bliss" (8.522). Compared to her everything else seems "mean" (473), and if he were to lose her, Adam has already said after seeing her in his dream, he would "other pleasures all abjure" (480). Adam lives in Paradise and shares the companionship of God himself; and yet he declares that he would give all this up if he could not have Eve as well. Is not Milton already at this point revising the orthodox account in a radical and indeed unacceptable way?

Genesis merely states that Eve offered Adam the fruit and he ate of it; and it is truly striking how little Augustine or Luther or Aquinas have to say about why Adam ate, as though his motive were essentially simple and transparent. But Milton wants to imagine the experienced reality of Adam's choice, the passional-erotic force of the love that makes Adam choose to die rather than lose Eve. Here we are once again involved in issues of literary history. It does not, it cannot, occur to Augustine or Aquinas to inquire so closely into the subjectivity of Adam; a lengthy literary elaboration of the language of erotic subjectivity, which Milton has at his disposal but they do not, is required before we can arrive at Milton's quasinovelistic representation of the nuptial intimacy of Adam and Eve.

But Milton goes further. He not only represents the complex and ambivalent detail of Adam's love for Eve, he presses the logic of his representation to its necessary conclusion. He sees that the physical act of love cannot be a mere adjunct to Edenic happiness; if love is eros in the fullest sense (as Adam makes Raphael admit), then lovemaking is its consummation—the full, final flowering of spiritual-physical delight, the zenith of satisfied desire. And if Eve is for Adam the sum of all delight, the Paradise of Paradise, without which all the rest would not be Paradise, then it follows that the essence of the Fall as loss of delight is for Adam the loss of their unfallen eroticism.

Milton thus represents the immediate effect of Adam's eating of the apple as an erotic transport that will leave them forever exiled from their earlier delight. Yet while they are actually in the midst of their intoxicated rapture, they experience their lovemaking as a pleasure beyond any previous pleasure. "Never did thy Beauty . . . so inflame my sense / With ardor to enjoy thee, fairer now / Than ever" (9.1029–32), says Adam, and Eve's eye in return darts "contagious fire" (1036). The zenith of fallen, like that of unfallen, pleasure, is sexual love. When Milton looks before the Fall and when he looks after, this is what he sees. The agony of the Fall, the essence of the loss that obsesses Milton's imagination, is the loss of that unfettered and unreproved, complete, physical/moral/intellectual pleasure of the body and being of Eve that Adam once enjoyed—a pleasure whose consummation or "Seal" is sex. It is this that puts the sharpest edge on Adam's suffering. If he had taken less erotic delight in

Eve, he would not have chosen to die with her; but then he would not have known ultimate delight, and Eden would not have been Eden. Nor would the Fall have the peculiar bitterness it has, as loss of ultimate delight. In proportion as Adam's unfallen erotic joy is powerful enough to be the fulfillment of Edenic delight, it is also powerful enough that he chooses to disobey God rather than give it up. But because he disobeys he loses what he disobeyed in order to keep.

Pre-Fall and post-Fall lovemaking: the two scenes are a matched pair. We are clearly meant to read them next to each other. They are opposites; but one leads to the other. The first scene does not *cause* the second; it is utterly spotless. And yet it is the sine qua non of the second. It is the scene of Adam's transport, matrix of the erotic blindness that will take hold of him at the crucial moment.

Despite his criticism of Augustine's view of sexuality, Milton is in some ways very close to Augustine. They both represent sexuality as something constitutive of the being of humanity in the deepest and most inescapable way.[32] Milton represents dramatically what Augustine articulates conceptually: that death is inscribed in the motions of sexual passion, that the self slips away from itself in erotic transport, which thus prefigures death. For Augustine this means that sexual passion must be abjured; but Milton in *Paradise Lost* tries to conceive a form of it that could be reconciled with unfallenness, an erotic intoxication that is not lust—even though while its spell lasts it shares with lust the ability to overthrow the hierarchy of reason. This unfallen passion is to be distinguishable in its essence from the passion that comes with the Fall; but it must communicate, also in an essential manner, with fallen passion. After all, what would any passion be that did not transport the self? And yet that is precisely what Augustine (with Christian orthodoxy in general) jettisons from his vision of Paradisal sexuality.

Milton must confront the essential communication between innocent and fallen eros because he must cross the threshold of Adam's choice, the choice that is motivated by "the acceptable ravishment of pre-lapsarian love" (Turner, 298). Milton knows that the choice of eros is necessarily the choice of death, that even in Paradise what he imagines is unimaginable except in relation to that excess that violates the conditions of eternal life, that opens a blank in consciousness, a space of forgetfulness in which the conscious subject's self-possession is broken and something passes that has no now, only a before and an after. The relation to God can only exist in that before and after; it is obliterated in the blank that comes between.

For Adam, thus, the moment of choice is elided, does not belong to conscious volition; the crucial moment, the crux of the entire poem, does not take place. It is announced retrospectively, as the foregone conclusion entailed by the present perfect of Eve's fall:

> some cursed fraud
> Of Enemy hath beguil'd thee, yet unknown,
> *And mee with thee hath ruin'd,* for with thee
> Certain my resolution is to Die.   (9.904–7; emphasis added)

Eve deliberates carefully before she eats the apple, but Adam not only does not deliberate, he does not, strictly speaking, decide; he finds that he has decided.[33] Adam discovers his choice rather than makes it. His motive is erotic love; but Milton conceives this eros not as an appetite, or as one passion among others. He sees it, rather, as that which springs from the essential constitution of Adam's being, or which is essentially constitutive of it, *even before the Fall.* Erotic passion is defined in the Christian anthropology as something that supervenes on the proper essence of the human, that afflicts or deforms it from the outside. It is a consequence of the Fall; and even though in fallen humanity it has wormed its way into the interior of the self, this fallen self is understood to be a deformation of the image of the creator that was in the beginning stamped on the creature as his and her own proper being. But Milton conceives what moves Adam and Eve, or at least Adam, before the Fall not as a supervening deformation but as the essence of the essence.

The "Bond of Nature" of which Adam speaks is not identical with the drive to genital consummation, though it is something of which that drive is a direct and essential expression. Adam chooses himself, his ownmost ownness, and in so doing chooses to die.

> So forcible within my heart I feel
> The Bond of Nature draw me to my own,
> My own in thee, for what thou art is mine;
> Our State cannot be sever'd, we are one,
> One Flesh; to lose thee were to lose myself.   (9.955–59)

It might appear, then, that, when push comes to shove, the male's narcissism comes to the fore, as the desire originating in lack unmasks itself in the imperious reassertion of ownership.

But if it is true that Eve's distinctness as other-than-Adam is in one sense effaced, this is not the whole story.

Adam's declaration to Eve that "what thou art is mine" is complicated in a crucial way by the fact that she, the missing and purportedly subordinate half, has now enjoyed an autonomous course of development; she has veered away on an eccentric trajectory of her own and is no longer the same as she was when she left.

I must remind the reader once more (the point is crucial) that, as Turner and McColley have shown, Milton goes strongly against the tradition of literary-artistic representation of Eve in his account of her fall. Eve's temptation was characteristically used as the occasion for diatribes accusing the female mind of "triviality, newfangledness, and even a love of what is prohibited and evil" (Turner, 290); Milton's Eve is, by contrast, won over by what appears to her the "Reason" and "Truth" with which the Serpent's words are "impregned" (9.737–38). Her sin is thus rooted not in the kind of corrupt desire associated with the demeaning cultural stereotype of women but in her independent-minded empiricism that trusts the evidence of her senses and her own reasoning procedures.[34]

That Eve's motive for desiring the fruit is in Milton primarily the desire for knowledge is manifest; what is not so obvious is the precise form of her understanding of what knowledge is and does, of why it is valuable. In her interior deliberation before she eats the fruit, Eve notes that God's prohibition "infers the good" communicated by the fruit, as well as Adam and Eve's "want" of it, and she then describes their "want" in this way:

> For good unknown, sure is not had, or had
> And yet unknown is as not had at all.   (756–57)

These lines echo the Platonic doctrine of the *Philebus* that a pleasure not consciously and rationally known as such would be no pleasure at all in the human sense but something appropriate to the lowest animals. Socrates in the *Philebus* speaks of a "whole life" lived Edenically "in the enjoyment of the greatest pleasures"; but even this life, he claims, would not be desirable if one were "without reason, memory, knowledge and true judgment," so that "you would . . . be unaware whether you were, or were not, enjoying yourself" (21a–d).

Milton knew the *Philebus*, which was one of the fundamental Platonic texts for the Italian Neoplatonists, and he may also have known Ficino's commentary on the *Philebus*, in which Ficino declares that "*to know* [*sapere*] is the common term" for the various faculties listed by Plato. The life of pleasure without *sapientia*, Ficino concludes, would be "the one closest to death, the one having the least of life to it."[35]

Plato and Ficino conceive the life without *sapientia* of pleasure as that of a very primitive organism—a jellyfish or oyster; the question of knowledge must be rearticulated at a higher dialectical level in the case of Adam and Eve, who obviously do possess the intellectual faculties of memory and reason. Thus in Eve's formulation it is not a simple pleasure of sensation but a "good" that is said to be nonexistent if "had . . . yet unknown." Milton's dialectical acumen in thus interpreting the motive of her fall is corroborated by Hegel, who also reads Genesis in terms of a reassertion at a higher dialectical level of the primitive distinction between immediate existence and knowledge. For Hegel, Adam and Eve possess a primary form of reason that does not know itself as such but is in some way still "dispersed into the multifariousness of its consciousness" and must now "become an 'other' to its own self," leaving its unity with itself—a unity that is innocent, not-nocent—in order to withdraw into itself in the "self-centeredness" of "knowing as such."[36] This withdrawal of the knowing self from the immediacy of consciousness in order that it may know that it knows is what Christianity condemns as evil, but Milton in his conception of Eve's motive comes close to grasping its dialectical necessity in Hegelian fashion.

But for Milton an essential aspect of this moment of the othering of itself of reason is the fact that it is a woman who accomplishes it—a fact altogether ignored by Hegel. This is a striking omission given that Hegel is, like Milton, commenting on Genesis. Indeed, Eve is not just *a* woman but *the* woman, the universal woman or archetype of womanhood. Milton reconceives the essence of this archetype as the drive to knowledge in the most fundamental philosophical sense of knowledge.

The drive to knowledge is tied up in a complex fashion with the question of gender and with that of Adam's desire for Eve. This is true because Eve's drive to knowledge, to the "self-centeredness" of "knowing as such," leads her not only to the "othering" of herself from her own self-immediacy but also to her separation from Adam—a separation he does not want and against which he struggles. Eve's dissatisfaction with the order of Paradise is evident from her first moments of consciousness, when she prefers the sight of her own face in the water to that of Adam.[37] Even though this initial division is quickly papered over, it manifests itself once more in her insistence to Adam that having to be always at his side is no Paradise (9.322–41). Adam himself suspects that her real reason for wanting to go off by herself is not the exigencies of gardening but that she gets tired of him ("But if much converse perhaps / Thee satiate, to short absence I could yield" [9.247–48]).

Thus it would be simplistic to see Adam's assertion that Eve is his own as a mere reabsorption of his "other half"; Eve has been from the outset a potentially dissonant force, a force that with her fall catastrophically ruptures the phallogocentric economy of Paradise.

What Adam accepts as his own is that which the woman has become on her own and against his will; within the limits of that moment, at least, he accepts her violation of the law of the father and the punishment that goes with it.[38] We must balance Adam's "what thou art is mine" with his earlier declaration to Raphael that his love for her is so overwhelming because she seems "so well to know her own" (8.548–49). Of course at that moment Adam had no inkling of the degree and kind of knowledge at which Eve would shortly arrive; but his initial response even then is to accept Eve's accession to this knowledge.

Here the structure and tonality of his mental and verbal deliberations become crucial. His first response to what Eve has done is horror; yet he never considers the possibility of leaving her in the lurch (9.896–916). When he finally opens his mouth to speak, he addresses her in a tone that, considering the circumstances, is astonishing. He comes across as consternated, but calm, and above all, courteous: "Bold deed hast thou presum'd advent'rous Eve. . . ." (921). The reproach implied in "presum'd" and perhaps in "advent'rous" is restrained by the tone of respect and is followed immediately by the relinquishment of all regret: "But past who can recall, or done undo?" For the next twenty-four lines, Adam tries to put the best light on the matter; but all this, we already know from his earlier, silent, declaration ("with thee / Certain my resolution is to Die"), is of secondary importance. His decision has already been made, even though when he speaks aloud he withholds it until last:

However I with thee have fixt my Lot,
Certain to undergo like doom.   (9.952–53)

"However" here means: however all that may be; whether or not the possible palliatives I have been voicing turn out or not; regardless, here is my decision.

When Adam now declares that it is his "own" in her that draws him, that *what she is is his,* the patriarchal drive to proprietorship over the female is pushed beyond its limit, undoes itself in its reassertion. This is so because, in refusing to give up ownership, Adam gives up that which ownership of women has always been designed to secure: that the woman be kept within bounds, restricted to the economy of the household, her sexuality and her own project of knowledge kept at bay so that they do not undermine the authority and drain the vital energy of the male.

That death consorts with the woman is certain, in *Paradise Lost* and in the main line of the Graeco-Hebraic-Christian tradition. That the male could preserve himself incorruptible by regulating his relation to the woman or by shunning her altogether is the corollary of this rule.[39] Adam has not yet eaten of the fruit but is already feeling the surge of compelling drive that will not bear sublimation, because now it is no longer all that is "wisest, virtuousest, discreetest, best" that is Eve's consort. When he beds Eve now, Adam knows, he will be bedding death. But he doesn't care, because he's in the grip of the erotic rapture that Diotima calls the lowest level of eros and that Nietzsche in one mood calls nobility.[40] This is also what Milton calls fallenness; but this does not prevent him from imagining it in the most consummate fashion.

When Adam makes his resolution to die with Eve, he takes precisely the step that the entire moral-ontotheological tradition is constructed to circumvent. He accepts the absolute expenditure that is entailed in mortal love. But he doesn't entirely know what he's doing, and he will not be able to stand by his choice. The condition of his being able to do it is that he still sees Eve through the veil of idealization, and that the pressure of the erotic drive is up. She's been gone all day, and Adam, who didn't want her to go in the first place (and as McColley argues, not just because he feared for her safety), has been "waiting desirous her return," weaving her a garland of flowers, while "Great joy he promis'd to his thoughts, and new / Solace in her return, so long delay'd" (9.839–44).[41] It is in this mood that he is suddenly and jarringly confronted with the possibility of being parted from Eve. Eating the fruit then strips away the courtly idealization of his view of Eve, but it heightens his erotic fervor into physical arousal, and in this state the veil of idealization is not missed. But when the pressure of the sex drive is released Adam is overwhelmed by what he now sees nakedly.

Of course it is *both* he and she who become aroused, and both are subsequently "naked left / To guilty shame" (1058). But this arousal and this shame have a different meaning for Adam than they do for Eve.

The first time Adam saw Eve she was naked and apparently open to his sexual desire. He approached her, and *immediately* pressed for sexual consummation (8.484–511). "And they shall be one Flesh, one Heart, one Soul" (8.499), Adam declared as he moved in on the newly glimpsed Eve, with this utterance sanctioning and sanctifying his exigent desire.

With Adam and Eve we are in unfamiliar erotic territory; none of the ordinary barriers to sexual consummation are evident. Yet the conventions of courtly lovemaking have such imaginative force for Milton that he must envision their spontaneous birth, in at least a minimal form, in the first Paradisal moment of erotic encounter. Eve must throw up a barrier of some sort, one that does not definitively push away Adam's desire but that slows it down, deferring his gratification and in the brief interim calling forth the ceremony of courtship. The naked directness of Adam's sexual excitement must be channeled into a mental/linguistic elaboration of the qualities of Eve that will mediate his approach to her. She must initially turn away, then after coming around she must blush and yield to Adam's impetuous ardor only with that "sweet, reluctant, amorous delay" which is a general characteristic of her "subjection" to Adam.[42]

> She heard me thus, and though divinely brought,
> Yet Innocence and Virgin Modesty,
> Her virtue and the conscience of her worth,
> That would be woo'd, and not unsought be won,
> Not obvious, not intrusive, but retir'd,
> The more desirable, or to say all,
> Nature herself, though pure of sinful thought,
> Wrought in her so, that seeing me, she turn'd;
> I follow'd her, she what was Honor knew,
> And with obsequious Majesty approv'd
> My pleaded reason. To the Nuptial Bow'r
> I led her blushing like the Morn.   (8.500–511)

There's no getting around it; in this tradition it's the woman who has to tame the impetuous desire of the man, purify and elevate his impulses. For the courtly tradition to face the truth of nature is to face the woman as knower in the full biblical sense of knowledge. When the veil is removed, it is from the woman that it is removed. The man was more or less unveiled already—that is, his desire was.

Milton does not scruple to represent the scene that is the undoing of all erotic idealization. It is not as explicit as what we are used to today, but it is explicit enough. The fruit "carnal desire inflaming hee on Eve / Began to cast lascivious Eyes, she him / As wantonly repaid; in Lust they burn" (9.1013–15); Adam "forbore not glance or toy / of amorous intent, well understood / of *Eve*, whose Eye darted contagious Fire" (1034–36). A naked man with an erection giving lewd signals to a naked woman who eyes his naked body with equal and unveiled desire: that's the picture, no mistake. And the woman is Mother Eve. It is as though Milton the regicide here dares even to unveil the primal scene.

If, according to the logic of doctrine, the second lovemaking scene is a fall from the first, according to a certain logic of representation everything else builds up to this moment; this is the moment of breakthrough or revelation. Revelation in what is perhaps the deepest sense, as unveiling of the truth of nakedness as the nakedness of the genitals. The signs of concupiscence are visible in their faces, but it is upward from the sexual parts ("most / to shame obnoxious" [9.1093–94]) that shame radiates; the genitalia are the physical locale of sinfulness and shame and the sense of disobedience.[43] Technically, of course, their sin is their disobedience in eating the apple; but the apple turns out to be an aphrodisiac, and it is the subsequent lovemaking that bears all the weight of the sense of fallenness: Milton calls this lovemaking the "Seal" of their mutual guilt (9.1043), as though this were what makes its nature fully manifest, both confirming it and making it irreversible.

Adam implies that the aphrodisiac effect of the apple is rooted in the pleasure of transgression: "if such pleasure be / In things to us forbidden, it might be wish'd / For this one Tree had been forbidden ten" (1024–26). This is a pleasure-in-dissolution, pleasure heightened by the violation of boundaries and restraints that it involves. It is true that ecstatic dissolution or liquefaction is as much the goal of the religious mystic as it is that of the sensual lover. That's why the mystic finds the language of erotic union so usable. Nevertheless, there is good liquefaction and bad liquefaction: only dissolution into the will of the father is guiltless. Bataille remarks that Christian mystics have noted without embarrassment their tendency to ejaculate in the midst of their godly transport,[44] which vividly demonstrates that unrestraint is not necessarily transgression, the dissolution of a boundary not necessarily the violation of an interdict.[45] Similarly, transport with a mortal lover might be justified provided it does not stop there, at the boundary of the beloved individual, but passes on to the source of all individuated beings.

Now, carnality is the essence of the perversion of love; to turn from God to created beings involves turning toward "the world" as the realm of physical bodies. And sexual desire, Augustine explains, is the essence of carnality, the most deeply seated, ineradicable, and disturbing of cravings— because it is excited by a pleasure surpassing all others (*CG* 14.16). But "it was not the corruptible flesh that made the soul sinful; it was the sinful soul that made the flesh corruptible" (*CG* 14.3); thus the evil in sexual lust must finally be understood not in terms of physicality as such but rather in terms of the question of *the direction in which love flows.* Sinful desire need not be "lustful" in the sense that its object is physical pleasure. Adam could love Eve with a courtly, idealizing love that did not involve sexual contact; and this love could still be, in Augustine's terms, "fornication against God" in proportion as it absorbed Adam's being and made him forgetful of God.[46] Thus even if we accept that Adam and Eve's fallen sex involves a carnal coarseness that was not there in their innocence, their unfallen lovemaking is not thereby exonerated of the stigma of culpable *passion* that was laid on it by Raphael when he reminded Adam that love should be "the scale / by which to heav'nly Love thou may'st ascend" (8.591–92). Adam's "passion" for Eve is consummated in the physical act of sex; but it is just as much present in his awe of her, in his feeling that, as he had said to Raphael, Eve is "absolute," "in herself complete" (8.547–48). In the context of the doctrine of Platonic-Augustinian eros, these words are decisive. They mean that *Eve is it,* she is the end point, the goal, not a rung on the ladder of eros; precisely what Raphael warned Adam against.[47]

But if unfallen lovemaking and even unfallen love was already passionate, unmeasured, ecstatic, thus already contained the seed of death within it, then what boundary is transgressed in Adam and Eve's passage to fallen eroticism? They are ashamed now, as they were not before; but what are they conscious of that makes them ashamed, if not of having turned from the creator to the creature, which is what Adam had already done?

There is no doubt that Milton is committed to the distinction between innocent and concupiscent sex; the question is exactly how he proposes to articulate the distinction. Recent apologists for *Paradise Lost* have been too willing to accept the author's intention for the actual deed; thus Turner scrupulously lists all the similarities in the description of fallen and unfallen sex and then infers from its very closeness that the similarity is self-consciously ironic (301–3). But C. S. Lewis was sure that this similarity simply meant that Milton had failed clearly to distinguish between lust and innocence. The one persuasive note that Lewis grants Milton is the sense that Eve is now becoming "a *thing*" to Adam, a sex object as we would say, and that "she does not mind" (*Preface*, 128). No doubt Lewis has his finger on something important here; Milton does in some measure suggest the transition to "mere fucking" by Adam and Eve. "Never did thy Beauty . . . so inflame my sense with ardor to enjoy thee," Adam says, and there is an unmistakable tone of coarseness in the appetitiveness of these words that contrasts sharply with his earlier language, if not with the exigency of his earlier approach. If Eve's lust meets Adam's, this does not necessarily resolve the ethical situation; the modern ideal of mutual consent does not automatically lay to rest the problem of the objectification of the other that always bedevils sexual relation.

Nevertheless, the plausible distinction between making love and merely fucking is indicated only by Adam's switch in linguistic register from courtly indirectness to appetitive frankness, and we do not know enough about Adam's or Eve's interiority to be able to carry through the detailed analysis of the change that takes place.[48] With respect to Eve's erotic subjectivity, indeed, we know nearly nothing; so it is mainly of Adam that we must speak. And concerning Adam we know that his unfallen desire for Eve was "passion" and "transport" even if, in some evident yet difficult to define sense (given the ineluctable fact of erection), it remained noncarnal.[49]

It seems, then, that the difference between fallen and unfallen eroticism in *Paradise Lost* is not the classical difference addressed by Raphael, the difference between moderation and transport, but that between idealization and de-idealization of the beloved woman. And the way to the de-idealization of Eve is prepared by the fact that her idealization was itself already fractured. It was fractured in its relation to the Christian axiomatics by its contamination with "courtly" erotic idealization in its non-Platonic form, as the idealization of the beloved herself, who was seen as "absolute" and "in herself complete" rather than as a step on the way to the true terminus of love.

For Christianity, both guilt, with its consequent shame, and death are the result of disobedience; and guilt is intrinsic to the sexual act insofar as this act violates the boundary of conscious rationality and unleashes an unmeasured pleasure. Milton accepts the linkage between sexual guilt or shame and death, but he also imagines a sexual transport *without guilt;* he posits the connection between transport and guilt as accidental and thus severable. By displacing the genesis of guilt from sexual transport onto the de-idealization of the object, Milton creates a persuasive account of how sexual guilt and death enter the scene at the same time. On this level of *Paradise Lost,* sexual guilt and death are essentially linked, and Milton imagines a world without sexual guilt as also, necessarily, a world without death.

What he cannot imagine, in the sense of holding it explicitly before his consciousness, is that guilt might not be essentially and necessarily linked to either sexuality or death and yet sexuality still be linked essentially to mortality, that the purest love imaginable might still and necessarily consort with death. And yet in another way, as we have seen, he does think it. On one side of the threshold of fallenness, Milton thinks in Adam an erotic resolve such that he will accept death itself—and thus also a mortal woman, an "advent'rous Eve" who knows good and evil and must die—as the corollary of his desire. And on the other side of this threshold he thinks in Adam a shattered, haunted sexuality that can bear the consequence of its own essential choice only by refracting its guilt as misogyny, piety, and the belief that it must all have been for the better. Adam after the Fall is a man who, as D. H. Lawrence might have said, has been "wounded in his sex."

The fallen Adam no longer has the courage of his earlier resolution. His guilt and shame make him pious and take away all his erotic nobility.[50] This is very strange. It is the fallen Adam who mouths the supposedly correct doctrine regarding Eve ("all was but a show / Rather than solid virtue" [10.883]), whereas the unfallen Adam had been so susceptible to this show, had doubted that it was a show. There are of course ways of translating this apparent contradiction into orthodox terms. Luther, for example, explains that Adam's eyes are opened to the truth of sin precisely as a consequence of the Fall (*Lectures on Genesis*, 164). But the narrative voice in *Paradise Lost* expressly tells us that it is from a "distemper'd breast" that Adam, "estrang'd in look and alter'd style" now speaks his reproachful words to Eve (9.1131–32). It is this same distempered Adam who now claims that before the Fall to behold the face of God was his "highth / Of happiness" (10.723–24), a sentiment unlike any that was voiced by the Eve-struck lover of before the Fall. It seems that the chief destructive effect of the Fall has been the shattering of the erotic spell that was the supreme, God-given delight of Paradise.

When Milton pursues the sexual urge all the way to its deepest roots, he finds that it entails death, and he recoils. For within the discourse of Christianity it is not possible to think this thought without becoming aware of the eye of the father that sees the guilty phallus, without feeling "soil'd and stain'd" (9.1076) and therefore ashamed, as though the "signs of foul concupiscence" were visible in one's face. And then it's all over; without the veil of idealization, no more erotic nobility, no more acceptance of a love that consorts with death.

Milton's Edenic desire is awesome in the degree of its self-assertion. He knows in his near-antinomian self-assurance that his desire is just and right; he knows what absolute delight must be, and he knows that his god is such that he will have intended the satisfaction of Milton's demand for such delight. "What next I bring shall please thee, be assur'd," God had said to Adam: "Thy wish, exactly to thy heart's desire." Raphael tells him that Eve has been made "so adorn for thy delight the more." And when Eve argues that they must work harder to keep the garden in order, Adam replies that "not to irksome toil, but to delight / He made us" (9.242–43).

But Milton's desire is ultimately baffled by the system in terms of which he attempts to think it through. In the end, Milton cannot extricate himself from the knot created by his own version of the Christian axiomatics. If death and sexual shame are a punishment for disobedience, and if it was for the sake of a woman, therefore because of the erotic imperative, that the man transgressed, then there is no exit from the maze, at least not in the direction of the ecstatic erotic fulfillment Milton tries to imagine. Milton imagines a man on the verge of embracing the fatality of his organic being when he imagines that Adam resolves to join himself irrevocably to the woman who consorts with death. But this resolve, which runs counter to the fundamental impulse of historical Christianity, is finally shattered, overwhelmed, humiliated by the unbreakable link that seems to hold between this resolve and shame. There is a higher perspective than that of organic fatality; there is the eye of the all-seeing father, who sanctions sexuality, but only within the limits of measure, short of the complete release that is isomorphic with death.

On the one hand, Milton loathes death and guilty sexuality. They were avoidable; they are the fruit of disobedience pure and simple. On the other hand, Adam's choice constitutes necessity in the only form in which the human race has ever known it. When he thinks Adam's choice, Milton thinks the essential constitution of his own being-as-fallen, which Milton did not choose, and thinks it as a choice.

The interplay on different discursive levels of freedom and necessity is subtle and complex.

Theologically, Adam was free not to fall, to remain immortal. According to Christianity, to the version of Christianity that won out, everything might have been different; there might have been no death.

But everything is not different. There is death, and therefore, because this is the story of how it came about that there is death, Adam must choose it, in Genesis and in Milton's poem. His choice is predetermined with a predetermination that has nothing to do with theology, that belongs rather to the conditions under which theology and all narrative are generated.

And yet the doctrine of free will has a profound role to play beyond theology, at the level of the fatality that constrains both Adam and Milton. Milton must die; he has no say in the matter. If there were an alternative, he would take it; but there is no alternative. Yet, when he thinks himself into Adam's being in order to repeat Adam's choice, Milton imagines a moment in which there *is* an alternative, but one that, as Adam, perfectly free to choose it, he will not choose. Nothing could be more agonizing for Milton than to reenact this choice—concerning which he, Milton, has no choice—and to reenact it precisely as freely chosen.

And this sets up a disturbing and irresolvable ambiguity. Isn't it true that Milton represents Adam's choice as an assent and affirmation of the condition of mortal love? Here once more are the crucial words that Adam speaks to Eve at the crucial moment, words that are unparalleled in literature up to Milton's time and for a long time after: "If Death Consort with Thee, Death is to mee as Life." There is no blame of the woman here as seductress, but also no Gnostic evasion of the body by treating Eve as a spiritual principle, principle of ascent from the physical.[51] It is something else altogether: the woman as pulling man down to the body and death, but assent to this as necessary and right, the goal of eros as lifedeath itself. Eros is wrested away from Plato, and Eve in her errancy from the phallogocentric law accepted as absolute terminus of desire: most difficult of feats for the Christian-Platonic inheritance.

And if Adam says yes to Eve and death from the depths of his being, and Milton impersonates Adam for the purpose, then doesn't Milton make the same affirmation?

This is an unanswerable question. Further distinctions would be necessary. Clearly not all of Milton assents; or if all of Milton does, then, apparently, only momentarily, experimentally, with the feigning freedom of the poet. Milton *traverses* the moment of this affirmation and leaves the track of this traversal inscribed in the text for us to retraverse. The moment of affirmation is in brackets, framed by the larger body of *Paradise Lost* as a whole, Milton's work as a whole, Christian doctrine; and this context is all on the side of the narratorial voice that judges Adam's choice as "compliance bad." Yet within the brackets, something takes place that is absolute—for us, yes, and even more so for Milton, who believes that this is more or less literally how death became our destiny.

PART THREE

TRAGICAL-EXISTENTIAL

CHAPTER SEVEN

Inflicting/Mourning: *Heart of Darkness*

"*H*EART OF DARKNESS" IS JOSEPH CONRAD'S MOST RADICAL EXPERI-
ment in the technique of narration and a milestone in the development of
modernist narrative.[1] Conrad here crosses two kinds of verisimilitude:
that of faithfulness to the matter narrated and that of faithfulness to the
limitations of a narrator who has been a participant in the events he
narrates. This doubled verisimilitude yields not twice the sense of reality
but its dissolution; when the narrator rejects the artifice of authorial
shaping and gives himself up to the vagaries of memory and language as
they "really" are, the narration tends to thematize narratability and to
open itself to a skepticism that is at once epistemological and moral.

It is tempting to think that the extreme nature of Marlow's subject, the
passage to a place where the conventions of European reality are sus-
pended, is essentially linked to the radicality of the narrative technique.
Yet Conrad's friend and sometime collaborator, Ford Madox Ford, a few
years later in *The Good Soldier* would carry the decentering implication of
the technique of doubled verisimilitude even further, demonstrating that
the disorientation that Conrad had gone to the jungle to find could be
located in the most genteel of settings.[2]

Despite the differences in setting and plot of these two novels, they
share a fundamental concern with the presence of unrestrained desire
beneath the constraining conventions of culture. Thus Ford's Dowell
wonders early on in his narration whether "the proper man with the right
to existence" is not "a raging stallion, forever neighing after his neighbor's

womankind" (14), a remark reminiscent of Marlow's notion of the "strong, lusty, red-eyed devils" that drive real men.[3] It is very striking, however, that Conrad's tale, which is nominally about the complete satisfaction of lust, only hints at the existence of sexuality, whereas Ford's focuses explicitly and exclusively on sexual passion. Even Dowell, who calls himself a "eunuch" early on, ends by declaring that he "should really like to be a polygamist; with Nancy, and with Leonora, and with Maisy Maidan and possibly even Florence [his wife, with whom he had never actually consummated relations]," and reasons that in this he is "no doubt like every other man" (257).

The Good Soldier, which at one point directly alludes to *Heart of Darkness,* is in crucial ways a rewriting of the earlier novel.[4] Not only is Ford's narrative technique influenced by Conrad's tale, but the psychic economy of the Dowell/Edward Ashburnham pairing echoes the Marlow/Kurtz doublet. In each case the relatively repressed narrator observes with a mixture of disgust and admiration the unlawful but manly exploits of the other; in each case the manly one wastes away and ultimately dies while the narrator is left to tell the tale. For Dowell, however, in contrast with Marlow, the secrets of the heart of darkness have to do with sexual desire and sexual infidelity.

Interestingly, Conrad himself wrote another story that is something like a domestic and eroticized version of *Heart of Darkness.* His early short story "The Return" is the tale of Alvan Hervey, who comes home one day to a letter from his wife informing him that she has left him for another man.[5] He drops the letter as though it were "hot, or venomous, or filthy" and rushes to the window, from which he sees "an illimitable darkness"; the sound of the city, in a description reminiscent of Marlow's impressions of the jungle, comes to him like "the deep mutter of something immense and alive" (126). At this point Hervey feels "very sick—physically sick—as though he had bitten through something nauseous" (128). Marlow will say in *Heart of Darkness* that lies make him sick "like biting something rotten would do" (29); the nausea Marlow assigns to the "taint of death" carried by lies is assigned in "The Return" to a woman's infidelity. Uncontrolled sexual desire, here referred to simply as "passion," is, Hervey thinks, "the unpardonable and secret infamy of our hearts, a thing to curse, to hide, and to deny" (130). "The contamination of her crime spread out, tainted the universe . . . caused a ghastly kind of clairvoyance in which he could see the towns and fields of the earth, its sacred places, its temples and its houses, peopled by monsters—by monsters of duplicity, lust, and murder" (135). In this and several other passages, the same kind of exaggerated sense of vileness and horrifying excess is inspired by the woman that in *Heart of Darkness* is inspired by Kurtz.

Hervey gradually arrives at the realization that what he really wants, what he has wanted all his life without realizing it, is to receive the "gift" of faith and love from a woman; but he also realizes that he will never receive this gift, that he can never really know her, never be *certain* of her inward response to him. "What did she think? What did she feel? And in the presence of her perfect stillness, in the breathless silence, he felt himself insignificant and powerless before her, like a prisoner in chains. The fury of his impotence called out sinister images." The realization that grieves Hervey almost past enduring is that she will never give him the response he craves: "To give her your thought, your belief, was like whispering your confession over the edge of the world. Nothing came back—not even an echo" (183).

In the end, Hervey confronts nothingness in the eyes of the Medusa head of a woman:

> He was in the middle of the room before he could see anything but the dazzling brilliance of the light; and then, as if detached and floating in it on the level of his eyes, appeared the head of a woman. She had jumped up when he burst into the room.
> . . . He looked into the unfathomable candour of her eyes. Nothing within—nothing—nothing.
> He stammered distractedly.
> "I want . . . I want . . . to . . . to . . . know . . ." (184–85)

Hervey's words are very nearly the same as those Conrad will place in the mouth of the Intended near the end of *Heart of Darkness* ("I want—I want—something—something— . . .").[6]

In "The Return," thus, the darkness of the heart and the horror of the existential abyss are probed strictly in relation to an anxiety and a need that the protagonist feels in relation to a woman.[7] In *Heart of Darkness,* by contrast, men go out adventuring for their dark truths, and women are supposedly confined to a world that is insulated from such truths. Yet everything will culminate in the drawing room of a woman, a woman with a "pale head" who comes "floating" toward Marlow in the dusk (72–73), and "mingled" with whose voice Marlow hears Kurtz's dying words (76).

Marlow's voice in *Heart of Darkness* is marked by an extraordinary reserve, a sense of unbridgeable isolation from other people; and this is true not only within the tale that is told but also, in a more complicated way, in the situation of the telling. Within the tale he tells Marlow draws an impermeable boundary between himself and certain others. Those excluded are, on the one hand, women, of which the chief examples are his aunt and Kurtz's Intended; on the other hand, those men who have no beliefs, no innards, no genuine masculinity. By the appeal he makes to his listeners' shared sense of this boundary, Marlow affirms the solidarity of the group he and they represent. Yet, even though Marlow and his listeners on the *Nellie* are committed to the same masculine ideals and idea of masculinity, the lines of community that hold Marlow to them are stretched very thin by the way in which he expands and eventually deforms the categories on which their agreement is based. Thus, the telling of the tale, Marlow's narrated journey to the limit of his experience, is up to a point also the journey of his narration farther and farther away from the shared premises of the narrative contract with his audience—a contract to which Marlow nevertheless skillfully and repeatedly appeals.

The Swedish captain who takes him up country, the stalwart boilermaker who shares Marlow's interest in rivets, even, less plausibly, the cannibal crew with their inexplicable restraint ("They were men one could work with" [36]), and, eventually, the harlequin (who calls Marlow "brother sailor" [53]): when Marlow narrates his encounter with each of them he reaffirms within his tale the manly bond that is the foundation of his listeners' identificatory investment in the tale. Marlow's exchanges with the Swedish captain and the boilermaker, for instance, are charged with unspoken intimacy of the sublimated type appropriate to men whose libidinal bond is that of shared labor. "I had my passage on a little seagoing steamer. Her captain was a Swede and knowing me for a seaman invited me on the bridge. . . . As we left the miserable little wharf he tossed his head contemptuously at the shore. . . . 'I wonder what becomes of that kind when it goes up country?' I said to him I expected to see that soon" (18). There is absolute confidence that their moral-sociological categories are shared; the depth at which community is presupposed by the contemptuous toss of the head and the elliptical reference to "that kind" is, as between two total strangers, breathtaking. And the listeners on the *Nellie* are included with Marlow as objects of the Swede's confidence.

But even this exchange is articulate and explicit by comparison with the charge of shared affect that is expressed by the single word *rivets* in Marlow's exchange with the boilermaker: "I slapped him on the back and shouted 'We shall have rivets!' He scrambled to his feet exclaiming 'No! Rivets!' as though he couldn't believe his ears. Then in a low voice,

'You . . . eh?' . . . 'Good for you!' he cried, snapped his fingers above his head, lifting one foot. I tried a jig. We capered on the iron deck" (32). By contrast, this same word functions as a mark of the distance, hostility, and incomprehension that holds between Marlow and the agent with the forked beard: "What more did I want? What I really wanted was rivets, by Heaven! Rivets. To get on with the work—to stop the hole. Rivets I wanted" (30). The word *rivets* thus pushes to its limit the compressive or inarticulate tendency of the language of work-centered masculine intimacy: a single word absorbs both the sense and the affect of an entire context and an entire ethos.

As Marlow goes farther into the jungle, however, the identifications he makes in his narration become more tenuous and problematic; neither the cannibals nor the harlequin fit without remainder into the privileged category of men who work in truth.

The rift between Marlow and his listeners first shows up in relation to his remarks on the humanity of the Africans who "howled and leaped and spun and made horrid faces" (37). At this moment in his narration Marlow appears to feel himself on unsure ground with his audience, because, in *anticipation* of dissent, he declares that only those with sufficient masculinity will be able to share his response to the Africans and attacks as a "fool" anyone who is incapable of sharing it. At this point one of his listeners responds with a grunt that Marlow interprets as ridicule:

> What thrilled you was, just the thought of their humanity—like yours. . . . Ugly. Yes, it was ugly enough, but if you were man enough you would admit to yourself that there was in you just the faintest trace of a response to the terrible frankness of that noise. . . . Let the fool gape and shudder—the man knows and can look on without a wink. But he must be at least as much of a man as these on the shore. . . . Of course, a fool, what with sheer fright and fine sentiments, is always safe. Who's that grunting? You wonder I didn't go ashore for a howl and a dance? Well, no—I didn't. (37–38)

"The man knows, and can look on without a wink"; this is the same ideological-rhetorical machinery that will be at work concerning Kurtz's vision and Marlow's relation to this vision. Marlow is here preparing his listeners for what is to come, pressing them in the direction of the more difficult boundary-transgression that will come later.

Marlow's response to Kurtz's response to the jungle and its people is the rhetorical crux of his narrative. Kurtz is neither one of "us" nor one of "them" (whether "them" is conceived as a European without ideals and masculinity, an African, or a woman); yet Marlow, for whom the boundaries of group identification are so important, finds himself indissolubly linked, by some profound affinity, to Kurtz.

Marlow's affiliation with Kurtz presents him with a moral problem that is also and necessarily a rhetorical problem. This affiliation is not simply a matter of the subjectivity of two individuals. It also has to do with the inclusion, or partial inclusion, of one individual (Kurtz) within the set of values that defines a community, that of men who work in truth, the community of which the other individual (Marlow) is already a member. This inclusion is problematic, and Marlow, in struggling with it, cannot make the determination in isolation from the judgment of the group whose values he is applying. Whatever his private struggles may have been with the question of his loyalty to Kurtz, it is necessary that he submit his deliberations, as he here does, to the scrutiny of his fellow sailors. He must also attempt to persuade them that his judgment of Kurtz is, if not the judgment they too would make, at least one that remains plausible, one they cannot rule out of order outright. His listeners sit as a mostly, but not entirely, silent jury as Marlow presents his case; their responses, few as they are, indicate very precisely the points of tension between them and Marlow.

Apart from their responses, however, we can also read the negotiation that takes place between Marlow and his listeners in the implicit and explicit appeals that Marlow directs at them. Marlow is intensely, almost despairingly, aware of the difficulty of bringing his friends to share his vision of Kurtz and of his jungle experience in general.

> You can't understand? How could you—with solid pavement under your feet, surrounded by kind neighbours ready to cheer you or to fall on you . . . how can you imagine what particular region of the first ages a man's untrammeled feet may take him into by the way of solitude— . . . by the way of silence—utter silence, where no warning voice of a kind neighbour can be heard whispering of public opinion. (49–50)

The rhetoric of this passage is on one level transparent and even crude. Marlow has already emphasized that manliness is required to look unflinchingly at the jungle mystery; his listeners can refuse him a hearing only on pain of accepting his contemptuous characterization of them. But Marlow here raises, as the limit-question of the problematic of group affiliation, the question of what happens to a member of the group when the group is entirely absent. Marlow invokes this vision of its own absence as an appeal to that very voice of public opinion (in the person of his listeners) that was not there to speak to Kurtz. He does so in order to persuade it that even a man who goes beyond all its "permitted aspirations" might still qualify as a partial member of the group or at least as not an absolute nonmember—and even as one who most profoundly confirms the values of the group by continuing to judge as the group judges at the very moment that he transgresses all its boundaries.

The appeal of manly group identification that Marlow makes to his listeners, and which must at the crucial moment stretch to include the difficult case of Kurtz, is initially established not by opposition with impercipient fools or faithless agents of empire but by opposition with women. Let us read the first appearance of this element of Marlow's rhetoric in his narration, attending in particular to Marlow's tone and what this tone implies. Only twice in his narration will he address his audience directly in such a tone of flustered self-exculpation, and we will see that the two passages, occurring far apart in the narration, are closely linked.[8]

Here is the first passage: "Then—would you believe it—I tried the women. I, Charlie Marlow, set the women to work—to get a job! Heavens!" (12). Marlow then introduces the figure of his aunt, who gets him the job he wants, and there follows his description of his "initiation" at the company headquarters. Then he returns once more to his aunt, and this is where the theme of "we men" as confronters of truth is first announced. Commenting on his aunt's sentimental views of colonialism, Marlow says:

> It's queer how out of touch with truth women are! They live in a
> world of their own and there had never been anything like it and
> never can be. It is too beautiful altogether, and if they were to set
> it up it would go to pieces before the first sunset. Some confounded
> fact, we men have been living contentedly with ever since the day
> of creation, would start up and knock the whole thing over. (16)

The resonances of this passage with the concluding scene of Marlow's narration are well known, and I will not restate them.[9] My interest is, rather, (1) in the way these remarks begin to tighten the threads of group identification between Marlow and his audience and (2) in the odd rift in this identification that already begins to appear in the nervously vehement tone of the remarks with which Marlow had first introduced his aunt ("I, Charlie Marlow . . . ! Heavens!").

His anxiety is even more evident in the second passage. "Good Lord!

Mustn't a man ever—," Marlow will say and be unable for some moments to continue his narrative; and this elliptical utterance has an unusually rich and extensive context that has to be filled in.

Marlow's remark occurs toward the end of his narration of the attack on the steamboat by the Africans, a narration that begins at very nearly the halfway point of his tale. Within the bounds of the narration of this "incident," located at the physical center of *Heart of Darkness,* there is a striking reduplication of the frame within which Marlow's narration takes place. Marlow's steamboat, unable to move because of the fog, anchored in midstream, mirrors the boat on which years later he tells his tale, anchored offshore as it waits for the tide to turn. This is only the most precise and literal mirroring of frame and narration in *Heart of Darkness,* and it serves as a focus for more general mirroring effects. Marlow describes Kurtz as a disembodied voice (48), and the frame narrator describes Marlow in the same way (30). And the group of listeners on the *Nellie* itself constitutes a microcosm of the legal-bureaucratic structure of the company in charge of the colonial exploitation of Africa: the helmsman is "Director of Companies," and the other two who are designated are "the Lawyer" and "the Accountant." There is no lawyer in Marlow's tale, but the lawyer-function is an important presence: the dying black men in the grove of death are said to have been brought there "in all the legality of time contracts" (20), and the starving cannibals on the steamboat are held there by "a piece of paper written over in accordance with some farcical law" (42). The Accountant on the *Nellie* is presented as a commentary on the role played within the deadly colonial structure by the seemingly harmless accountant Marlow meets in the jungle: his game with dominoes is described as "toying architecturally with the bones" (7).

I am considering the ways in which the frame mirrors and clarifies certain elements of what it frames, and I am focusing on the fact that there is one moment of the framed narration that bears a privileged relation to the frame. It is "pitch dark" (30) on the *Nellie* as Marlow tells his tale, and the friends have anchored the boat in the Thames to wait for the ebb. As Marlow sits in the anchored *Nellie* he narrates how he anchored the steamboat in the middle of the African river and its occupants were "struck blind" by the night (41). In the African scene, however, there is complete silence as well as complete darkness: "not the faintest sound of any kind could be heard." The silence intensifies the value of sound, amplifies its impact on the sensorium: "About three in the morning some large fish leaped, and the loud splash made me jump as though a gun had been fired."

Then, strangely, this whole stage-setting is repeated in a different key. Night comes to an end, and the sun rises, but the ship remains paralyzed by "a white fog, very warm and clammy, and more blinding than the night" (another of those transfers of significance between darkness and light, black and white, that commentators have noticed).[10] And then again, the fog rises long enough that the crew starts to weigh anchor— but suddenly redescends. Three times, then, the steamboat is isolated in the blind and silent blackness or whiteness of its anchorage.

Suddenly, into this floating isolation that the splash of a fish can startle like a gunshot comes a clamor so extravagant and piercing that to Marlow it sounds "as though the mist itself had screamed." Here is the entire description of this extraordinary sequence of sounds, which occurs at very nearly the precise halfway point of the story:

> a cry, a very loud cry as of infinite desolation, soared slowly in the opaque air. It ceased. A complaining clamour, modulated in savage discords, filled our ears. The sheer unexpectedness of it made my hair stir under my cap. I don't know how it struck the others: to me it seemed as though the mist itself had screamed, so suddenly and apparently from all sides at once did this tumultuous and mournful uproar arise. It culminated in a hurried outbreak of almost intolerably excessive shrieking which stopped short, leaving us stiffened in a variety of silly attitudes and obstinately listening to the nearly as appalling and excessive silence. (41)

Thus is announced the presence of the Africans who a few hours later will mount a desperate "attempt at repulse" against the steamship.

I count as a single structural unit the stretch of narration from the decision to drop anchor for the night up to the disposal of the body of Marlow's native helmsman. The action for which the stage is set by the anchoring of the boat is not complete until that point; there is a quite conventional coherence of narrative sequence here, from the ominous silence preceding the uproar, through attack and repulse, to the concluding disposal of the dead body. But the effect of this conventional action-adventure sequence is to a considerable degree frustrated by the character of its telling, which is even more digressive and disruptive of chronology than the narration is elsewhere. Between the opening tumult and the attack there is the long digression on cannibals; between the death of the helmsman and his hasty burial there is the even longer digression on Kurtz.

The coherence of the entire sequence at the level of the telling is, however, secured by a leitmotif that recurs three times after its initial appearance: the motif of the mournful cry of the Africans that shatters the mist-enclosed silence.

1. It is by means of this cry that we return to the main narration after the digression on the cannibal crew:

> It takes a man all his inborn strength to fight hunger properly. It's really easier to face bereavement, dishonour, and the perdition of one's soul—than this kind of prolonged hunger. Sad, but true.
> And these chaps too had no earthly reason for any kind of scruple. Restraint! . . . there was the fact facing me . . . a mystery greater— when I thought of it—than the curious, inexplicable note of desperate grief in this savage clamour that had swept by us on the river- bank behind the blind whiteness of the fog. (43)

Marlow here voices again his deepest conception of masculinity, as something beyond ideals and beliefs, an ungraspable, mysterious essence that is a man's most proper and inalienable possession—the essence that, we have seen, he wants to propose to his listeners as capable in some way of transcending even the moral community within which it is nurtured. Then, with the mention of the cry, Marlow resumes his main narration.

2. Marlow now narrates the discussion on board the steamboat concerning whether the natives will attack, and once more the question of the cry or cries recurs. He delivers a "regular lecture" on the nature of the Africans' cries to the "pilgrims," who think that Marlow has "gone mad":

> What made the idea of attack inconceivable to me was the nature of the noise—of the cries we had heard. They had not the fierce character boding of immediate hostile intention. Unexpected, wild, and violent as they had been they had given me an irresistible im- pression of sorrow. The glimpse of the steamboat had for some rea- son filled those savages with unrestrained grief. The danger, if any, I expounded, was from our proximity to a great human passion let loose. (44)

I do not think the strangeness of this moment in the tale has ever been properly appreciated. The severe, self-controlled Marlow is so over- whelmed by a conviction concerning the nature of the natives' affect that he raves, as if inspired, to people he despises and from whom he normally conceals his interiority with an "unresponsive attitude" (30–31). And as he recounts the events to the listeners on the *Nellie*, Marlow retains this conviction, even in the face of the fact that his prediction was wrong and the natives did in fact attack. Marlow insists nevertheless that what he said to the pilgrims was "absolutely true to fact," because "what we afterwards referred to as an attack was really an attempt at repulse." And he makes this subtle distinction: "The action was very far from being aggressive; it was not even defensive in the usual sense; it was undertaken under the stress of desperation and in its essence was purely protective" (44).

Marlow's interest is not in the attack or "attempt at repulse" itself but in the character of the affect that motivates the attackers. The danger, "if any," is from "proximity to a great human passion let loose," and specifically the passion of "unrestrained grief" (44).

3. There follows the account of the fighting and of the helmsman's death, and we come almost to the conclusion of the affair; but just before we get there, Marlow evokes for the third time the unrestrained grief of the natives, and it is this evocation that results directly in the major rift between Marlow and his audience that we have been approaching for some pages. The helmsman dies, but for the moment the "dominant thought" (47) that grips Marlow is that Kurtz must be dead, too, and this thought overwhelms him with grief: "We are too late; he has vanished—the gift has vanished by means of some spear, arrow, or club. I will never hear that chap speak after all—and my sorrow had a startling extravagance of emotion, even such as I had noticed in the howling sorrow of these savages in the bush. I couldn't have felt more of lonely desolation somehow had I been robbed of a belief or had missed my destiny in life." Here Marlow is interrupted by the response of one of his listeners, to which he responds, "Why do you sigh in this beastly way, somebody? Absurd? Well, absurd. Good Lord! Mustn't a man ever. . . . Here, give me some tobacco" (48).

We are still within the resonance of that moment when, with Marlow's steamboat floating blind and deaf in the middle of the river a cry of "infinite desolation" had shattered the silence. Marlow's response to this cry has dominated his sense of everything that has happened from that point to the death of his helmsman and the disposal of his body. And finally Marlow himself has experienced a moment of what he takes to be the same kind of "unrestrained grief" as that of the natives—in fact, as he knows in the time of narration, for the same person the natives are mourning.

This is when the second, and far more marked, moment of Marlow's discomfiture before his audience occurs. It is not with respect to the question of Kurtz's unrestraint that the agreement between Marlow and his listeners will be strained; it is with respect to a certain unrestraint of

Marlow's. "Good Lord! Mustn't a man ever—." Marlow is so deeply disturbed by the ridicule of his listener, to whom we apparently should ascribe the *absurd* that Marlow picks up, that he interrupts his narrative for some moments, and even when he tries to resume it his agitation is extreme. Four more times (for a total of six) he will repeat the offending word, the word that informs him, as he believes, that what he has described is for his audience something a man "mustn't ever." As before, Marlow takes the offensive, hurling at his listeners the reproach that they are not qualified to judge what (as he had earlier said) "the man knows" and can look at "without a wink" (38): "'Absurd!' he cried. 'This is the worst of trying to tell . . . Here you all are each moored with two good addresses like a hulk with two anchors, a butcher round one corner, a policeman round another, excellent appetites, and temperature normal— hear you—normal from year's end to year's end. And you say, Absurd! Absurd be—exploded. Absurd!'" (48).

But already Marlow has begun to hedge. It's not just that he was out there in the jungle where a man sees strange and disturbing things, but, as he has mentioned earlier, that he wasn't his *normal* self, he "had often 'a little fever'" (43); hence his reference to his listeners' "temperature normal." And now he very quickly begins to recuperate his agreement with his listeners: "My dear boys, what can you expect from a man who out of sheer nervousness had just flung overboard a pair of new shoes?" Thus Marlow revises his account, minimizing and even rendering ridiculous the "extravagance of emotion" that had dominated his entire narration of the encounter with the natives since the moment of that initial cry when "it seemed the mist itself had screamed." And in fact he proceeds to transmogrify his moment of weakness into a moment of strength, of manly restraint in the most primitive sense of that restraint as it is learned from earliest boyhood: "Now I think of it, it is amazing I did not shed tears. I am, upon the whole, proud of my fortitude."

And now that Marlow has regained his composure, denigrating his moment of emotional extravagance and reestablishing the boundaries by which "we men" cohere together, we are just around the corner from the corresponding reassertion of the major category by opposition to which manliness is defined. After a few lines on Kurtz, Marlow is suddenly, and as if out of nowhere, reminded of a woman: "Voices, voices—even the girl herself—now. . . ." (49).

Here occurs the second suspension of his narrative. "He was silent for a long time."

When he speaks again, he will repeat five times the idea that women are "out of it." This repetition suggests that the agitation of Marlow's earlier self-defense has not entirely spent itself; especially because the lie he now mentions will have resulted in the terrible cry of mourning of the Intended—the cry that repeats the cry of the savages with its extravagance of grief, that very extravagance that Marlow himself has experienced, like the natives and the Intended, in regard to Kurtz. "'I laid the ghost of his gifts at least with a lie,' he began suddenly. 'Girl! What? Did I mention a girl? Oh, she is out of it—completely. They—the women I mean—are out of it—should be out of it. We must help them to stay in that beautiful world of their own lest ours gets worse. Oh, she had to be out of it'" (49).

We cannot call Marlow's attitude toward Kurtz—the attitude that he somewhat defiantly proposes to his audience for its approval—admiration, exactly. Marlow is too severe, too ascetic for that. And yet Kurtz makes an irresistible claim upon his loyalty by reason of his manly potency. He has inspired devotion in lesser men and fear in his enemies, and he has "conquered" a woman worth winning, a woman of a type whose possession even the restrained man might well envy him:

> But then, you see, I can't choose. He won't be forgotten. Whatever he was he was not common. He had the power to charm or frighten rudimentary souls into an aggravated witch-dance in his honor, he could also fill the small souls of the pilgrims with bitter misgivings—he had one devoted friend at least, and he had conquered one soul in the world that was neither rudimentary nor tainted with self-seeking. (51)

Marlow's definition of masculinity is thus curiously equivocal. Whereas he most often identifies masculinity with restraint, efficiency, and devotion to work, there is an alternative or "safety valve" definition that opens in another direction: the definition that allows for the possibility of a violently disruptive form of masculinity. This "red-eyed devil" type of man, although not by any means identical with the restrained type, will nevertheless be assigned a place beside the restrained type as an opposite of the "flabby," inefficient type. "I've seen the devil of violence, and the devil of greed, and the devil of hot desire; but by all the stars these were strong, lusty, red-eyed devils, that swayed and drove men—men, I tell you. But as I stood on this hillside I foresaw that in the blinding sunshine of that land I would become acquainted with a flabby, pretending, weak-eyed devil of a rapacious and pitiless folly" (19–20). "Strong, lusty, red-eyed devils"—"we are not like that ourselves," the men on the *Nellie* might feel; "yet we can see, as men, that there is nothing in this that is essentially unmasculine, that it corresponds to an aspect of that which we accept as 'being a man.'" But beyond this, the question Marlow appears implicitly to pose to them is whether the devil of violence, greed, and hot desire is not in fact the core or essence of masculinity, an essence that it is masculine to repress but that in certain circumstances can overpower masculine restraint, and do so precisely out of an authentically masculine impulse.

On the one hand, then, Marlow feels something like admiration or respect for Kurtz as a "devil of hot desire"; on the other hand, it is this that makes Kurtz an obscene figure of rapacity from the truth of which the Intended must be protected ("Oh, she had to be out of it"). By shifting the focus of his narration to the eminently manly problems of Kurtz's truth and the Intended's weakness, Marlow brings it back away from the, let us say, feminine strain with which he has been struggling since the moment of the natives' mournful uproar.

But what of that moment in which Marlow's narration sputtered to a stop, in which the categories that constitute his narrative contract with his audience were momentarily ruptured? This is not a mere aberration, a moment of weakness from which Marlow pulls himself back together; his narration has another economy than the one enforced by the terms of his agreement with his listeners, another economy in the web of which Marlow's response to the Africans is bound in an essential fashion to his response to the Intended.

I will now let go of the thread of the rhetoric of Marlow's tale in order to trace the functioning of this other economy, a functioning that is inscribed in Marlow's language in a more tacit way than that which I have traced so far. We will be working our way toward the culminating cry of the Intended that is, with the mournful tumult of the natives, the second major pole around which Marlow's narration is structured.

Why does Marlow go to visit the Intended? The "ascetic" Marlow has nothing to do with women; his libido flows into work and, through work, into his bonds with other men. But he is haunted by the memory of the man who has poured out all his vital energy in the satisfaction of his lusts.[11] More specifically, he is haunted by the juxtaposition of the image of Kurtz's depravity with that of the perfect purity he sees in the Intended.

He draws the opposition between her purity and Kurtz's defilement as sharply as possible; the Intended must be as free from taint as Kurtz is corrupt. But if the soul of the Intended is "as translucently pure as a cliff of crystal" (70), nevertheless it will be from her that Marlow will hear the "echo" of Kurtz's dying whisper. There is thus in the end in some sense a transgression of the line that separates purity from defilement. The transgression occurs only in Marlow's consciousness and never touches that of the Intended, but Marlow seems to be compelled by a need to bring what remains of Kurtz into immediate proximity to the purity he thinks must be protected from it. As he passes through her doorway he is possessed by near-hysteria at the feeling that he is conveying to her the "conquering darkness" in an "invading and vengeful rush" from which he will have to protect her (72); and yet he proceeds.

We know from his own words that he comes to speak to her about Kurtz believing that she will take deeply, completely, without resistance, the impress of Kurtz's memory, the horrific memory he comes to deposit with her. It is this apparent receptivity of hers that Marlow presents as the immediate incentive to his visit: "She seemed ready to listen without mental reservation, without suspicion, without a thought for herself. I concluded I would go and give her back her portrait and those letters myself" (71).

Two impressions in Marlow's imagination, then: of a devouring, obscene, dominating Kurtz (who has also in manly fashion, in his final moment, passed judgment on himself) and of a translucently pure, utterly selfless, endlessly receptive feminine substance onto which Marlow, horrified by what he is doing, is compelled to transfer the impress of Kurtz's image. It is his *prior* fascination with the juxtaposition of these two images that leads to his visit and to the ensuing vision, which merely inserts the physical presence of the Intended into a scenario that is already prepared in Marlow's imagination and in this way gives it a hallucinatory reality.

The scene with the Intended and Marlow's narration as a whole will climax in her "exulting and terrible" cry of "inconceivable triumph and unspeakable pain." Does it also fulfill the desire that drove Marlow into her presence? Doesn't Marlow come to see her precisely in order to wring her heart to the utmost and make her cry out in this way? But then— what of the "exulting" side of her cry, her "inconceivable triumph"?

Let us recall Kurtz's last declared intention. He is on the boat headed downriver, his life waning: "'Close the shutter,' said Kurtz suddenly one day; 'I can't bear to look at this.' I did so. There was a silence. 'Oh, but I will wring your heart yet!' he cried at the invisible wilderness" (67). The phrase "I will wring your heart yet" does not occur in the manuscript

version of *Heart of Darkness*; in its place, as Robert Kimbrough's edition
notes, Conrad had initially written "I will make you serve my ends." The
revision brings in an ambiguity where there was none in the manuscript;
in addition to the utilitarian meaning that it preserves, the new phrase
can express a desire to inflict suffering, and specifically the suffering of
grief. And, as Conrad may well at least subliminally have been aware, the
latter meaning of the phrase is peculiarly strongly marked by literary
history. Hamlet addresses it to Gertrude as he prepares to remind her of
her failure properly to mourn her dead husband:

> Leave wringing of your hands. Peace, sit you down,
> And let me wring your heart, for so I shall
> If it be made of penetrable stuff. . . .   (*Hamlet*, 3.4.34–46)

(This is, incidentally, perhaps the first use of "wring" with "heart"; its
earliest citation in the *Oxford English Dictionary* is 1766, and the expression apparently becomes common only after 1780.)

Does Kurtz's exclamation thus suggest a desire to elicit by violence a
response of anguish or grief from the wilderness? But if that is the case,
then the question of Kurtz's phallic masculinity is here being broached in
a way that seems to have little to do with the way Marlow has explicitly
posed it.

Now, the story is manifestly full of wrung hearts: those of the natives in
general and the savage mistress in particular, that of the Intended, and,
for one moment, that of Marlow—all of them wrung with grief over the
real or imagined loss of Kurtz. But it is said to be the *wilderness* to which
Kurtz addresses his intention, and the wilderness is heartless, "pitiless"
(56), and "unmoved" (57).

Yet sometimes, in connection with Kurtz, Marlow allows himself to
elide the difference between the wilderness and its inhabitants. In this
way he creates the illusion of that very phenomenon the desire for which
Kurtz apparently expresses when he says "I will wring your heart yet."

> . . . to me it seemed as though the mist itself had screamed, so sud-
> denly and apparently from all sides at once did this tumultuous and
> mournful uproar arise. (41)

> The bush began to howl. (46)

> . . . from the depths of the woods went out such a tremulous and
> prolonged wail of mournful fear and utter despair as may be imag-
> ined to follow the flight of the last hope from the earth. (47)

And at the precise moment that he first sees Kurtz, Marlow hears a cry (source unspecified, possibly Kurtz's African "mistress") of which he says that its "shrillness pierced the still air like a sharp arrow flying straight to the very heart of the land" (59).

Marlow later explicitly indulges the fantasy that is only implied in the foregoing passages when he allows himself to describe the savage mistress as the personification of the "colossal body" of the jungle. The impression of her "wild sorrow" is sufficient for Marlow for at least one moment to call the land itself "sorrowful" and to attribute to it (if only in a simile) a "passionate soul" (60).

What is curious about all this is the implied connection in Marlow's imagination between Kurtz's violent aggressiveness and his ability to arouse mourning for his death in the hearts of women and even, almost, of nature itself.

Marlow, the man of restraint and devotion to work, cannot help being tempted to admire the prick who "conquers" not only jungle empires but the souls of women. It is not the conquest as such that most compels him, and certainly not the form that the enjoyment of its fruits takes, but rather the tribute of affect that attends upon the lapsing of Kurtz's presence, a tribute that comes to Kurtz as a consequence of his ability violently to impose on others the impression of his being.

In the end, Marlow will lie to a woman, and when he does, he will wring her heart with an overwhelming access of grief for the dead Kurtz, thus in some strange and unexpected modality satisfying the desire Kurtz had voiced before he died.

The woman's cry brings to its sharpest point the expression of unreserved grief that appears to be the consummation Marlow seeks from her. But it is going to be an ironic consummation, for it will be not only a cry of mourning but also a cry of triumph. She will be ecstatic at the thought that Kurtz, at what Marlow calls the "supreme moment of complete knowledge" (68), knew only her, that his being was absolutely focused on hers at the moment when he died. Kurtz's death will be her triumph, because it seals her appropriation of his being, but also her absolute loss—a loss from which Marlow likes to believe she will never recover.

Here are the precise words with which Marlow reports her astonishing cry: "I heard a light sigh and then my heart stood still, stopped dead short by an exulting and terrible cry, by the cry of inconceivable triumph and of unspeakable pain" (75–76). It is a Dionysian cry, and it releases the accumulated pressure of affect generated by all the major antitheses of the story.[12] But it is not so easy actually to imagine such a cry, especially coming from an upper-class woman having a formal interview with a stranger in a Victorian drawing room.

Easy or not, however, it is not a question of *realism*. Critics' frequent expressions of dissatisfaction with the characterization of the Intended miss the mark, because the whole scene and especially the cry are motivated by textual forces that are deeper and more far ranging than those generated by the requirements of verisimilitude. The very fact that she is known only as the Intended already functions to place her in an allegorical or quasiallegorical register. And the "last words" *topos* that structures the scene is one of the oldest in literature, present already in the *Iliad* in Andromakhe's lament over Hektor:

> . . . for me passing all others is left the bitterness
> and the pain, for you did not die in bed, and stretch your arms to
>   me,
> nor tell me some last intimate word that I could remember
> always, all the nights and days of my weeping for you.   (24.742–45)

But the scene also opens on a more subtle and generalized textuality. For if the cry of the Intended is not exactly orgasmic, it is disquietingly situated in proximity to a field of sexual-libidinal forces with which it resonates in a complex fashion.

I will now interrupt this reading of the text of *Heart of Darkness* in order to map a portion of the more extensive textual topography against which this complex resonance can be rendered audible. The *topoi* of this topography do not belong to any officially accredited literary system; they are the crisis-points of the libidinal dialectic the textual coherence of which I have been attempting to define in this book.

I have previously noted that *Heart of Darkness* verges on a field of representation that it does not explicitly enter, that of sexuality. We are now going to move laterally from *Heart of Darkness* to several other texts whose exploration of the sexual-libidinal field will show up as contiguous, at a certain level, with *Heart of Darkness*. I have already briefly touched on the medical discourse on sex of William Acton,[13] and there is in Conrad's time already another, unofficial discourse on sex Steven Marcus judges isomorphic "at all points" with the medical discourse: that of pornography (Marcus, 27).

What is available in pornography, at least as a fantasy, is the passionate sexual response of a woman that Acton tells us is in reality both necessary to the male's excitement and also rarely to be met with. On the one hand, "all that we have read and heard tends to prove that a reciprocity of desire is . . . necessary to excite the male": but on the other hand, Acton believes, "the majority of women (happily for them) are not very much troubled with sexual feeling of any kind. What men are habitually, women are only exceptionally" (cited in Marcus, 30–31).

I turn now to Marcus's account of *The Lustful Turk*, a pornographic novel of 1828. Whether Conrad read pornography is not the issue; the significant fact is the existence in his time of certain *topoi* of a widespread fantasy-discourse on nature and desire, *topoi* that are interestingly reconfigured in *Heart of Darkness*.[14]

The male sexual fantasies that are represented in *The Lustful Turk* are primarily of the sort that dominate pornography to the present day (and not only pornography, as we saw in the climax of Dante's *Rime petrose*): fantasies of aggressive dominance. And it is already typical in its own time; according to Marcus, already in the nineteenth century the "overwhelming majority" of pornographic books focus on such representations (211–12).

But Marcus also reinserts *The Lustful Turk* into the broad intellectual debate over the question of "sensibility," and he does so in terms that enable us to see how *Heart of Darkness* may be read in relation to this same larger context. In *The Lustful Turk* "sexuality is itself largely represented in the language, the diction, of sensibility" (204). In particular, according to Marcus, the term *nature* is deployed in a characteristically eighteenth-century fashion: "It slumbers, but it can be alarmed; and then it is 'too powerful.' It is implicitly connected with the 'recesses' of the heart. It makes itself felt through the senses, through 'new and wild sensations,' and it produces at first not pleasure but disorder, confusion, 'a complete tumult'" (205). At the limit-point of the male fantasy of arousal of the female, the woman responds with "a fury of pleasure and ravishment" (206) that is absolutely overpowering, a "pure delight [says one of the women in *The Lustful Turk*], I may even say agony, of enjoyment" (213). "That is to say," Marcus comments, "feelings of pleasure and pain are copresent in a state that is larger, more intense, more overwhelming than either could be alone" (206).

Now, if we were to consider the concluding scene with the Intended in direct relation to the pornographic *topos* of woman's pleasure-at-the-limit, it seems that it could only be as an ironic undoing of the fantasy this *topos* represents. The masterful male who could make the woman come is absolutely absent; his absence, indeed, is a necessary condition of her transport. And if her cry resembles a cry of sexual consummation in its mixture of pain and exultation, it is not as pleasure crossing the threshold that divides it from pain but as the inverse: at the limit of grief, as in Nietzsche's account of the Dionysian cry, exultation and triumph erupt. Here the balance seems to shift all the way to the other extreme from the situation of the Turk: Marlow wants to believe that here it is all "spiritual," all loving recognition—an absolute, eternal, mourning recognition of Kurtz, himself—that is proffered, however misguidedly, by the Intended.

And yet, within this spiritualized scene of mourning, the lustful, violent, dominating male remains a ghostly presence, and for the narrating Marlow all the irony flows the other way: it is the sublimities or sublimations of the Intended that are made to seem illusory by the ghostly presence that represents the reality of which the woman cannot be made conscious.

Furthermore, already in *The Lustful Turk* the question of the woman's response is complex. Our Turk is not entirely satisfied with the merely natural potency by means of which he transports his women with voluptuous pleasure; he desires a more profound or far-reaching consummation. Marcus interprets the following passage as a mechanical effect of the "conversion of the terminology of sensibility into the terminology of . . . sexual reverie" (205); but considering that it manifests an aspect of male sexual anxiety that is documented elsewhere, by Hegel for instance, one may doubt whether it is a mere slip, or how narrowly it may be historicized:

> how strange it is [muses the Turk] . . . that these slaves, whose destinies depend on our will, rarely give that fervent return to our pleasure, so absolutely necessary to the true voluptuous energy of enjoyment. It is true, nature will always exert its power over the softer sex, and they frequently give way to its excitement, but the pleasure they experience is merely animal. Thus it is with Zelia . . . even in the height of our ecstasies, a cloud seems to hang on her beauteous countenance, clearly indicating that it is nature, not love, that creates her transport (cited by Marcus, 204–5).

It is necessary, these lines imply, not only that the woman be transported with pleasure, but that it should be *her lover as such* whom she experiences as the origin and end of her pleasure; what is required, in other words, is a reciprocity of desire that would include recognition in something like a Hegelian sense. But in the Turk's view it is precisely such recognition that is not to be had from a woman in the experience of sexual pleasure. The more the male exercises his potency the more he forces her resistance to fall away as he causes an irresistible pleasure to rise in her; and it seems as though by pushing her pleasure past the boundary at which it becomes indistinguishable from pain he would be absolutely impressing his being upon her as source of her ecstasy. But the greater the transport of pleasure, the more thoroughly she is in the grip not of his power, of him *as such*, but of the power of "nature."

When the woman takes her pleasure, Hegel declares, "her interest is centered on the universal and remains alien to the particularity of desire."[15] The universality in which the woman is interested is of course not the *true* universality toward which the man tends; it is that of "the relation of the *individual* member of the family toward the *whole* family as the substance," whereas "what is truly universal" is not the family but the political community (269). Also, the relationships of mother and wife, even though oriented toward the universal, are partly determined "in the form of something natural pertaining to desire" (274). But even if the ethical life of the wife "is not pure" (275), the form of universality toward which it is oriented dictates that for her "the particular individual is . . . a contingent element which can be replaced by another individual. . . . it is not a question of *this* particular husband, *this* particular child, but simply of husband and children generally" (274).

We must, I think, understand what Hegel says here in relation to the remarks in the section on Reason, subsection on Pleasure and Necessity, in which he describes in a very explicit way the annulment of the individual being in sexual *jouissance*. The subject of pleasure that Hegel here describes is not explicitly identified as male, but Hegel indicates by a citation that the model he has in mind is Goethe's Faust. Neither is the pleasure he describes explicitly identified as erotic, although the account is transparent enough, as Jean Hyppolite's reading shows.[16] Finally, neither does Hegel identify the annihilation that befalls the individual in the moment of the fulfillment of pleasure as originating in the character of the feminine principle. But we have seen that woman's pleasure is "centered on the universal," and it is the power of universality that is unleashed in erotic consummation and on which the pleasure-seeking (male) individual founders.

The passages in which Hegel describes the hedonic project of desire are at least as crucial in the overall design of the *Phenomenology* as are those that concern the master-slave dialectic. In fact, as Hyppolite notes, the discussion of pleasure and necessity takes up "at a higher level" the dialectic that had culminated in the encounter of master and slave (*Genesis and Structure*, 281). Yet this moment in the *Phenomenology* has been, so far as I know, completely ignored in poststructuralist debate. In the

case of erotic desire, the desiring subject does not seek the destruction/
consumption of the object; rather, the subject recognizes the other as a
consciousness, but, not recognizing the other as autonomous, it takes the
other to be *"in principle* the same essence as itself, or its selfhood."

> It attains therefore to the attainment of *pleasure,* to the consciousness
> of its actualization in a consciousness which appears as independent,
> or to the vision of the unity of the two independent self-conscious-
> nesses. It attains its End, but only to learn there what the truth of
> that End is. It comprehends itself as this particular individual who
> exists *for himself,* but the realization of this end is itself the *Aufhebung*
> of the latter. For it is not as *this particular* individual that it becomes
> an object to itself, but rather as the *unity* of itself and the other self-
> consciousness, hence as an individual that is *aufgehoben* or as a *uni-
> versal.* (*Phenomenology of Spirit,* 218)

This annulment of the individual is what Hegel calls necessity (*Notwen-
digkeit*) or fate (*Schicksal*), the fatality by which individuality necessarily
passes into universality and thus reveals its essential nothingness (219);
but this is an abortive passage into universality, because it takes place in
mere feeling rather than in thought, and the subject of pleasure therefore
cannot recognize its "purpose and action [*Tun*] in fate, and fate in its
purpose and action" (220). The undergoing of fate in the consummation
of erotic desire thus remains something purely passively undergone.

Hegel thus articulates what the lustful Turk cannot, the nature of the
abyss of individuated being that is purported to be the male's erotic
relation to a woman. And then, by a necessity the structure of which
should by now be familiar, Hegel turns to *Antigone* to identify in a
woman's mourning the culmination of the only relation in which true
mutual recognition is possible between a man and a woman.

It is true, however, that Hegel's emphasis is on the ritual of burial as
expression of familial piety and hence as a raising of the dead individual
above the mere destructiveness of natural reduction (270–71), not on
Antigone's affect of grief as such. Grief is mere subjective feeling and as
such has no power to transform the passivity of death in the required way;
the sister performs the burial rites as a representative of the family, and
the family is the "*natural* ethical community," the threshold of the transition from mere nature to the genuinely ethical sphere of the political
community. "Because the ethical principle is intrinsically universal, the
ethical connection between the members of the Family is not that of
feeling, or the relationship of Love" (269).

Hegel thus assigns an essential structural privilege to the mourning of a woman while yet neutralizing all the elements in this mourning that would drag it down to the level of the merely natural—which is to say, to the level of that which woman as such represents, for Hegel and for the thanatoerotophobic tradition in general. Devoid of desire, acting only out of the sense of familial piety and of a duty toward the brother that is "of the highest" (275), Antigone recognizes her brother as the individual ethical self that he is and performs in the Symbolic the essential act of mourning memorialization. By this act she preserves him from the natural reduction that threatens to return the individual to the meaningless negativity of natural process.[17]

Hegel thus neutralizes as well the misogynistic violence that is aroused when the woman is blamed for the infinite passivity of death that overtakes the (male) individual. Yet what if a man were completely unphilosophical about all this, completely absorbed in aggrieved resentment at the foundering of his individuality, and interested only in finding compensation for his suffering? What, that is, if one were Marlow/Kurtz, or Akhilleus?

In the *Iliad* the struggle of lordship and bondage is intimately tied up with an erotic violence of which Hegel does not speak, even though it may well be, as Thomas McCary has argued, that the Homeric heroes provide the model for Hegel's account of lordship and bondage.[18]

If indeed the Homeric heroes are Hegel's model, it must be said that he has radically simplified the outlines of their struggle. In the *Iliad*, sexual desire is put at the disposal of a will to power that is itself motivated by a vengeful urge to seek compensation for the natural reduction that is every warrior's ultimate portion (*moira*). The enemy is to be killed, but the triumph over him is completed, first, by inflicting grief on his wife and parents, and then by raping his wife. And all this is underlain by the unassuageable affect of self-loss, of the warrior's pity for his own death—the ultimate passivity that no human will to power can overcome, but that the warrior can transform momentarily into an illusion of activity when he inflicts the pathos of loss on others, and especially on women.

What is unrepresented but inescapably implied by the *Iliad*, the horizon of its representability, is the realm of the most pornographic of pornography. There is no longer any question of the woman's pleasure: Andromakhe's husband will be killed, her son will be murdered, her city destroyed, and she will be thrown into slavery; and in the midst of all this she will be raped—like all the Trojan women. "Let no man be urgent to take the way homeward / until after he has lain in bed with the wife of a

Trojan / to avenge Helen's struggle and groans" (2.354–56), wise old Nestor exhorts the Greeks. The Greek warrior will satisfy his vengefulness and his lust in one and the same act, upon a woman who at that very moment endures the most total agony of grief over her loss of everything except physical existence, an agony that is itself the effect of the violent power of the man who is now raping her. To make women cry out, their hearts wrung with suffering: there is some emotional luxuriance in this for the vengeful male in the grip of automourning, as though he had been denied something that is his and it were a woman whom he holds responsible, so that only her suffering could satisfy his vengefulness. But, at the same time, it is as though, beyond blame and vengeance, only in and through a woman, in the unlimited flow of a woman's affect, could the flood of a man's grief over the loss of what is most intimately his find the outlet it requires.

We can now approach the cry of the Intended once more, this time by way of a relay through which pass all the active/passive forces of inflicting/mourning that circulate in the jungle portion of Marlow's narrative. This relay is the shutter in relation to which Marlow, Kurtz, and the native helmsman by turns occupy the same position.

The native helmsman. He is the only person killed by the attack that is not an attack, gashed in the side by a spear that comes in through the shutter of the pilot's cabin that Marlow had closed, but that the helmsman foolishly reopened in order to shoot at the bush (46).

Marlow. Just before the helmsman is killed, Marlow looks out through this shutter and sees the wilderness resolve itself into a swarming mass of humanity: "I saw a face amongst the leaves on the level with my own looking at me very fierce and steady, and then suddenly, as though a veil had been removed from my eyes, I made out deep in the tangled gloom, naked breasts, arms, legs, glaring eyes—the bush was swarming with human limbs in movement" (46). Then Marlow closes the shutter.

Kurtz. It is this very same shutter through which Kurtz cannot bear to look, which he asks Marlow to close, and through which he cries at the "invisible wilderness" his intention or desire to wring its heart. That the shutter is an associative link between the helmsman and Kurtz is confirmed by Marlow: "Poor fool!" he exclaims, concerning the helmsman. "If he had only left that shutter alone. He had no restraint, no restraint—just like Kurtz" (51).

Kurtz threatens violence against the wilderness through the shutter, but it is the wilderness that accomplishes violence through the same shutter. And this violence results in Marlow's moment of extravagant grief that echoes the grief of the natives themselves that begins the entire sequence and that thus already at the beginning fulfills the intention Kurtz will voice only later.[19]

Who or what is subject and what is object in all this? When Marlow first looks through the shutter at the jungle, he sees, as in a (Lacanian?) mirror, another (black) face that looks back into his. Black and white, darkness and light, action and passion, mourning and murder circulate in an unbroken flow across all the boundaries that constitute the official rhetoric of Marlow's narration.

This is true of all except the boundary between male and female. Is it that something must stand firm so that everything else can circulate? The aggressive-defensive-protective inflicting/mourning that invades the house of the Intended in a "vengeful rush" (72) does at last find its response in the cry of a woman who mourns Kurtz-for-Marlow with the unmeasured grief that the desire to be mourned requires. Marlow is not seduced by the sexual urge as it is ordinarily understood, nor by desire in any form that he is prepared to name, but by an erotic desire that takes him unawares, that he never recognizes—the desire to inflict mourning on a woman and then to drink of her grief.

But the allure of the woman's grief turns out to be the springe that catches the woodcock, and there is at best a standoff between the triumph of the potent (if ghostly) stiff and that of the receptive female.

Marlow, Pentheus-like, voyeur of "cruel and absurd mysteries not fit for a human being to behold" (73), but also double of the dead man who elicits the woman's cry ("it is his extremity I seem to have lived through" [69]), sees two scenes at once, superimposed in one moment: "I saw her and him in the same instant of time—his death and her sorrow—I saw her sorrow in the very moment of his death" (73). In this "supreme moment of complete knowledge" (68), Kurtz whispers, "The horror, the horror," and the woman, thinking that it is her name that this moment brings from his lips, cries out in agony, but also in exultation.

The ironies are balanced.

On the one hand, in the end a woman will in the most classic fashion be the *hyle* that lends itself to the masculine form the impress of which it will henceforth bear (*hyle* is what the Greeks called 'matter' or substance-without-form, from a base sense as wood or timber, hence 'stuff', 'material').[20]

But in proportion as the Intended tends in Marlow's consciousness to blend with Kurtz's African mistress whose gesture of mourning she repeats, and thus with the wilderness itself, she evokes the form-dissolving power of nature, the power that had caressed Kurtz and consumed his substance (*hyle* also means 'woods', a 'forest'). In *Heart of Darkness* there is no Hegelian neutralization of the woman's "vocation as individual," or of her desire; she is not a sister but a lover, and her mourning does not operate as an ethical intervention that would guard against the process of natural reduction but belongs to the realm of nature that does the reducing. Hence the death of the male that the woman mourns is also inscribed in masculine anxiety as her "inconceivable triumph"; she evokes for Marlow the matrix of primordial mud and the nauseating foulness of corruption that reabsorb the individuality of the male after its momentary flight in pursuit of the ethical.[21] From the outset, the stench of mud and mortality had haunted Marlow's experience of the wilderness:

> in and out of rivers, streams of death in life, whose banks were rotting into mud, whose waters . . . thickened into slime. (17)

> The smell of mud, of primeval mud by Jove, was in my nostrils. (29)

> a provision of hippo-meat . . . went rotten and made the mystery of the wilderness stink in my nostrils. Phoo! I can sniff it now. (36)

> I felt an intolerable weight oppressing my breast, the smell of the damp earth, the unseen presence of victorious corruption. (62)

All these references converge on the taste of lying, that taste that is "like biting something rotten" (29), hence on the culminating lie Marlow tells the woman, the lie *she forces him to tell*.[22]

Nevertheless, the woman's "power" that excites Marlow's anxiety belongs as little to an autonomous feminine subjectivity as does the pure passivity to which Marlow's fantasy of her eternal grief reduces the Intended.[23] The woman as force of generic life is here a male fantasy, and it may be that it is the force of such a fantasy that motivates the attempt to contain women within the constraints of a straitened "separate sphere."[24]

The fantasy at work here, and its specific effect in terms of the attempt to control women, is restricted neither to Conrad's tale nor to the Victorian milieu out of which it comes. The triumph in the cry of the Intended resumes that of the *alaladzo* or *ololuge*, the cry of the maenads as they set upon their sacrificial victim. Like *Heart of Darkness*, Euripides' *Bacchae* was concerned with "natural" impulse that overpowers cultural restraint, and with masculinity that seeks to shore up its boundaries against the upsurge of nature that it construes as "feminine." (The Athenians, of course, restricted the sphere of women to a degree unimaginable by the Victorians.)

Thus as with *Heart of Darkness* we reach modernity we find that in certain quarters nothing has changed in Western history with respect to the question of thanato-erotic anxiety. When (masculine) thought plumbs the depth of existence, what it discovers, as always, is the unendurable embrace of a corruptible and corrupting body of love—one that characteristically is imaged as female.

CHAPTER EIGHT

The Bride Stripped Bare,
or Lacan *avec* Plato

*B*EYOND THE LACANIAN IMAGINARY AND SYMBOLIC, THERE IS AL-
ways the beyond of the true subject.[1] In the "Rome report" this beyond is
evoked as "the immediate particularity of desire"; in book 7 of the Seminar it is gestured toward in terms of "the second death"; in book 11, most
surprisingly and enigmatically, it is identified with *lost immortality.*

I do not imagine that there is some absolute privilege to the moment at
which Lacan tells us that immortality is the object commemorated in the
nostalgia of lack; he is endlessly fertile in the creation of new articulations
for his *via negativa,* each of which displaces in subtle ways aspects of
whatever seemed to have been set reliably in place by previous articulations. Yet Lacan himself privileges the trope of lost immortality in a
rather startling way when, taking as his point of departure Plato's *Symposium,* he tells us that immortality is to be understood as the *real* lack. The
other lack, the one that is commonly taken to be at the very foundation of
Lacanism, *supervenes* upon this "real, earlier lack":

> Two lacks overlap here. The first emerges . . . by the fact that the
> subject depends on the signifier and that the signifier is first of all in
> the field of the Other. This lack takes up the other lack, which is the
> real, earlier lack, to be situated at the advent of the living being, that
> is to say, at sexed reproduction. . . . This lack is real because it relates
> to something real, namely, that the living being, by being subject to
> sex, has fallen under the blow of individual death. (11.204–5)

In terms of this "real lack," we get a surprisingly positive account of the mysterious "*objet a*": "all the forms of the *Objet a*" are "representatives" or "equivalents" of the "immortal life" that is lost at birth (198).

If Lacan is not to be taken quite literally when he tells us that the *objet a* is the representative of immortal life, neither is it a matter of undecidable "speculation" of the sort Derrida has analyzed in Freud's *Beyond the Pleasure Principle*.[2] Lacan is expressing an ethical stance, a judgment on libidinal being, and this moment in his text is of a piece with the ethical architecture of his entire system, which in turn is solidary, at a crucial level—the level in which I have been interested in this entire book—with Platonizing Christianity. Hence the *objet a* is readily translatable into Christian language: "the religious tradition," Lacan tells us in his reading of *Hamlet*, calls the *objet a* a "*vanitas*". "This is how all objects are presented, all the stakes in the world of human desire—the *objets a*."[3]

An intriguing question arises around such moments in Lacan's text. Lacan operates what appears to be an unparalleled negativity in the movement of his thought, a negativity of which Mikkel Borch-Jacobsen has recently given a masterful representation.[4] Holes and absences, and behind these, holes and absences: Lacan seems to deny satisfaction to the nostalgia for presence in what might be taken as a most scrupulously "deconstructive" fashion. This aspect of his doctrine is well known and no doubt constitutes a crucial element in its attractiveness for poststructuralist theory. What interests me here, however, is that in and through this movement of negativity Lacan preserves in a sophisticated new fashion the Christian/Platonic depreciation of the worldly libidinal object as a "*vanitas*," a deceptive appearance that lures the subject away from her ontological destiny.

For Lacan as for the tradition, the annulment of this allure, the relegation of the libidinal object to the realm of nonbeing, is the necessary condition for the liberation of the subject's *true desire*, a desire the aim of which cannot be realized by means of any empirical object—a *vanitas* or *objet a*. In recognizing the truth of her desire, the subject recognizes her own truth, becomes the true subject that she really always was but from which she had been alienated. For Lacan this true subject is no longer a "presence," because the self-propriation or reappropriation that is aimed at involves the annulment of the self that is reappropriated; and this marks an important break with the idealizing tradition, which promises another, fuller reality beyond the sacrifice of the empirical self or ego. Nevertheless, we will see that the point of annulment/reappropriation is the point of the *beyond* that always reemerges out of the rubble of Lacanian negativity, and—this is what I want most of all to emphasize—always at the expense of the libidinal object.

The beyond of the subject that constitutes its ownmost propriety is not to be comprehended within the dialectic of self and Other; it is, rather, what is always left over from any such entanglement. "There is, in effect, something radically unassimilable to the signifier. It's quite simply the subject's singular existence" (3.179). Quite simply: it isn't often that Lacan authorizes the use of one of his concepts in this way. The subject's "singular existence" is nothing, but an absolutely determinate nothing, because it is the nothing of this particular destiny. Particularity in its absoluteness is necessarily nothing, because it is outside of both the identifications of the Imaginary and the significations of the Symbolic; yet this nothingness is not the mere negativity of the void but the affirmation of an absolute self-proximity and self-propriety. This negative affirmation is the source of a tragical/existential pathos of authenticity that makes Lacan's tale of bleeding eye sockets something other than a mere vision of horror; for Lacan, Oedipus has "a beautiful attitude, and, as the madrigal says, it's twice as beautiful on account of its beauty" (7.306). Human desire is for Lacan, at the limit, a desire to contract into the infinite particularity of one's own being as a being of nothingness. This means that, all the while that the various dialectics of desire and identification are being played out at the level of the mirror, the other, and the Other, there is an entirely different level, an ontological or transcendental level, at which the real destiny of the subject is decided, at which in a sense it has always already been decided. The Being of the subject is *never*, at this ontological level, implicated in the images or signifiers in which it is alienated.

That is why it is possible ever to speak of alienation in the first place. Only that can be alienated which has a "proper" to begin with; hence the mirror stage in which the subject first begins to come into being is, by an apparent paradox, already a movement of alienation ("armour of an alienating identity" [*E*4], "image that alienates him from himself" [19]).

Similarly, in the process by which desire emerges out of the subtraction of need from demand, there is a strong sense that desire manifests the *reappearance* of some mysterious essence that was already there at the beginning, the mysterious "it" that turns up "alienated in needs" (ce qui se trouve aliéné dans les besoins) when they "return" to the subject after being submitted to demand:

in so far as his needs are subjected to demand, they return (*reviennent*) to him alienated. . . .

That [?] which is thus alienated in needs constitutes an Urverdrägung (primal repression), an inability, it is supposed, to be articulated in demand, but it [?] *re-appears* [*apparait:* but Sheridan's "re-" seems faithful to Lacan's sense] in something it [?] gives rise to that presents itself in man as desire. (E286/690)

In one sense need is what can be satisfied, as for example hunger by food; but in another, more complex sense, it is the bearer of unsatisfiable desire in its archaic, inchoate form. The emergence of desire is a question of *Aufhebung* in the strict sense, as the realization of the *truth of need* in its cancellation. Desire is "already there" in need in a complex metaphysical modality, no doubt, and we have to make all the necessary concessions to the negativity of Lacan's discourse. The "before" of the particularity of the subject is projected retrospectively, *nachträglich,* and as a nothingness. Yet it was indeed there at the beginning, before being re-cognized in the mirror, as "original desire, unconstituted and confused" (1.170). There is an *absolute priority* within the movement of Lacan's discourse to this "it"- that-returns; it accrues to itself the most highly valorized predicates and orients the sense in the final analysis of all the other terms. In "The Signification of the Phallus," as elsewhere, it is the term *particularity* (*particularité*) that signals the residual positivity of Lacan's beyond, the Being of the "re-":

In this way, demand annuls (*aufhebt*) the particularity of everything that can be granted by transmuting it into a proof of love, and the very satisfactions that it obtains for need are reduced (*sich erniedrigt*) to the level of being no more than the crushing of the demand for love. . . .

It is necessary, then, that the particularity thus abolished should reappear *beyond* demand. It [i.e., the abolished particularity] does, in fact, reappear there, but preserving the structure contained in the unconditional element of the demand for love. By a reversal that is not simply a negation of the negation, the power of pure loss emerges from the residue of an obliteration. For the unconditional element of demand, desire substitutes the "absolute" condition: this condition unties the knot of that element in the proof of love that is resistant to the satisfaction of a need. Thus desire is neither the appetite for satisfaction, nor the demand for love, but the difference that results from the subtraction of the first from the second, the phenomenon of their splitting (*Spaltung*). (*E* 286–87/691)

Part of the difficulty of this much-quoted passage comes from the fact that the "particularity" that reappears is not, or not exactly, the one that was *aufgehoben*. In the reappearance beyond demand of this abolished particularity what reappears is not the object-as-*aufgehoben* (milk, or the breast) but the *subject* who had formerly demanded, and identified with, the now-abolished object.[5] This reappearance is described obscurely, as the transition from the particularity of a thing to a particularity of which we know only that it "preserves" a "structure" originally "contained" in the "unconditional element" of demand; and what can Lacan mean when he says that this structure is *reversed* into the "absolute condition" of desire?

That the particularity preserved here is that of the subject is confirmed in Lacan's redescription of the genesis of desire two years later in "Subversion of the Subject and Dialectic of Desire." Here, he refers to the "margin" between demand and need in which "desire begins to take shape" as "a subjective opacity" (*opacité subjective*) (*E* 311/813). This "subjective opacity" is linked to the subject's "anxiety" at the threat of the fantasized omnipotence of the Other—that is, the mother—to whom the subject is subjected. What "Subversion of the Subject" makes clear is that the Law of the Father comes not to deny the child access to the mother but to *rescue* him from the "elephantine feet" of the mother's "omnipotent" whim. "It is this whim that introduces the phantom of the Omnipotence . . . of the Other in which his demand is installed . . . , and with this phantom the need for it to be checked by the Law" (311).[6] And Lacan now also sheds some light on the "absolute condition" of desire: in the "unconditional element of the demand for love," the subject remains "in subjection to the Other," but in "rising" to the "absolute condition" the subject attains "detachment," evidently from the Other/mother (ibid.). The account of "subjective opacity" in "Subversion of the Subject" thus suggests that what is involved in the transition from need to demand to desire is above all the preservation of the "particularity" of the subject from an Other—the mother—that makes it anxious and threatens to overwhelm it.

In the background of both of the passages I have just considered is the account of the child's *fort-da* of *Beyond the Pleasure Principle* that Lacan had developed in the "Rome report" of 1953. According to this account, the child in Freud's anecdote or fable detaches himself from his dependence on the presence of the mother by transposing his desire onto the play of a signifier (a bobbin on a string) by which he plays out the relation of presence and absence. The child's action, Lacan wrote, "negatives the field of forces of desire [i.e., as a field involving real others] in order to become its own object to itself"; desire is thus raised "to a second power" (*E* 103) as it lifts itself free of the reality of the object and sets itself in relation to a signifier. What is in question in the "Rome report," as in Lacan's later accounts, is the "absoluteness" of desire that implies "detachment" from the Other whose presence or absence agonizes the subject. Yet, as we will see, the subject jumps from the frying pan of the mother only to land in the fire of the Symbolic. What is always in question is the autonomy of a self whose *particularity* as desire is constantly exposed to alienation or annulment.

Now, the subject as pure desire cannot have the particularity of a thing in the world but only that of pure structure or form, as is the case, Lacan observes in "Kant avec Sade" (an important essay not included in the English selection of the *Écrits*), with Kant's moral law, the "form" of which is "its sole substance" (*E* 770). Yet structure is normally the element of transparticularity or universality, whereas the structure of Lacanian desire has to be understood precisely as the structure of *absolute particularity*, of individuation beyond that which matter can bestow. Desire is nothing but the self-attraction or re-turn to itself of a mortal particularity, the pull of its death as that by which it knows itself, beyond the *cogito*, to be that very being of nothingness that it is.

This particularity is the primordial and recurrent (non)substance out of which is woven Being-toward-death in the final pages of the "Rome report." Here Lacan describes the suicide of the vanquished in the master-slave struggle as "the supreme detour through which the immediate particularity (*particularité immediate*) of desire, reconquering its ineffable form, rediscovers in negation a final triumph" (*E* 104/320). This negation, Lacan affirms, is "that desperate affirmation of life that is the purest form in which we recognize the death instinct." As we will see, in Seminar 7 Lacan valorizes this same "desperate affirmation" of the death instinct as the path of tragical-existential heroism. The suicidal slave of the "Rome report" must thus be understood as incipiently heroic in his negation.

This heroism involves the negation of *the Symbolic itself* in the interest of the immediate-particularity-beyond-thingness of the desiring subject: "The subject says 'No!' to this intersubjective game of hunt-the-slipper in which desire makes itself recognized for a moment, only to become lost in a will that is will of the other. Patiently, the subject withdraws his precarious life from the sheeplike conglomerations of the Eros of the symbol in order to affirm it at last in an unspoken curse" (104–5). It is true that

Lacan then proceeds to describe this moment of negation as one pole of an "endless circularity": The dialectic of Lacanian psychoanalysis is "not individual," and it is only within this dialectic that "the subject brings his solitude to realization" (105). Yet between the Symbolic and the "centre exterior to language" (ibid.) that makes possible its transformation into full speech—the center constituted by the individual's relation to a death that Lacan, citing Heidegger, calls one's "ownmost" and "unsupersedable" possibility (103)—there is a more destructive, less dialectical relation than Lacan's pacifying (and uncharacteristic) remark here about "the satisfaction of everyone" (105) suggests.

There is a modification of desire, a sort of reflex, that accompanies it wherever it goes, right up to the point of death; and this reflex of aggressivity or hatred, which Lacan in Seminar 7 calls "the *destrudo*" (7.194), is always waiting in the wings to wreck any accommodation with the Symbolic that Lacan might momentarily hold out.

Lacan, who sometimes gestures at historicizing his theories, seems to believe in the intrinsic character of jealous, aggressive rivalry; he is fond of quoting Augustine's famous remark from book 1 of the *Confessions* about the infant in arms who already glares with hatred "at another baby sharing his milk."[7] Anyone who thinks it strange to encounter in Lacan the Augustinian view of "human nature" has not attended to the faithfulness with which he ties his text to the dialectic of mourning elaborated by the Platonizing tradition. In the final analysis, desire is not for Lacan a matter of anything that this or that empirical instance could either show or refute; the level of empirical demonstration or "clinical experience" is always only an intermediate moment on the way to the definition of a transcendental structure. The "Freudian experience" starts "by postulating a world of desire. It postulates it prior to any experience" (2.222). The aggressivity unleashed at the level of imaginary relations must be *derived*, but it cannot finally be derived, even by way of *Aufhebung*, from anything like a biologically given urge or energy. The mysterious "tension" experienced in the premirror stage and catalyzed into aggressivity by the mirror-experience (*E* 19) must, in the last instance, be derived ontologically, at the level of the Being of the subject. Thus Lacan implies already in 1948 that the aggressivity associated with the ego is rooted in a primordial disharmony, that the "negative libido" (21) unleashed by the mirror stage has something to do with Heraclitus's notion of a primal Discord (21); by the time of Seminar 7 he will cite Luther on the existence of "a hatred that existed even before the world was created" (7.97).[8]

The notion of aggressivity plays an absolutely crucial role in Lacan's theory of clinical technique. Aggressivity is the force that drives the analysis. The analyst in his neutrality waits for the explosion of the patient's aggressivity that is the negative transference, the "initial knot of the analytic drama" (*E* 14). Once the negative transference is activated, the analyst knows that the subject is launched on the "regression" that will take him through the stages of "decomposition" of the ego's structure (*E* 44), because the aggressivity tapped by the negative transference is precisely that which has sutured the self to its ego-relations.

But the significance of the destructive impulse of aggressivity goes beyond its role in narcissism; it is linked, Lacan argues in Seminar 7, to that ultimate impulse of self that wants to negate *all created being*. What is "modestly called the negative therapeutic reaction," he now declares, is identical with what "at the more remarkable level of literary generality" he terms the "malediction" of Oedipus, the curse against existence implied in his *me phynai* 'rather not to be', as Lacan translates it (313, 306). This curse shows us the path of uncompromising desire. Oedipus's malediction is the word of "true being-for-death" (309), and his negation demonstrates the "true subsistence of a human being, the subsistence of the subtraction of himself from the order of the world" (306). This is where Lacan comments that "it's a beautiful attitude." Beautiful because it is not, as Mikkel Borch-Jacobsen gives us to think, ultimately a matter of void-beyond-void, but of that empty-yet-full *particularity* of the own-most. "If analysis has a meaning," desire is "the very articulation of that which roots us in a particular destiny (*destinée particuliere*)" and which keeps us on "the track of something that is specifically our business (*proprement nôtre affaire*)" (319/368).

In Seminar 7 Lacan uses the example of Sophocles' *Antigone* to articulate once more the paradoxical relation that the particularity of an individual destiny has to the order of language. Antigone's brother is "something unique"; that is why Antigone distinguishes him from a husband or children, who might be replaced (7.279). The value of his being is purely and simply its uniqueness or particularity, "without reference to any content." Whatever Polynices has done, the predicates that one might attach to his being are irrelevant; yet the "register of being of someone who was identified by a name has to be preserved by funeral rites." The "unique value" involved cannot exist outside of language; it is precisely the fact that this was a linguistic being that shelters his uniqueness from the universality of the animal species (ibid.). And yet this uniqueness is precisely the beyond toward which language can only gesture, the "center extrinsic to language" of the "Rome report." "Involved is an horizon determined by a structural relation; it only exists on the basis of the language of words, but it reveals their unsurpassable consequence" (278).

On the one hand, the Symbolic captures the desire of the subject in the endless round of signification, keeps him at a distance from *jouissance* by subjecting him to the pleasure principle. "The function of the pleasure principle is, in effect, to lead the subject from signifier to signifier, by generating as many signifiers as are required to maintain at as low a level as possible the tension that regulates the whole functioning of the psychic apparatus" (7.119). But, on the other hand, in some mysterious way, at the limit of its elaboration by certain profound practitioners, say Sophocles or Lacan, "the signifier in its most radical form" (295) can put "man" "in relationship" with that which is absolutely transcendent to the signifier, the transcendent void that is the correlative of the desire of the subject in his authentic particularity (119). Lacan in Seminar 7 calls this void "the Thing," *das Ding*. The Thing is the transcendent or transcendental non-object, the negative of the Platonic Idea in whose place it nevertheless stands, at the summit of the hierarchy of desires. Since "this Thing will always be represented by emptiness" (129), the function of the Symbolic as route of access to authentic desire involves fundamentally the annulment of the particularity of all empirical objects of desire. This annulment reveals the Thing for which objects can be only the stand-ins or reminiscences and thus reveals as well the unspeakable particularity of the subject.

At the core of the pursuit of *jouissance* as transgressive approach to the forbidden Thing, then, is the transcendent *destrudo*. At the limit, "the unspeakable field of radical desire" is "the field of absolute destruction, of destruction beyond putrefaction" (7.216); it seeks to annihilate "the very cycles of the transformations of nature" (248). Along the way to this apocalyptic culmination (which Lacan, following Sade, calls "the second death" [211, 248]), however, what is involved is the more modest, and from the present perspective more consequential, annulment of all libidinal objects in the ordinary worldly sense. Thus, taking up the themes of Seminar 7 and of "Kant avec Sade," Lacan tells us in Seminar 11 that "in its pure state" desire "culminates in the sacrifice, strictly speaking, of everything that is the object of love in one's human tenderness—I would say, not only in the rejection of the pathological object [in Kant's sense, as object of feeling] but also in its sacrifice and murder" (275–76). This is what the function of aggressivity or destructiveness comes to at the limit— the "sacrifice and murder" of the object.

Lacan is not of course speaking of actual physical sacrifice and murder, but of the need to "renounce the object" through the intervention of the "paternal metaphor" (11.276). He is rearticulating the question of the game of Fort-Da and of the resolution of the Oedipus complex. Yet it is striking that only in the extremities of violence does he find the suitable figures for what he perceives as the ultimate tendencies of desire.

This is especially striking because Lacan's account is rooted from the outset in a condemnation of a thoroughly classical type that Lacan levels against libidinal investment.

As we shall see, Lacan's critique of the allure of the "pathological" object is not free of the thanatoerotophobic misogyny of the tradition from which it springs; and this raises questions about the nature of the urge to "destroy" the object that Lacan perceives at the core of *jouissance.*

The entire problematic of imaginary captivation, let us recall, is elaborated in relation to sexual allure at the level of the animals; this is one of Lacan's most insistently repeated themes in Seminar 1. "In the animal world, the entire cycle of sexual behavior is dominated by the imaginary" (1.138); it is in fact the very "essence of the image" that it is "invested by the libido" (141). To be captivated by libidinally invested images is to be trapped like an animal at the level of "the cycle of sexual behaviour," of the "mechanical throwing into gear of the sexual instinct" (122). Of course the critique of love-as-imaginary-capture is precisely that one doesn't see the Other as such, but only one's own image in the other (142)—but this "egomorphic" character (2.166) is also what the Christian tradition found to blame in all mortal love. The problem with egomorphic love, for Augustine and for Lacan, is that it *misses the self;* the subject falls for a cheap substitute and loses his ownmost propriety in the process. "The libidinal captation has an irremediably fatal significance for the individual" (1.148); "the individual is so much a captive of the type that, in relation to this type, it is annihilated" (145). This is the death of mere animal nature, the death that has been conceived at least since the Greeks at once as organic cessation, the tremor of sexual conjunction, the passage of the individual into the universality of the species, and the reduction of the form of the individual by what Hegel calls the "unconscious forces of nature." Lacan evokes this death in the "Rome report" as well, with Hegel and Hegel's Antigone apparently in mind though they are not mentioned:

> This [human] life is the only life that endures and is true, since it is transmitted without being lost in the perpetuated tradition of subject

to subject. How is it possible not to see how loftily this life tran-
scends that inherited by the animal, in which the individual disap-
pears into the species, since no memorial distinguishes his ephemeral
apparition from that which will reproduce it again in the invariability
of the type. (*E* 104)

Lacan, who rarely mentions Nietzsche, is actually very close to him in
some ways, at least to the Nietzsche who defends to the last the boundary
of his absolute particularity, who fears most of all *to be torn* by sexual
desire, by a woman, by the universality of the species, and who, at least in
his earliest phase, developed the pathos of *sparagmos*, like Lacan, into an
interpretation of tragedy and a "tragic sense of life" (7.313).[9] "It is in the
nature of desire to be radically torn," says Lacan, because the subject is
"irremediably separated" from the object, an object that "by essence
destroys him" (2.166). "The perfect woman always tears to pieces when
she loves," Nietzsche wrote in *Ecce Homo*, in what Lacan might have
recognized as a profound insight into the nature of *das Ding*.

We have already seen that it is first of all the mother who threatens the
subject with destruction, the mother who, apparently, can never be, in
D. W. Winnicott's hopeful term, "good enough." She is structurally or
essentially condemned, no matter which way she goes, to threaten with
destruction the absolute particularity of the subject. For if satisfying need
is a way of crushing the demand for love, *satisfying this demand would be
even worse*. There is the case in which

> the Other, which has its own ideas about [the subject's] needs, inter-
> feres, and in place of that which it does not have, stuffs him with the
> choking pap of what it has, that is to say, confuses his needs with the
> gift of its love.
>
> It is the child one feeds with most love who refuses food and plays
> with his refusal as with a desire (anorexia nervosa).
>
> Confines where one grasps as nowhere else that hate pays the coin
> of love. (*E* 263–64)

Feminist readings of Lacan have tended to interpret the infant's pre-
Oedipal relation to the mother as a pleasurable symbiosis that is disrupted
by the father,[10] but we have seen that what Lacan calls the "privileged
mode of presence" of the law represented by the father "originates in
desire" out of the need for the Other/mother to "be checked by the Law"
(311). In fact, as Marcel Marini notes, "the mother as origin" is, for Lacan,
"an unthinkable figure."[11]

This is so even though Lacan also says that "the desire of the mother is the origin of everything" (7.283). Rigorously speaking, the mother is only the first empirical occupant of the transcendental place of *das Ding*, which is itself the unattainable object of desire that can in truth only be represented by an emptiness (129). Everything that has to do with "mother/child interpsychology" is rooted in the incest taboo, but the incest taboo itself only expresses "the essential character of the maternal thing, the mother, insofar as she occupies the place of that thing, of *das Ding*" (67; cf. 106, where Lacan comments on Melanie Klein). *Das Ding* itself is absolutely inaccessible, a reminiscence like that of immortality; it is "the prehistoric Other that it is impossible to forget" (7.71). The law of the father comes to save us from the "choking pap" of the mother's love so that the transcendental form of desire may be revealed behind the empirical beings that stand in for it.

This transcendental form was revealed in a particularly profound and important way, Lacan believes, by the troubadours. Troubadour love is a "historical modification of Eros" (7.99) the effects of which on us have been "decisive"; it has "left traces in an unconscious, . . . a whole imagery, that we continue to inhabit as far as our relations with women are concerned" (112). What is so significant about "courtly love" is that by surrounding the lady with "cultural elaborations" which posit her as "inaccessible" and "depersonalized," "emptied of all real substance" (149), the courtly lover "elevates" his object "to the dignity of the Thing" (112). But *das Ding* can only be represented as a void or emptiness; to manifest emptiness is why, for example, pottery was invented (120); this is also the fundamental secret of architecture (136). So it should come as no surprise that, at the highest point of elevation of woman, where she attains the "dignity" of signifier of *das Ding*, it should be "her thing" denuded that manifests "the emptiness of a thing in all its crudity" (163).

Lacan arrives at this conclusion on the basis of a poem of disputed authorship, most commonly attributed to Arnaut Daniel: the notorious *sirventes* "Pois En Raimons ni Truc Malecs."[12] The poem is an obvious satire on the notion of courtly love service. The lady has asked her lover, one Bernard de Cornilh, that he do to her something called "cornar," which is variously interpreted as anal intercourse or, in the more likely reading, as oral-anal contact. The word "cornar" is thus to be rendered as "blowing her horn" or "putting one's mouth to her horn." The author, let us say Arnaut, contributes this poem to a satirical debate on the question of whether Bernard de Cornilh had been right to refuse his lady's request. Two other poets, the Raimon and Truc Malec of Arnaut's first line, condemn Bernard's refusal; but Arnaut, taking Bernard's side, opines that *cornar* does not constitute a valid trial of love: "There will truly be other practice tests (*assais*) / More beautiful and of greater value" (18.19–20).

The debate on the question comprises three extant poems and part of a fourth, and, as Pierre Bec points out, the "internal cohesion" of the cycle is guaranteed by the repetition of the identical rhyme scheme, "which is moreover exclusively specific [in the troubadour corpus] to these four pieces" (139). This scheme involves the repetition within each stanza of the identical rhyme at the end of each of the stanza's nine lines, which gives a rollicking, comical effect to the whole. What we have in this cycle is an example of the dialectic of troubadour formalism, and an extraordinarily high-spirited one; here the burlesque of the conventions of *fin'amors* is pursued in a completely overt fashion.

Truc Malec in one of the poems to which Arnaut is apparently replying declares that Bernard has been a fool to disdain the lady's anus or *corn* 'horn', the sight of which she had vouchsafed him, and that, for his own part, he would joyously have "put his mouth to her horn" (ieu lai volgr' aver cornat / Alegrament); in the other poem, by Raimon de Durfort, the lady is quoted, even if only fictively, as saying that she has thoroughly washed herself so that her lover will smell no noxious odor: Qu'ien l'ai fach lavar e forbir / E ja no'l sentiretz pudir (23–24). As we saw in chapter 4, the dialectic of troubadour formalism regularly generates transgressions of the forms it sets up, even within the genre of the *canso* 'love poem'. Thus Arnaut's poem can be accounted for on purely formal grounds, as a satirical inversion of the poems to which he is replying, when he describes the lady's "horn" as "rough and soiled and hairy" (12), a "swamp" (14) of which "the stench would shortly have killed you" (33). For all we know, Arnaut might have been known to his friends as an enthusiastic sexual experimentalist—a possibility supported by Dante's placement of him among the sodomites in the *Purgatorio*—such that his audience would have howled with delight to hear him adopt this finicking stance.

Lacan, however, ignores the properly literary level of the play of the signifier and (as in the case of *The Purloined Letter*) goes straight to the message that he finds embodied here, which he translates as the utterance of a woman. In so doing, he also ignores the fact that, unlike Raimon, Arnaut does not even pretend to cite the woman's voice but explicitly uses the male voice throughout. Because this lady is no actual woman but a culturally constructed signifier, Lacan feels free to ventriloquate her utterance from the place he tells us is defined by Arnaut's poem.

The idealized woman, the Lady, who is in the position of the Other and of the object, finds herself suddenly and brutally positing, in a place knowingly constructed out of the most refined of signifiers, the emptiness of a thing in all its crudity, a thing that reveals itself in its nudity to be the thing, her thing, the one that is to be found at her very heart in its cruel emptiness. (7.163)

... at the extreme point of his invocation to the signifier, she warns the poet of the form she may take as signifier. I am, she tells him, nothing more than the emptiness to be found in my own internal cesspit, not to say anything worse. Just blow in that for a while and see if your sublimation holds up. (7.215)

One might ask: How can emptiness be accused of crudity? When was a cesspit ever empty? And how does the woman's "thing" come to be located at her *heart*? Here we are, once again, only more candidly than in Conrad, at a certain male fantasy of the heart of darkness, the cruel emptiness of a woman's heart that is equivalent to her "internal cesspit."

But where are we in the Lacanian topography? The lady is not an imaginary lady; if she were, all her lover would perceive would be the egomorphic reflection of his own narcissism. This lady is no image; she is made out of words, and we find her at the level of the Symbolic order, all the way into the network of signifiers at its most complexly elaborated. "It is only when the person involved is transformed into a symbolic function that one is able to speak of her in the crudest terms" (7.149). These terms, in evoking the real of the body, rupture the Symbolic and open it out into its beyond as the field of the Thing. What Lacan is interested in, once again, is the paradox of how the relation to the signifier, which traps man at the level of the pleasure principle, can lead "man" to the beyond, how it can "put him in relationship with an object that represents the Thing" (119). Hence the special significance of courtly love. "Courtly love marked the rise to the surface in European culture of a problematic of desire as such" (235). The place of the thing that, in the empirical genesis of the psyche, is originally occupied by the mother is occupied at the other end of the symbolic ascent by the Cruel Lady. And, at the limit of this symbolic elaboration, at the very verge of the passage to the pure nothing that desire desires, we find the nausea of a stinking female aperture.

Of course Lacan does not, strictly speaking, refer to a female aperture but to an aperture indifferent to gender, a cloaca that belongs to no woman, or man either, but to a "terrifying, inhuman" being (150) who is figured as female. And the Thing that the lady, or the lady's "cesspit," figures is even more inhuman and ungendered than the cloaca itself.

Lacan would have it, apparently, that if the lady, and the mother before her, stand in for the Thing, there is no *necessary* connection between the Thing and femininity. There is an empirical condition of near-universal extension that situates the mother as the first Other, but this does not give her a logical or transcendental privilege. The "primal dyad" of the game of *fort-da* must be understood in a general sense, as a relation to the Other, but not necessarily, even if in the original example and in general that's who it is, the mother. The mother is only an example: "It is in the interval between these two signifiers that resides the desire offered to the mapping of the subject in the experience of the discourse of the Other, of the first Other he has to deal with, *let us say, by way of illustration*, the mother" (11.218; italics added).

Yet the mother and the female sex that she embodies are not just one possible example among others. The whole question of castration arises for the young child, Lacan insists, primarily out of the discovery of the mother's castration, of the fact that there is only "an absence, a void, a hole" (3.176) where the phallus should be. So there is something about the female body that suits it, at the level of the Real and the Imaginary, for representing the "central void," precisely that same fact that assures that the woman's sex will be subtracted from the Symbolic order, for "strictly speaking there is no symbolization of woman's sex as such" (ibid.). But this dubious privilege of feminine anatomy is, metaphysically speaking, accidental. At the more sophisticated, symbolic level of representation attained by the troubadours, we find that the anus serves just as well, perhaps even better, insofar as it is a *transsexual* hole; also in that the anus, as Lacan informs us in a curious passage, feels more like a ring, and is thus closer to "signifying value," whereas the vagina feels purely natural, "more like a mollusk than anything else" (316–17).

And yet it remains that at certain highly privileged moments in Lacan's text, it is on the support of a woman's body that Lacan descries the void. Not only in the culturally "decisive" posing of the problematic of desire by the troubadours, but also in "the initial dream, the dream of dreams, the inaugurally deciphered dream" (2.147) that lies at the very origin of psychoanalysis: Freud's dream of Irma's injection. In one of his most brilliant and persuasive interpretations of a text, Lacan argues that what Freud discovers in this dream, and which is most crucially represented in the chemical notation for trimethylamine, is the secret of the symbolic structure of the dream and of the unconscious (157–60). But in order to arrive at this insight, Freud has to traverse a "moment of great anxiety," the moment at which Freud *forces* Irma to let him look into her throat. Here is Freud's own account of what he sees: "I find on the right a large white spot, and elsewhere I see some remarkable curled structures which evidently are patterned on the nasal turbinal bones, extensive white-grey scabs."[13] Now here is Lacan's interpretation:

> What he sees in there, these turbinate bones covered with a whitish membrane, is a horrendous sight. This mouth has all the equivalences in terms of significations, all the condensations you want. Everything blends in and becomes associated in this image, from the mouth to the female sexual organ, by way of the nose [N.B.]. . . . There's a horrendous discovery here, that of the flesh one never sees, the foundation of things . . . the flesh from which everything exudes, at the very heart of the mystery, the flesh in as much as it is suffering, is formless, in as much as its form in itself is something which provokes anxiety. Spectre of anxiety, identification of anxiety, the final revelation of *you are this . . . this which is the ultimate formlessness.* (154–55)

Here is the hyperliteral vision in the hysterical mode once again. As in Hamlet's hysteria, what is at issue here is the identification of the body as such with the body of dissolution, ultimate formlessness as the hidden secret of the form of the body, and somehow, beyond form—there where my chapfallen lady is no longer distinguishable in her sex from Yorick—the form of the female. Death is neither male nor female, it is the undoing of the distinction; and yet in these texts it is more female than male (even to the point at which the nose can be inverted or subincised into the female genitalia).

Notice the special force of Lacan's declaration that this is the "final revelation of *you are this.*" "You are this" is a phrase that has a crucial significance for Lacan. "It's the foundation or foundational speech—*you are this, my woman, my master*" (3.279); but in the dream of Irma's injection the *you are this* occurs at the limit of all speech and all relation, there where we peer into the *beyond.*

Must there not be a direct relation between this moment of total anxiety in which Freud looks into the putrescence of the nose-womb-tomb, and from which he then emerges by access to the Symbolic order, calling upon "the congress of all those who know" (Freud: "*I quickly call Dr. M., who repeats and confirms the examination. . . . My friend Otto now*

also stands next to her, and my friend Leopold percusses her bodice") so that
"another voice can be heard," the voice of the one who writes *Mene,
Mene, Tekel, Upharsin* on the wall (2.158–59)—must there not be a direct
relation, if not a complete identity, between this moment of anxiety and
the one from "Subversion of the Subject" in which desire brings forth the
law in response to the threat of the omnipotence of the Other/mother?

One begins to wonder just what kind of mothering Lacan must have
had as a small child. How can anyone who has learned to read psycho-
analytically not wonder whether something from Lacan's own personal
history is pulling the strings of his discourse at certain moments when he
speaks in universalizing terms of the infant's relation to the mother? And
if Lacan's account is only the story of one such possible relation, grounded
in the vicissitudes of a particular childhood—a merely contingent, empirical possibility, even if one that might be actualized with some fre-
quency in Lacan's culture—then many of Lacan's claims fall by the way-
side, as does the portentous tonality of much of his discourse.

Eloquence, profundity, and philosophical sophistication are not scientific demonstration. Of course Lacan claims to penetrate the pretenses of
scientific method and to supersede ordinary science by his own "science of
desire"; but the persuasiveness of that claim itself rests on the persuasiveness of his account of the moment of origin of desire, the moment we
have been considering.[14]

In this account Lacan repeats practically verbatim the main themes of
the thanatoerotophobic tradition. One might wish to follow him when he
does so, but at least one should know to what metaphysics one is declaring allegiance—as Lacan most certainly knows, even if many of his
followers do not. Lacan consciously brews a mixture of Platonism and
Augustinianism when he writes that "every object relation" is "infected
with a fundamental uncertainty" because the empirical object is "only
ever graspable as a mirage" (2.169) and warns us that "in effect, when we
are in another's power, we are in great danger" (7.84). And we confirm
once again that this danger, which is the danger of the libidinal object *in
general*, has a peculiar relation to women: the words "damage" and "danger" are etymologically related to "domination" and to "dame in the
archaic French sense, our lady" (ibid.).

Lacan frequently ridicules the notion other psychoanalysts champion
of a mature genital sexuality, an erotic "oblativity" that would provide the
grounds of an enduring and satisfying sexual relation. Yet at times he
holds out another ideal of such love, a more mature maturity and a more

generous oblativity, that would operate at the level of the Symbolic order. This love is described in Seminar 1 as the "active gift" that is to be contrasted with the love that is an "imaginary passion" (1.276). Imaginary passion is "an attempt to capture the other in oneself, in oneself as object"; not as an object with these or those characteristics but in "the absolute particularity of oneself as object," in "whatever may be most opaque, most unthinkable in this particularity." We recognize the terms—*opacity, particularity*—with which Lacan elsewhere names the unspeakable beyond of the subject. Yet if here they are associated with narcissistic love, this does not at all mean that it is against an illusion indicated by these terms that his critique is directed. On the contrary, love on the "symbolic plane," "beyond imaginary captivation," is directed precisely at this "particularity," which Lacan equates (as in his account of Antigone's love for Polynices) with the "being of the loved subject," "beyond what he or she appears to be." Narcissistic love and authentic love are thus grounded in the same "particularity" beyond "specificity"; but with two differences. The authentic variety is active whereas the other is passive; and authentic love only loves the other insofar as the other maintains an authentic self-relation, for "when the loved being goes too far in his betrayal of himself and persists in self-deception, love can no longer follow" (ibid.).

This account is early and relatively undeveloped, but it indicates a persistent strain in Lacan's thought.[15] Ten years later, at the end of Seminar 11, he invokes a "limitless love" that can only live "outside the limits of the law" (11.276). One can attain such love only after having passed through the experience of "the opaque relation to the origin, to the drive" (273), the experience that involves the "sacrifice and murder" of the object. The function of opacity appears to have here the sense that it has elsewhere, as the limit-point of the particularity of the subject.[16] Thus the experience of the "radical phantasy" that makes possible this relation to the origin seems to be Lacan's version of ultimate self-knowledge.

Everything in Seminars 7 and 11 implies that the radical fantasy involves transgression of the incest taboo; but because the mother is only the stand-in for the Thing, and because the unconscious sexual drive has nothing to do with genital sexuality, but with the relation to lack and to death (11.204), the most profound sense of this experience would apparently be the relation to transgression and absolute destruction as transcendental structure of the relation between desire and the law. In this experience one would touch the *destrudo* that is the core of *jouissance*; the "pathological object" would be murdered in order to reveal the absolute nonobject that is the true correlate of desire as relation to the contentless particularity of the self-that-is-nothing or, as final mediation on the way to nothing, the self-that-is-shit (11.268). And then, on the other side of this experience, one would at last be capable of real love.

It might, then, be argued that Lacan is still, in Seminar 11, pursuing that "pacification" of aggressivity that he invoked in "Aggressivity in Psychoanalysis." He does not denigrate love but recognizes its difficulty; he does not apotheosize destructiveness but confronts the profundity of its grip on humanity. Only the journey to the absolute core of destructiveness can issue in the final beyond that is "limitless love," the love whose name in the tradition is agape (here once again Anders Nygren's *Agape and Eros* is a crucial reference for us).

"Limitless love" here, as in the tradition, involves the downgrading of those ordinary loves in which humanity dissipates and has always dissipated its being, and which there seems little prospect of its ever ceasing to do. Lacan, like other moralists of an absolutist stripe, seeks to make us feel that the lives we lead are a degraded version of the real thing. But isn't it a little late in the day for making such sharp divisions between darkness and light, such a clean break with the creaturely?

Lacanian *agape* seems unattainable or just barely attainable. One must be an initiate into the innermost mysteries of psychoanalysis if one wishes to attain it, those mysteries to which Lacan holds the key. The "beyond" of analysis "up to now" has been approachable

> only at the level of the analyst, in as much as it would be required of him to have specifically traversed the cycle of the analytic experience in its totality.
>
> There is only one kind of psycho-analysis, the training analysis—which means a psycho-analysis that has looped this loop to its end. The loop must be run through several times. (11.273–74)

The one who has looped this loop several times and thus delivered his desire "in its pure state" becomes capable of guiding others to the absolute consummation.

This consummation is specifically in competition with that other one associated with women. The analyst is the mystic bride/groom who alone can offer the "active gift," beyond all imaginary captivation, that Lacan had envisioned in Seminar 1.

> What the analyst has to give, unlike the partner in the act of love, is something that even the most beautiful bride in the world cannot

outmatch, that is to say, what he has. And what he has is nothing other than his desire. (7.300)

Truth of the nullity of the subject and the object: In some ways Lacan's is a very traditional truth, as we have seen. But perhaps, depending on how we read him, not entirely traditional. It may be that for Lacan (at least in certain portions of his text) the price of authenticity is confrontation with the *absolute* nothingness of the self, and thus with something never before approached in the tradition, the frustration of all desire for self-presence.

Nevertheless, when Lacan in Seminar 11 describes the *object a* as the representative of the vanished immortality of the sexed individual he indicates that the desire for infinite self-presence *is operative,* that the gulf of nothingness into which authentic desire ultimately hurls itself is opened out by the force of a desire that is vain indeed, but vain because of its idealism, its urge to transcendence of all worldly allure. Lacanian desire is not the negation of Platonic desire; it is Platonic desire disabused of the illusion of self-presence and nevertheless obeying its imperative of self-propriation, where self-propriation means the return to itself of a nothingness.

My question is whether Lacan's project of negativity does not in its entirety continue to be motivated by the forces of the dialectic of mourning—which is to say, by forces that arise from the ineluctable character of the libidinal relation to an object that, whatever it may be in itself, has only too exigent a reality for the desiring subject. So exigent and so dangerous is this reality that even the annulment of the self, so long as this annulment confirms the authenticity and is the autonomous activity of that same self that is annulled, may be a price willingly paid in order to extricate the self from the embrace or abyss of the object.

In order even to approach this question we must allow the full field of the dialectic of mourning to unfold from the texts of the tradition, from Homer and Plato on, the texts in which the pathways of this dialectic have been opened, and without prematurely submitting these texts to the grid of the Lacanian system which itself belongs to the interior of the field they define.

Notes

Preface

1. Hence the first volume of John Bowlby's monumental study of mourning is dedicated entirely to the process of attachment. John Bowlby, *Attachment,* vol. 1 of *Attachment and Loss* (New York: Basic Books, 1969).

2. Jacques Derrida, *Of Grammatology,* trans. Gayatri Chakravorty Spivak (Baltimore: Johns Hopkins University Press, 1976), 155.

3. Juliana Schiesari has recently argued that in the patriarchal tradition, mourning is suppressed by melancholic longing for a transcendent object. Juliana Schiesari, *The Gendering of Melancholia: Feminism, Psychoanalysis, and the Symbolics of Loss in Renaissance Literature* (Ithaca: Cornell University Press, 1992). Schiesari's powerful book regrettably appeared too late for me to make full use of here. I want to register my admiration for Schiesari's work and my sense that she and I are working on critiques of the same "privileged intuition," that of "a nameless and transcendental 'what' that has been lost" and that is "concomitant with a denial of the 'what' that is explicitly represented as lost in the ritual of mourning" (Schiesari, 131).

Chapter One: The Argument

1. Plato's *Symposium,* trans. Michael Joyce, in *The Collected Dialogues of Plato,* ed. Edith Hamilton and Huntington Cairns (New York: Pantheon, 1961), 206a. Except where otherwise indicated, citations of Plato are to this edition.

2. Cited from Ebreo's *De l'origine d'amore,* in John Charles Nelson, *Renaissance Theory of Love* (New York: Columbia University Press, 1958), 86–87.

3. Cited in Paul Oskar Kristeller, *The Philosophy of Marsilio Ficino,* trans.

Virginia Conant (Gloucester, Mass.: Peter Smith, 1964), 207–8. For an extended treatment of Ficino's thought focusing on the questions of mourning and melancholia, see Juliana Schiesari, *The Gendering of Melancholia: Feminism, Psychoanalysis, and the Symbolics of Loss in Renaissance Literature* (Ithaca: Cornell University Press, 1992).

4. Augustine tells us in the *Confessions* (7.9) that it was his reading of "some books of the Platonists" that motivated his decisive turn away from Manichaean materialism. I will cite throughout the lucid translation of the *Confessions* by Rex Warner (New York: New American Library, 1963). Modern scholarship has established by examination of textual parallels that the books Augustine refers to must have been primarily the *Enneads* of Plotinus, in particular the treatise on beauty (*Enneads* 1.6). See Carol Harrison, *Beauty and Revelation in the Thought of Saint Augustine* (Oxford: Clarendon Press, 1992), for an account, with extensive bibliography, of Augustine's development from a fairly pure Neoplatonism toward what Harrison calls an "incarnate aesthetic" (35) in his later work.

5. Socrates: "You will lay down the law in the city . . . that the lover may kiss and pass the time with and touch the beloved as a father would a son, for honorable ends . . . but there should never be suspicion of anything further. . . . Surely the end and consummation of culture is love of the beautiful [etc.]" (*Republic,* 303b–c).

6. I cite here and following the English translation of the *Republic* by W. H. D. Rouse (which is more vivid on the topic in question than the translation in the Hamilton-Cairns *Collected Dialogues* from which I elsewhere cite), in *Great Dialogues of Plato,* ed. Eric H. Warmington and Philip C. Rouse (New York: Mentor Books, 1956).

7. There is evidently a nonphilosophical animus alongside Socrates' philosophical argumentation concerning poetry. Plato is in competition with Homer and competing at an unfair disadvantage. Homer's greatest hero, Akhilleus, weeps and wails in a way that is utterly unbecoming to a good man and unworthy to be represented (388 a–b); but this is the type of character who best admits of imitation, whereas "the wise and calm character, being nearly always the same and self-composed, is not easy to imitate, and when imitated is not readily understood." Hence "the imitative poet is clearly not naturally suited to imitate this part of the soul . . . if he is to be popular with the multitude, but rather to imitate the resentful and complex character, because that can be imitated well" (604c–605a). Plato appears to be commenting on the difficulty of his own task in having as his protagonist the wise and calm Socrates, as opposed to the crowd-pleasing baby, Akhilleus. I do not want to speculate concerning the degree to which Plato's condemnation of the Akhillean type of protagonist might be determined by his own ambitions as a writer, but Plato's critique of the tragic and epic hero does cohere well with the tradition reported by Diogenes Laertius according to which Plato as a young man was a poet but burned his poems when he came

under the influence of Socrates. Diogenes Laertius, *Lives of Eminent Philosophers*, vol. 1, trans. R. D. Hicks (Cambridge, Mass.: William Heinemann, 1966), 3:5–6.

8. *Marcus Aurelius: Meditations* and *Epictetus: Enchiridion*, trans. George Long (South Bend, Ind.: Gateway Editions, 1956), 171–72.

9. See William J. Bouwsma, "The Two Faces of Humanism: Stoicism and Augustinianism in Renaissance Thought," in *Itinerarium Italicum: The Profile of the Italian Renaissance in the Mirror of Its European Transformations*, ed. Heiko A. Oberman with Thomas A. Brady, Jr. (Leiden: E. J. Brill, 1975), 3–60.

10. Michel Foucault, *The Care of the Self: The History of Sexuality*, vol. 3, trans. Robert Hurley (New York: Vintage Books, 1986), 227, 224.

11. For a very thorough and detailed historical conspectus of the question of eros in European thought, see the essential work of Anders Nygren, *Agape and Eros*, trans. Philip S. Watson (New York: Harper Torchbooks, 1953). See especially Nygren's account of the pervasiveness of the "eros-motif" in Augustine's thought (449–562). Nygren's stance toward the question of eros is the antithesis of my own; he takes even Platonic "heavenly Eros" to be too earthly, too "motivated," and attempts to disentangle Christian *agape* in its true divine purity from its historical entanglement with "heavenly Eros." Nevertheless, Nygren's historical analyses consistently focus on precisely the issues that are of the most pressing significance for this book.

12. Saint Augustine, *On Free Choice of the Will*, trans. Anna S. Benjamin and L. H. Hackstaff (Indianapolis: Bobbs-Merrill, 1964), 3:23.

13. Saint Augustine, *Concerning the City of God Against the Pagans*, trans. Henry Bettenson (Baltimore: Penguin Books, 1972), 14:25.

14. The *Iliad*, brutal as is its depiction of the possession and exchange of women, is free of the sexual denigration that is so prominent in Shakespeare's *Troilus and Cressida*. Not for lack of any opening: even if Briseis is blameless, Helen *could* be blamed, as she is in Shakespeare and indeed in Aeschylus. But in the *Iliad*, Helen remains valuable beyond measure, because those who fight over her believe in possession and thus think that she can be repossessed. (This is the problematic of value that Shakespeare takes up with a jaundiced eye. There is nothing in the *Iliad* that corresponds to the acid, moralizing satire of the disputants over Helen that Shakespeare puts in the mouth of Diomedes, a speech that also contains the most pointed denigration of her in the play.) Akhilleus operates according to the logic of absolute desire, which desires the inviolability of possession. It is possession itself that is perfidious as soon as it is no longer absolute, and for absolute desire if possession has no absolute value it has no value at all. Akhilleus thus comes to the very threshold of the Platonic problematic.

15. Here we cross paths momentarily with Lacan, who observes that "the first object [the subject] proposes for this parental desire whose object is unknown is his own loss—*Can he lose me?* The phantasy of one's death, of one's disappearance, is the first object that the subject has to bring to play in this dialectic,

and he does indeed bring it into play—as we know from innumerable cases, such as in anorexia nervosa. We also know that the phantasy of one's death is usually manipulated by the child in his love relations with his parents" (11.214–15). I do not know of any text of Lacan's in which he develops this notion further.

16. Kathryn Bond Stockton, *God Between Their Lips: Desire Between Women in Irigaray, Brontë, and Eliot* (Stanford: Stanford University Press, 1994), 193–249.

Chapter Two: Before Transcendence

1. The Iliadic warriors have a conception of an afterworld to which the shade of the dead goes, but this scarcely constitutes an afterlife. After Akhilleus sees in a dream the shade of Patroklos, he exclaims (23.103–4) that "in the house of Hades" there remains a *psykhē* and an *eidolon* (a 'soul' and an 'image') but without a *phrēn*, the center of vital physical existence. Citations of the *Iliad* in English from Homer, *The Iliad*, trans. Richard Lattimore (Chicago: University of Chicago Press, 1961). Erwin Rohde commented thus on these lines: "Down in the murky underworld [the dead] now float unconscious, or, at most, with a twilight self-consciousness, wailing in a shrill diminutive voice, helpless, indifferent. Of course, flesh, bones, and sinews, the midriff [*phrēn*], the seat of all the faculties of the mind and will—these are all gone forever. . . . They can hardly be said to *live*, even, anymore than the image does that is reflected in the mirror; and that they prolong to eternity their shadowy image-existence—where in Homer do we ever find that said?" *Psyche: The Cult of Souls and Belief in Immortality Among the Greeks*, trans. W. B. Hillis (New York: Humanities Press, 1925), 9.

It is true that the Homeric hero desires a "deathless glory" and perhaps also, as Gregory Nagy has argued, the immortality of cult worship; but these are earthly forms of transcendence that Christianity will know how to value. See Nagy, "The Death of Sarpedon and the Question of Homeric Uniqueness," in his *Greek Mythology and Poetics* (Ithaca: Cornell University Press, 1990), 122–42.

2. The *Iliad* was, by the way, in the 1950s already the focus of a famous discussion concerning the emergence of the unified subject; Bruno Snell called it "the discovery of the mind" and located its beginnings in archaic Greece. But since the subject that is claimed to be missing at one level of analysis might always be rediscovered at another level, we now "know" that Akhilleus is thoroughly and finely individuated in this poem in terms of rhetorical style. A recent book by Richard P. Martin (*The Language of Heroes: Speech and Performance in the Iliad* [Ithaca: Cornell University Press, 1989]) summarizes and pushes farther the contemporary debate over the individual style of Akhilleus. His conclusions, grounded in ethnography, should disturb the confidence of those who nostalgically appeal to precapitalist cultures as an alternative to individualism. According to Martin, "ethnography, other literatures, and the *Iliad* itself concur to convince us of the necessity and consciousness of individual style in traditional society. The heroes of the Homeric poems surely possess individual styles; furthermore, I suggest that these are not mere literary constructs, but are based on a

deeper social reality" (98). This matter of individual style is not an innocuous matter of display but fundamentally *agonistic;* individual heroes in the epic, like individual singers in a native oral tradition, operate "in a context where authority is always up for grabs and to be won by the speaker with the best style" (238). Martin's research shows the limitations of Anthony Easthope's distinction between two "opposed kinds of discourse: one collective, popular, intersubjective, accepting the text as a poem to be performed; the other individualist, elitist, privatized, offering the text as a representation of a voice speaking" (*Poetry as Discourse* [London: Methuen, 1983], 77). Even if there is some value to Easthope's characterization as applied to the difference between folk ballads and the verse of Milton, Martin's work suggests that the claims of the individual voice are already at work in the poetry of societies of the most traditional sort.

3. Gregory Nagy, *The Best of the Achaeans: Concepts of the Hero in Archaic Greek Poetry* (Baltimore: Johns Hopkins University Press, 1979); Berkley Peabody, *The Winged Word: A Study in the Technique of Ancient Greek Oral Composition* (Albany: State University of New York Press, 1975). These seem to me the most impressive of the neo-Parryist works of the past two decades.

4. The present reading is thus as far as possible from finding in the *Iliad* that "harmony of man and nature" that Lukacs and other Marxist critics have found in the Homeric poems.

5. Emile Benveniste, *Indo-European Language and Society,* trans. Elizabeth Palmer (Coral Gables: University of Miami Press, 1973), 334.

6. Robert Redfield, *Nature and Culture in the Iliad* (Chicago: University of Chicago Press, 1975), 167.

7. W. Thomas McCary, *Childlike Achilles: Ontogeny and Philogeny in The Iliad* (New York: Columbia University Press, 1982).

8. J. T. Kakridis, *Homeric Researches* (Lund, Sweden: C. W. K. Gleerup, 1949), 20.

9. Kakridis argues that the Meleager story is the matrix of the events of book 6 involving Hektor and Andromakhe. Whether or not we are to admit a role as source of book 6 to a conjectural "Meleagris," the crucial point for our purposes is Kakridis's demonstration that the ascending scale of affection is a basic structuring device of which we must take account if we are to understand the farewell of the Trojan couple. It occurs in canonical form in Hektor's words to Andromakhe: "But it is not so much the pain to come of the Trojans / that troubles me, not even of Priam the king nor Hekabe, / not the thought of my brothers who in their numbers and valour / shall drop in the dust under the hands of men who hate them, / as troubles me the thought of you, when some bronze-armoured / Achaian leads you off, taking away your day of liberty, / in tears" (450–56). It also occurs transformed into a figure of speech in Andromakhe's words to Hektor: "Hektor, thus you are father to me, and my honoured mother, / you are my brother, and you it is you who are my young husband" (429–30). And, most strikingly, it is concretized in the sequence of Hektor's meetings with friends and

family as he goes through Troy, leading up to his meeting with his wife (first the Trojan women, then Hekabe, then Paris and Helen, then Andromakhe [238–394]), whom he seeks out with difficulty only for the purpose of saying farewell.

What the work of Kakridis shows is that the ascending scale of affection is a structure operative at the level at which the text is generated, a structure that belongs to what Nagler calls the "semiotic system" underlying the "surface of the narrative" and providing generative capacities such that the resultant poetry "resembles living speech in the dynamics of creativity." M. Nagler, *Spontaneity and Tradition: A Study in the Oral Art of Homer* (Berkeley: University of California Press, 1974), xxiv, 16.

10. Strictly speaking, it is historically inaccurate to refer to the women, or the other exchange objects in the *Iliad*, as "commodities." We are dealing here with what Louis Gernet calls "the substance of a noble commerce," "premonetary signs" whose function as bearers of value is rooted in the contests of a warrior nobility and not in the idea of profit. Louis Gernet, "The Mythical Idea of Value in Ancient Greece," in his *The Anthropology of Ancient Greece*, trans. John Hamilton and Blaise Nagy (Baltimore: Johns Hopkins University Press, 1981). Thus the word for goods or possessions, *ktēmata*, refers primarily to "things acquired as a result of war, the games, or gift-giving. The term never gives primary emphasis to the idea of commercial gain" (76). This technical difference does not of course make any more humane or less brutal the treatment of the human beings who are regarded as exchange objects.

11. This is not to say that the *oikos* is an organic unity that completely absorbs the individuality of its members; on the contrary, the *oikos* is full of tensions and conflicts of various sorts. And some of the worst of these tensions are sexual—as in the story of how Phoinix's father, Amyntor, banished him and cursed his seed because Phoinix, in obedience to his mother's behest, seduced Amyntor's concubine (9.454–56). This is a very extreme case of the tearing apart of the sacred *oikos*: in cursing his son in this way, Amyntor denies himself the continuation of his own line.

12. As Cedric Whitman pointed out, there is also a synchronic or "geometric" structural relation between the opening situation and the closing situation; the latter "inverts" the former as part of the overall "ring composition" of the poem. Cedric H. Whitman, *Homer and the Heroic Tradition* (Cambridge: Harvard University Press, 1958), 259–60.

13. Cf. the discussion of *geras* and *timē* in Benveniste, 341–42. Benveniste draws a careful distinction between the sense of the two words, but it remains clear that *geras* is fungible *timē*, as is implied by Benveniste's own remark that "Achilles was deprived of his *timē* when his captive girl was taken away."

14. Of course by the time Phoinix says this, Akhilleus has already pronounced his thundering rejection of Agamemnon's *apoina*. He cannot very well change his mind on the spot; but Phoinix's words have an effect on Akhilleus, for though he still declines the gifts, he softens his previous declaration that he is leaving, saying instead that "we shall decide tomorrow" (619). Phoinix's words are the explana-

tion of the much debated lines 84–85 of book 16 in which Akhilleus declares his hope that thanks to Patroklos's work in the battle the Akhaians will return Briseis "and give the shining gifts in addition." There is no mystery in this remark when we realize that the gifts are fungible *timē* and thus attract Akhilleus's reawakening interest in his "honor." He clearly has taken to heart Phoinix's admonition that loss of the gifts would lessen his *timē;* and it is consistent with this concern that he should warn Patroklos not to do more than drive the Trojans from the ships, for "so you will diminish my honor" ("render me *atimoteros* '*timē*-less'," which could mean 'deprive me of my compensation').

15. *Apoina* and *poinē* are strictly distinct forms of reparation, but they are explicitly linked by Aias when he contrasts Akhilleus's refusal of Agamemnon's *apoina* to the acceptance of *poinē* by a man who has lost a brother or a son. Leonard Muellner has pointed out that the link is also implied by the judicial scene that is pictured on Akhilleus's shield. As Muellner says, "the question on Achilles' divinely wrought shield is whether the murdered man's kinsman has the right actually to *refuse* the murderer's offer of *poinē* in the same way as Achilles himself has refused the embassy's *apoina*." Leonard Muellner, *The Meaning of Homeric EYXOMAI through Its Formulas* (Innsbruck: University of Innsbruck, 1976), 106. The analogy between the two cases brings out the role of both *apoina* and *poinē* as forms of compensatory value that come to assuage vengefulness and to make unnecessary the regress to violence.

16. *Poinē* can mean either 'blood money' or 'vengeance', 'punishment.' Both are forms of compensation for a wrong incurred.

17. Homer, *The Iliad,* trans. Robert Fitzgerald (Garden City, N.Y.: Anchor Books, 1975), 215.

18. In these remarks Akhilleus is nominally complaining against his treatment by Agamemnon, but he slides into a complaint against warrior destiny itself. The first line is ambiguous: *Moira* might mean either 'the warrior's share' or 'fate'; but by the third line the reference is to fate alone, as the death that awaits all.

19. A Lacanian reader would see in this structure of desire the succession of *objets a,* but to collapse our analysis into the Lacanian system at this point would result in a predetermined reading of a familiar type: Akhilleus's grief would become, like Hamlet's, mourning for the missing phallus, of which Briseis would be (as *objet a*) the representation, and so forth (see Jacques Lacan, "Desire and the Interpretation of Desire in *Hamlet*," in *Literature and Psychoanalysis,* ed. Shoshona Felman (Baltimore: Johns Hopkins University Press, 1982), 11–53. The structure I have called automourning is not mourning for the phallus; it involves an obsessive speculation upon the affect of an other who, far from being a "void" in the trajectory of the mourner's desire, is the site within which the self-affection of the mourner is constituted (as we are about to see).

20. Gregory Nagy, *Comparative Studies in Greek and Indic Meter* (Cambridge: Harvard University Press, 1974), 255–61.

21. For more on *kleos* and "hearing," see Nagy, *Meter,* 244–46.

22. But this only means that old men are no longer truly masculine. McCary has shown in detail the consistent relegation of old men in the *Iliad* to the category of unmasculine powerlessness that also includes women and children (210–14).

23. In Socrates' critique of Homer in *Republic,* book 3, where he clearly has Akhilleus in mind, he says that "we should be right in doing away with the lamentations of men of note and in attributing them to women." Paul Shorey, trans., *The Collected Dialogues of Plato,* ed. Edith Hamilton and Huntington Cairns (New York: Bollingen Foundation, 1961), 387c–388a.

24. Sigmund Freud, "Mourning and Melancholia," in *The Standard Edition of the Complete Psychological Works,* ed. and trans. James Strachey, 24 vols. (London: Hogarth Press and the Institute of Psycho-analysis, 1953–74), 14:255.

25. Pietro Pucci, *Odysseus Polutropos: Intertextual Readings in the Odyssey and the Iliad* (Ithaca: Cornell University Press, 1987).

Chapter Three: How the Spirit (Almost) Became Flesh

1. Rudolph Bultmann, *The Gospel of John: A Commentary,* ed. R. W. N. Hoare and J. K. Riches, trans. G. R. Beasley-Murray (Philadelphia: Westminster Press, 1971), 43. Except where otherwise noted, all citations of Bultmann will be from this work.

2. For Bultmann, "Heidegger's existentialist analysis of the ontological structure of being would seem to be no more than a secularized, philosophical version of the New Testament's view of human life. . . . One should . . . be startled that philosophy is saying the same thing as the New Testament and saying it quite independently"; *Kerygma and Myth: A Theological Debate,* ed. Hans Werner Bartsch, rev. ed. Reginald H. Fuller (New York, 1961), 24–25.

3. This history is magnificently recounted by John Henry Newman in his *Essay on the Development of Christian Doctrine* and *History of the Arians.* No retelling can exceed the lucidity and drama of Newman's narrative; but from a purely scholarly standpoint an authoritative recent account of the early centuries of Christianity is Jaroslav Pelikan, *The Emergence of the Catholic Tradition (100–600)* (Chicago: University of Chicago Press, 1971).

4. The adjectival form of *sarx* is *sarkikos,* which does not naturalize well into English; hence my simpler coinage 'sarctic.'

5. Edward Schillebeeckx, *Christ: The Experience of Jesus as Lord* (New York: Seabury Press, 1980), 426.

6. Birger Pearson, *The Pneumatikos-Psychikos Terminology in I Corinthians* (Missoula, Mont.: Scholars Press, 1973).

7. Thus Raymond Brown, who insists that there is in John a final, in addition to a realized, eschatology, nevertheless concedes that "Bultmann, Dodd, and Blank are . . . correct in insisting that the main emphasis in the Gospel is on realized eschatology." Raymond E. Brown, *The Anchor Bible: The Gospel According to John,* 2 vols. (Garden City, N.Y.: Doubleday, 1966), 1: cxx. The debate on

this issue is too complex to describe here; but it may be remarked that, in general, the fixing of the "intention" of the text as a whole depends on how the exegete interprets the provenance of the various historical strata of the text, a decision that in turn tends to be decided on the basis of a preunderstanding of the intention that awaits fixing. Bultmann, for example, feels free simply to excise as an interpolation any passage that does not support his interpretation, declaring that it does not belong to the authentic Johannine intention even if John himself "took it over from the tradition of the church" (Rudolf Bultmann, *Theology of the New Testament* [New York: Charles Scribner's Sons, 1955], 2:54). Conversely, C. K. Barrett argues in reply to Bultmann's excision of the "last day" references that they may belong to the authentic text even if added by a redactor: "For someone has incorporated these references in the Gospel as it has been transmitted to us, and if this person was not John I then he was John II—or John III or IV"; and the addition may be accepted as authentic because the redactor "understood what the Gospel was intended to convey" (C. K. Barrett, "Christocentric or Theocentric? Observations on the Theological Method of the Fourth Gospel," in Barrett, *Essays on John* [Philadelphia: Westminster Press, 1982], 5). Bultmann and Barrett stand on the same ground. Each believes that he can make out the essence of the thing across the sedimentation of strata, then judges the character of the strata according to this essence. Only they see the essence differently on the crucial point, the question of eternal life.

8. Robert Kysar, *The Fourth Evangelist and His Gospel: An Examination of Contemporary Scholarship* (Minneapolis: Augsburg Publishing House, 1975), 69.

9. This summary leaves over two miracles, the transformation of water into wine at the wedding in Cana and the walk on the water. I discuss the former toward the end of this essay; as for the latter, its status is obscure in various ways. It lacks the precise rhetorical-metaphorical sense of most of Jesus' miracles; hence Barrett concludes that "John included the narrative primarily because it was in the source—in all probability, Mark—he used for the preceding narrative." C. K. Barrett, *The Gospel According to St. John,* 2d ed. (London: SPCK, 1978), 281. Furthermore, Barrett admits the possibility that John intended here no miracle at all. The question turns on a grammatical point: the genitive *epi tēs thallassēs* could conceivably be translated 'by the sea' instead of 'on the sea' (280–81).

10. I rely primarily on the *Jerusalem Bible: Reader's Edition* (Garden City, N.Y.: Doubleday, 1968) for the English text of John.

11. According to the orthodox interpretation asserted by Barrett against Bultmann, "Martha's belief is in no way discredited but rather confirmed by the extraordinary events that follow" (Barrett, *Gospel,* 395). She already believes, quite properly, in the resurrection of the last day of Pharisaic Judaism, and she already believes that Jesus has the power to bring Lazarus back to life ("Even now," she has said to Jesus, "whatever you ask of God, he will grant you"); Jesus' words merely bring out "the Christological basis and interpretation of the miracle" (394). For Barrett, thus, the significance of the miracle is both present and futural:

the resurrection of Lazarus is "an acted parable of Christian conversion," but the movement of the resurrection which begins in conversion "is to be completed only at the last day" (395).

12. Ludwig Feuerbach, *The Essence of Christianity*, trans. George Eliot (New York: Harper Torchbooks, 1957), 243. In reality, according to Feuerbach, nothing happens to the bread and wine, which simply remain what they are; they only acquire a new significance: "this state of being flesh is not that of real flesh; . . . it has only the value, quality, of a significance, a truth conveyed in a symbol" (244). Hence, Feuerbach concludes, the entire thing really exists only in the faith, which is to say the feelings and imagination, of the believer, and if this is so the whole process of the Lord's Supper "can quite well . . . be accomplished in the imagination," without the mediation of the bread and wine. Indeed, precisely this is accomplished in those "devout poems" that take the blood of Christ as their theme:

> In these we have a genuinely poetical celebration of the Lord's Supper. In the lively representation of the suffering, bleeding Saviour, the soul identifies itself with him; here the saint in poetic exaltation drinks the pure blood, unmixed with any contradictory, material elements; here there is no disturbing object between the idea of the blood and the blood itself. (245)

Whatever the differences between him and Hegel, Feuerbach follows the master on this point, that the bread and wine are a "disturbing object" between the mind and the true ideal-imaginative object of its meditation. In the sacramental feast, according to Hegel, "there is a sort of confusion between object and subject rather than a unification."

> Something divine, just because it is divine, cannot present itself in the shape of food and drink. In a parable there is no demand that the different things compared shall be understood as a unity; but here the thing and the feeling *are* to be bound together; in the symbolical action the eating and the drinking and the sense of being one in Jesus are to run into one another. But thing and feeling, spirit and reality, do not mix. Fancy cannot bring them together in a beautiful image. The bread and wine, seen and enjoyed, can never rouse the feeling of love; this feeling can never be found in them as seen objects since there is a contradiction between it and the sensation of actually absorbing the food and drink, of their becoming subjective. (G. W. F. Hegel, *The Spirit of Christianity*, in *Early Theological Writings*, trans. T. M. Knox (Philadelphia: University of Pennsylvania Press, 1981), 251–52)

13. His arguments here are not among his most closely knit. He insists that these references treat the Eucharist as a *pharmakon athanasias*, a magical antidote to death; but they can easily be interpreted in a more orthodox sense. See Barrett, *Gospel*, 82–85, 283, 297. A particularly satisfying argument, from both a theological and formal-literary point of view, for the authenticity of 6:51–58 and for its

placement precisely here is given by Edward Rensberger in his *Johannine Faith and Liberating Community* (Philadelphia: Westminster Press, 1988), 75–78.

14. Barrett, who says that this moment in John's text manifests its "anti-docetic interest," argues that "the event as described is physiologically possible": "Blood might flow from a corpse if only a short time had elapsed since death; and a fluid resembling water might issue from a region described as *pleura*" (*Gospel,* 556). Bultmann, however, without argument dismisses considerations of such a possibility as merely "odd" (678n).

15. Indeed, even the significance of the crucifixion and death of Jesus, upon which Bultmann lays so much stress, is subtly and perhaps contradictorily minimized. It is really in the resolution of the "decision for death" that Jesus declares in 13:31 that the whole of the Passion is anticipated, and this in turn is already contained in the fact of Incarnation itself; the crucifixion is thus necessary only to make the full significance of the Incarnation visible and thus comprehensible (632); it is merely a "demonstration": "the demonstration of his victory over the world which had already been wrested from it" (634).

16. In fact, the interpretation of Jesus' death that Hegel suggests in *The Spirit of Christianity* as properly *spiritual* is simply that of the Gnostics and docetists: "The form of a servant, the humiliation in itself, as the veil of divine nature, would present no obstacle to the urge for religion if only the real human form had been satisfied to be a mere veil and to pass away" (293).

17. Heidegger appears to say the same: "The ownmost, nonrelational possibility is *not to be outstripped* (italics in original). Being towards this possibility enables Dasein to understand that giving itself up impends for it as the uttermost possibility of its existence. . . . Anticipation discloses to existence that its uttermost possibility lies in giving itself up, and thus it shatters all one's tenaciousness to whatever existence one has reached" (*Being and Time,* trans. John Macquarrie and Edward Robinson [Oxford: Basil Blackwell, 1980], 308). But Heideggerean authenticity involves the elimination of Dasein's "relation to any other Dasein" (294); the "giving oneself up" that is involved here is a way of returning to oneself in a purer modality, beyond mere "presence."

18. Bultmann feels some discomfort at the apparent sense of Jesus' utterance in 12:2–4: "Admittedly the promise that the servant will follow him, and that he will be where Jesus is, is peculiarly ambiguous. The meaning in the foreground conveys a promise to the servant to follow him [sc. Jesus] into death" (Bultmann, 426).

19. Jesus is *"Deus revelatus;* not the whole of the abyss of Godhead, but God known" (Barrett, "Christocentric?" 12).

20. Thus far I follow Bultmann; but we have seen that Bultmann himself clings to the essential "spiritualizing" kernel of the old distinction in his reformulation.

21. In Jesus' mixing of saliva and earth Irenaeus saw an allusion to Genesis 2:7, where Jaweh breathes life into a man made of dust; "but this is improbable" (Barrett, *Gospel,* 358). Besides John, only Mark records Jesus' use of spittle. "The

Marcan spittle miracles seem to have been deliberately omitted by Matthew and Luke. The use of spittle was part of the primitive tradition about Jesus but left him open to a charge of engaging in magical practice" (Brown, 372).

22. Bultmann moves quickly to spiritualize this language; he informs us that "'Food,' 'nourishment' is that which maintains life, existence; *this* constitutes its essence, and not the fact that in general it is a material substance which is chewed with one's teeth." And he drives his conclusion home: "The use here is therefore *not figurative,* but it is used in its *proper sense*" (195, n. 1; emphasis added). "Proper sense": the essence of nourishment detached from the material process by which it is only incidentally achieved. Thus Bultmann pulls the teeth (figuratively or properly?) from his own insistence on the scandalous character of Jesus' *logos.*

23. It appears that the people of Jesus' time recognized a contrast between Jesus and John the Baptist precisely on the question of ingestion: Mark 2:18–19 records that Jesus was asked by the people why his disciples did not fast as did John's disciples and the Pharisees. In a context where John the Baptist was known for his asceticism, it would be especially striking to move directly from his ministry to Jesus' attendance at the wedding at Cana (attested only in John).

24. As we have seen, orthodox Christianity has understood the logic of this return in terms of a compromise formation in which the *sarx* is allowed an innocuous or merely transitional place; it is in part a moment through which the spiritual pendulum passes on its way back up, in part something that is retranslated as the principle of individuation of the immortal self purified of everything fleshly.

25. William Robertson Smith pointed out in his great work on ancient Semitic religion that in archaic Israel there was a "deeply marked" distinction between bread and flesh, with the former drawing its sacrificial significance from its association with the latter:

> Among the Hebrews vegetable or cereal oblations were sometimes presented by themselves, but the commonest use of them was as an accompaniment to animal sacrifice. When the Hebrew ate flesh, he ate bread with it and drank wine, and when he offered flesh on the table of his God, it was natural that he should add to it the same concomitants. . . .
>
> Of these various oblations animal sacrifices are by far the most important in Semitic countries . . . so that among the Phoenicians the word zébah, which properly means a slaughtered victim, is applied even to offerings of bread and oil. (222)

> The difference between cereal and animal food was . . . deeply marked, and though bread was of course brought to the sanctuary to be eaten with the zebahim, it had not and could not have the same religious meaning as the holy flesh. . . . At all events no sacrificial meal could consist of bread alone. All

through the old history it is taken for granted that a religious feast implies a victim slain. (242)

The predominance assigned in ancient ritual to animal sacrifice corresponds to the predominance of the type of sacrifice which is not a mere payment of tribute but an act of fellowship between the deity and his worshippers. (224)

The value of the Arabian evidence is that it supplies proof that the bond of food is valid of itself, that religion may be called in to confirm and strengthen it, but that the essence of the thing lies in the physical act of eating together. (271)

Lectures on the Religion of the Semites: The Fundamental Institutions, 3d ed. (New York: KTAV Publishing House, 1969). (The first edition of the lectures was published in 1889.)

26. The incident of the raising of Lazarus does not take us, as the Bread of Life discourse does, all the way to the penetralia of Jesus' teaching; but even there the hyperliteral reference is present. Just before Jesus raises Lazarus, his sister cautions him: "Lord, by now he will smell; this is the fourth day." We are not told whether Jesus in resurrecting Lazarus also takes away the smell of death.

27. As E. R. Dodds points out, Dionysus was the god of the *hygra physis,* of the movement of life through its various manifestations as the transformations of a universal liquid flow ("not only the liquid fire in the grape, but the sap thrusting in a young tree, the blood pounding in the veins of a young animal, all the mysterious and uncontrollable tides that ebb and flow in the life of nature"), and it was as a consecrated feast on the living flesh of a sacrificial victim that this flow was transmitted to the communicants. Introduction to *Euripides: Bacchae,* ed. Dodds (Oxford: Clarendon Press, 1960), xii.

There was a precise parallel to the Dionysian *omophagia* in Semitic tradition. Here is how the Semitic ritual was described by Robertson Smith:

In the oldest known form of Arabian sacrifice, described by Nilus, . . . the whole company fall on the victim with their swords, hacking off pieces of the quivering flesh and devouring them raw. . . . The plain meaning of this is that the victim was devoured before its life had left the still warm blood and flesh . . . and that thus *in the most literal way* all those who shared in the ceremony absorbed part of the victim's life into themselves. One sees how much more forcibly than any ordinary meal such a rite expresses the establishment or confirmation of a bond of common life between the worshippers and also . . . between the worshippers and their god.

. . . In later Arabian sacrifices, and still more in the sacrifices of the more civilized Semitic nations, the primitive crudity of the ceremonial was modified, and the meaning of the act is therefore more or less disguised, but the essential type of the ritual remains the same (338–39).

28. As elsewhere at crucial moments, John's is the only gospel that attributes this utterance to Jesus.

29. *Agapēsas eis telos*, says the Evangelist in 13:1, which Bultmann glosses as loving not only 'right to the end' but as 'right to its completion', 'to the culmination', 'completely' (487).

Chapter Four: Cruel Lady

1. Since the realm of literature is precisely that of mortal libidinal investment, from the perspective of the Platonizing tradition all of literature, whether "tragic" or "comic," belongs to the realm of mourning. Thus Guillaume de Conches remarks in his commentary on Boethius:

> Some muses are sound, others are "wounded" [*alie integre, alie lacere*]. The declarations of philosophy are sound because they preserve man in the soundness and constancy of reason. Those of poetry, that is, of the art which invents and depicts things in meter, are wounded, because they tear apart men's hearts, and deal faithlessly with them by recalling pleasure or sorrow to the memory, rather than guiding or consoling them.

For Guillaume it is a matter of indifference whether poetry reminds us of pleasure or sorrow, because sorrow is the hidden essence of earthly pleasure. Guillaume's commentary is cited from Winthrop Wetherbee, *Platonism and Poetry in the Twelfth Century: The Literary Influence of the School of Chartres* (Princeton: Princeton University Press, 1972), 93.

2. Gregory Vlastos, "The Individual as Object of Love in Plato," in his *Platonic Studies* (Princeton: Princeton University Press, 1973), 31. Cf. Martha Nussbaum, *The Fragility of Goodness: Luck and Ethics in Greek Tragedy and Philosophy* (Cambridge: Cambridge University Press, 1986), chap. 6, 165–99. For Socrates, Nussbaum says, "Alcibiades is just one more of the beautifuls, a piece of the form" (195).

3. Plato's *Symposium*, trans. Michael Joyce, in *The Collected Dialogues of Plato*, ed. Edith Hamilton and Huntington Cairns (New York: Pantheon, 1961). All further citations of Plato refer to this edition.

4. Joseph Anthony Mazzeo, *Medieval Cultural Tradition in Dante's Comedy* (Ithaca: Cornell University Press, 1960), 92.

5. As Mazzeo remarks, the *Divine Comedy* manifests a "striking resemblance" to "some of the most important ideas in Plato's *Phaedrus* and *Symposium*." Mazzeo, *Structure and Thought in the Paradiso* (Ithaca: Cornell University Press, 1958), 121. Mazzeo notes that in the Renaissance Ficino and Landino interpreted the *Commedia* "as a platonic work" (208n).

6. On the intricacies and contradictions of the Christian doctrine of the resurrection of the body, see chapter 3.

7. "We must make ourselves indifferent to all created things," declares Ignatius Loyola. *The Spiritual Exercises of St. Ignatius*, trans. Anthony Mottola

(Garden City, N.Y.: Image Books, 1964), 47. According to Thomas à Kempis, the heart must be altogether "severed from earthly liking," to the point of withdrawing even from one's "dearest friends." *Imitation of Christ*, trans. Richard Whitford (New York: Pocket Books, 1953), 3:53, 226. One is reminded of Augustine's confession to God as a sin the fact that he wept for "a small portion of an hour" when his mother died (*The Confessions of St. Augustine*, trans. Rex Warner [New York: New American Library, 1963], 9:12); Anders Nygren cites a passage from Augustine's commentary on the Gospel of John in which Augustine says that "if we love God as we should, we should not love anything at all in the world" (O si Deus digne amamus, nummus omnimo amabimus). Anders Nygren, *Agape and Eros*, trans. Philip S. Watson (New York: Harper Torchbooks, 1953), 510. The tortuosities of the attempt to reconcile love of God with love of neighbor are well manifested in the debates over the distinction in Augustine between *uti* love, love of something as a means toward a further enjoyment, and *frui* love, love of something as an end in itself. For a brief survey of recent views on this question, see Carol Harrison, *Beauty and Revelation in the Thought of Saint Augustine* (Oxford: Clarendon Press, 1992), 245–53. See also Nygren's trenchant analysis in *Agape and Eros*, 503–12.

8. Roger Valency, *In Praise of Love: An Introduction to the Love-Poetry of the Renaissance* (New York: Schocken Books, 1982), 247.

9. Hence Pietro Bembo's Platonizing discourse on love, as represented by Castiglione, evades the precise sense of this initiating move, while otherwise remaining as close to the *Symposium* as possible. The first, "courtly" phase of love that he describes is presented in the terms not of the *Symposium* but of the *Phaedrus*, whose erotic doctrine is in certain respects incompatible with that of the *Symposium*. The incorporeal form of beauty is recognized immediately in the beauty of the beloved, without generalization to the beauty of all bodies, and this recognition then subserves devotion to the single individual in whom it is recognized (334). But whereas in the *Phaedrus* this devotion is lifelong and leads to the desired attainment of ideality, Bembo treats it as the first stage in an ascent of the *Symposium* type, in this way bringing that ascent into line with the requirements of courtly idealization. Even when the time comes to leave behind the individual beloved, the movement of abstraction is discretely revised; the lover does not pass through love of all bodies but goes straight to the uniting of "all possible forms of beauty in his mind" to form the "universal concept" of beauty. *The Book of the Courtier*, trans. George Bull (Bungay, England: Penguin Books, 1976), 338–39.

10. Charles Singleton identifies Dante's focus on the death of the beloved in the *Vita Nuova* as his distinctive contribution to the troubadour or "courtly" theory of love: *An Essay on the Vita Nuova* (Baltimore: Johns Hopkins University Press, 1977), 94–101.

11. Some remarks by Collin Hardie manifest clearly the character of the Christian strategy by which the body is *aufgehoben*. In the *Commedia*, Hardie argued, "Dante's love for Beatrice is spiritualized, but not . . . thereby made incorporeal,

but rather more corporeal." By "more corporeal," however, Hardie understood the "acceptance and transformation" of matter such that "individuation no longer is due to matter but to formal principles" ("Dante and the Tradition of Courtly Love," in *Patterns of Love and Courtesy; Essays in Memory of C. S. Lewis*, ed. John Lawlor [London: Edward Arnold, 1966], 43). This strange logic, according to which the body is rendered "more corporeal" by the annulment of its materiality, is characteristic of Christianity at least since Paul. The most sophisticated modern version of this logic that I know is in Rudolf Bultmann's critique of Paul's distinction between a spiritual *sōma* and a fleshly *sōma*. For Bultmann, this distinction remains too closely bound to physicality, failing to eliminate entirely the element of the *sarx* 'flesh' from the thought of the resurrection body:

> Since Paul's capacity for abstract thinking is not a developed one, and he therefore does not distinguish terminologically between *soma* in the basic sense of that which characterizes human existence and *soma* as the phenomenon of the material body, he connects the idea of somatic existence in the eschatological consummation with a mythological teaching on the resurrection (I Cor. 15). In it *soma* must appear somehow or other as a thing or a material substance, or as the "form" of such a thing. And since the substance of the resurrection body cannot be "flesh and blood" (I Cor. 15:50), the unfortunate consequence is that *pneuma* must be conceived as a substance of which that *soma* consists. In distinction from this mythology the real intention of Paul must be made clear.

What Paul is really getting at by the notion of the spiritual *sōma*, claims Bultmann, is the idea of "the ontological structure of human existence," a structure that must be preserved from one life to the next if the continuity of the mortal and resurrected individual is not to be disrupted. This "ontological structure" is not a substance but a "self-relation" that can be "appropriate" or "perverted." Rudolf Bultmann, *Theology of the New Testament* (New York: Charles Scribner's Sons, 1954), 1:197–98.

12. *Purgatorio* 32.1–6. I cite the verse translation of the *Divine Comedy* by John Ciardi (New York: New American Library, 1970). Italian text of the *Divine Comedy* cited from the edition by John D. Sinclair (New York: Oxford University Press, 1972). There is a clear allusion in this *troppo fiso* to the last of Dante's *Rime petrose* ("Così nel mio parlar"), where in the sexual fantasy that ends the *canzone*, the speaker imagines himself giving the lady a fixed stare, up close: "Ancor nelli occhi . . . guarderei presso e fiso" (80.74, 76). All quotations of Dante's lyric poetry in Italian and English, including the *Rime petrose* and the *Vita Nuova*, will be from K. Foster and P. Boyde, *Dante's Lyric Poetry*, vol. 1, *The Poems* (Oxford: Clarendon Press, 1967). I consider more closely the significance of the *Rime petrose* later in this chapter.

13. Nancy Vickers points out that Dante's citations of Lamentations 1.1 (in the *Vita Nuova* and in Epistle 8) "relate Florence without Beatrice to Rome without

Christ—yet additional witness . . . to the Christological marking of the Beatrice experience." "Widowed Words: Dante, Petrarch, and the Metaphors of Mourning," in *Discourses of Authority in Medieval and Renaissance Literature,* ed. Kevin Brownlee and Walter Stephens (Hanover, N.H.: University Press of New England, 1989).

14. I am not thinking here in terms of either the actual mourning of a historical Dante for a real woman named Beatrice or of a mere "technical exercise" or "poetic artifice" that could be simply opposed to "real life." It is a question, rather, of the working out on the symbolic level of a problem in libidinal economics. It is clear and, I think, widely recognized today that the old distinction between real life and poetic artifice is too simple. For an interesting reconfiguration of the question of reality in the *Vita Nuova* see Robert Harrison, *The Body of Beatrice* (Baltimore: Johns Hopkins University Press, 1988).

15. Indeed, the theme of *amor de lonh* seems to characterize troubadour love from its earliest beginnings. In the songs of the first troubadour, Guilhem de Poitou, "there is clear evidence . . . that some concept of *amor de lonh* already existed." Gerald A. Bond, Introduction to *The Poetry of William VII, Count of Poitiers, IX Duke of Aquitaine,* ed. and trans. Bond (New York: Garland, 1982), lix.

16. *The Poetry of Arnaut Daniel,* ed. and trans. James J. Wilhelm (New York: Garland, 1981), 5:32.

17. The "love game," James Wilhelm wrote, with specific reference to Bernart, was on the one hand "deadly serious"; but on the other hand, insofar as it was really about sex, it was "pure jest." James Wilhelm, *Seven Troubadours: The Creators of Modern Verse* (University Park: Pennsylvania State University Press, 1970), 116–27. Frederick Goldin goes so far as to theorize that Bernart's audience itself was divided into groups, such that his discourse would shift in register from courtly to lustful as his eye moved from the group that was friendly to idealization to the "carnal sector." Frederick Goldin, *Lyrics of the Troubadours and Trouvères: An Anthology and a History* (Gloucester, Mass.: Peter Smith, 1983), 112–16. The notion that the troubadour makes a "bawdy wink at the audience" when he alludes to sexual desire is voiced by Simon Gaunt in connection with Giraut de Bornelh (Simon Gaunt, *Troubadours and Irony* [Cambridge: Cambridge University Press, 1989], 154). Sarah Kay, too, in her *Subjectivity in Troubadour Poetry* (Cambridge: Cambridge University Press, 1990), treats sexuality in the troubadours in general as a guilty and furtive element that only shows itself in symptomatic ways. Kay's challenging and important discussion suffers from her blending of such diverse figures as Marcabru, Bernart, and Raimon de Miraval to produce a homogeneous picture of sexual loathing in troubadour poetry. Kay, Gaunt, and others seem to have accepted Marcabru's cynical moralism as their own view of troubadour love. According to Gaunt, Marcabru "often portrays sex as an act of masculine aggression perpetrated against another man, whilst generally seeing women's sexuality as either completely passive or utterly voracious, and he is clearly preoccupied with the male organ, its size and its performance. All

these are elements which are typical of pornography" (60). This is the view of a troubadour who rather than celebrating courtly eroticism attacks it as immorality, and Gaunt wonders whether Marcabru was not "subconsciously titillated by constantly talking about sex," "repelled and fascinated by illicit sex, torn between the condemnation of certain activities and a troubling obsession with describing them" (ibid.). This guilty doubleness is on my reading quite alien to Bernart, Giraut de Bornelh, Arnaut Daniel, or Bertran de Born.

18. Laura Kendrick, *The Game of Love: Troubadour Wordplay* (Berkeley: University of California Press, 1988).

19. L. T. Topsfield, *Troubadours and Love* (Cambridge: Cambridge University Press, 1975), 127–28, 135.

20. Amelia van Vleck says that "joy" in troubadour poetry refers to "the creative impulse of poetry, and that "few scholars would still translate it as *"jouissance."* Amelia E. van Vleck, *Memory and Re-Creation in Troubadour Lyric* (Berkeley: University of California Press, 1991), 20. But compare the compendious earlier discussion by Martín de Riquer, in whose opinion the definition of *joi* that comes closest to the mark is that of Jean Frappier. After listing the various forms of exaltation conveyed by the word, Frappier concludes that "despite the somewhat esoteric sense of the term . . . the idea of carnal felicity is never quite erased in it." Martín de Riquer, *Los Trovadores: Historia Literaria y Textos* (Barcelona: Editorial Planeta, 1975), 90. Riquer cites Frappier, *Vues sur les conceptions courtoises dans les littératures d'oc et d'oil au XIIe siècle,* Cahiers de Civilisation médiévales (1959), 2:140–41.

21. As Mariann Regan points out, it is a "Robertsonian" hangover to think that "praise in religious terms of profane love must be ironic"; perhaps, Regan suggests, the sexual undertone in a troubadour poem might be part of "a richer, more comprehensive game of self" than some critics have been able to see. Mariann Sanders Regan, *Love Words: The Self and the Text in Medieval and Renaissance Poetry* (Ithaca: Cornell University Press, 1982), 87.

22. Bernart himself does not explicitly discuss the theory behind his practice, but we do find such discussions in other poets whose erotics are similar to his. In the *sirventes* of Giraut de Bornelh, "Be·m· plairia, seingner en reis" (58), there is a debate between the poet and the king of Aragon in which the poet accuses rich men like the king of wanting "only enjoyment" from love, *Non voles·mas lo iauzimen* (24), for they ask to lie with the lady without first doing love service (37–38). *The* cansos *and* sirventes *of the Troubadour Giraut de Borneil: A Critical Edition,* ed. Ruth Verity Sharman (Cambridge: Cambridge University Press, 1989), 389–94. The art of wooing, says the poet, "suffers great harm" when the lover does not undergo the emotional and imaginative experience of deferral *enan del iazer* 'before getting into bed' (33–36).

The "most candid commentary" on *iazer* or *jazer* 'lying together', according to Glynnis Cropp, is from a *partimen* by Gaucelm Faidit and Peirol, in which Peirol asks Gaucelm which lover has the most pleasure, the one who lies with his lady all night without "doing it" (*e non lo fai*), or he who only has enough time with his lady to "do it once" (*d'una vetz faire*) and then has to leave. Gaucelm's reply is that the former has twice as much joy (*joi*) as the latter, "for in just lying with her there are a hundred pleasures, if he knows how to awaken them." Glynnis Cropp, *Le Vocabulaire courtois des troubadours de l'époque classique* (Geneva: Librairie Droz, 1975), 374.

These examples are rich in implication. On the one hand, both poems insist on the *primacy* of the pleasures of deferred consummation, of courtship and foreplay. But on the other hand, they are concerned with an explicitly sexual joy, a joy for which sexual consummation glows on the horizon and is achievable. (As Riquer observes, the entire genre of the *alba* presupposes that the lovers have already consummated their love [*Los Trovadores*, 91].)

23. I have just this once provided my own translation here in an effort to retain something of the rhythm of Bernart's beautiful lines. There is no poetry that loses more in translation than does that of the troubadours. Any reader with a knowledge of even one Romance language would be well rewarded by attempting the troubadours in the original.

24. The *asag* or *asais* was the "trial" or "proof" of love, the ultimate test of the lover's service, which consisted in sharing a bed with the beloved, yet without sexual consummation. According to René Nelli, the *asag* corresponded to the fourth and highest degree of *drudaria* 'love service'. *L'Érotique des Troubadours* (Toulouse: Eduard Privat, 1963), 181, 196–202.

25. For a particularly radical view of the turn from the doctrine of the *Symposium* to that of the *Phaedrus*, see Nussbaum's remarkable chapter 7 in *The Fragility of Goodness*, 200–233. On the physicality of Platonic love, see also Vlastos, "The Individual," 39–40. A. W. Price, however, rejects the notion that unconsummated physicality is a component of "Platonic love": "It is hard to conceive how a perilous policy of deliberate mutual arousal without gratification could actually further a life of happiness and harmony, of self-control and inner peace. Even if it came off, it could only generate an obsessive sexual heroism. . . . The bad horse must be reduced again to a state of fright, which is not one of titillation induced by petting" (*Love and Friendship in Plato and Aristotle* [Oxford: Clarendon Press, 1989], 90).

26. Jörn Gruber, *Die Dialektik des Trobar: Untersuchungen zur Struktur und Entwicklung des occitanischen und französischen Minnesangs des 12. Jahrhunderts* (Tübingen: Max Niemeyer Verlag, 1983).

27. Sarah Spence, *Rhetorics of Reason and Desire: Vergil, Augustine, and the Troubadours* (Ithaca: Cornell University Press, 1988), 103–27.

28. According to Gaunt, Raimbaut d'Aurenga appears to have written a courtly *canso* ("Braiz, chans") to his own wife, the only instance of its kind (137). On my reading, the poem shows the possible transformability of the conventions of courtly love to the condition of marriage: "My heart says to me, 'Why am I reviled by her?' 'Because she knows I consider no other woman worthy of my

love, because of which she values me little.'" This could mean that his wife no longer values his love because she rests so secure in her possession of him. This is precisely why, Andreas Capellanus tells us, passionate love cannot exist in marriage, because jealousy, "nurse and mother of love," is absent; but Raimbaut appears to re-create the conditions for passion out of the convention of the unresponsive lady. For Gaunt, however, the fact that the poem is addressed to his wife "undermines the sincerity of the whole poem" (127).

29. When Peire d'Alvernhe considers death in "De Dieu non pense" (17), he does so in classical Christian fashion, as the stench that ought to make us distrust the beauties and desires of this world. But Peire is one of the least courtly of troubadours.

30. Joan M. Ferrante, *Woman as Image in Medieval Literature* (New York: Columbia University Press, 1975), 10–12.

31. The traditional corpus of the *trobairitz* has been made available, with English translations, in Meg Bogin, *The Woman Troubadours* (New York: Paddington Press, 1976). For critical commentary on the *trobairitz*, see Bogin's introductory chapters; Marianne Shapiro, "The Provençal Trobairitz and the Limits of Courtly Love," *Signs* 3 (1978): 560–71; and the essays collected in *The Voice of the Trobairitz: Perspectives on the Women Troubadours*, ed. William D. Paden (Philadelphia: University of Pennsylvania Press, 1989). The recent appearance of Angelica Rieger's comprehensive *Trobairitz: Der Beitrag der Frau in der altokzitanischen höfischen Lyrik, Edition des Gesamtkorpus* (Tübingen: Max Niemeyer Verlag, 1991) should open a new epoch in the assessment of the poetic activity of women in the troubadour period.

32. Kay and others note that the poems of Castelloza offer a particularly anguished picture of a woman's experience of love. Rieger, however, reminds us of the "highly precarious" nature of the identification of the lyrical "I" of Castelloza's poems with the *trobairitz* herself. Castelloza "gives expression in her songs to the unhappy and hopelessly enamored woman—without necessarily being this woman herself." Her *vida*, Rieger reminds us, describes her as "very learned" and "very gay," *mout gaia e mout enseingnada* (568–69).

Like every aspect of the feminist critique of history and ideology, the assessment of the *trobairitz* is fraught with ambiguity. To treat Castelloza as a suffering, repressed woman who voices her anguish in her poems may underrate the art and intellect of a gay and learned woman; but to emphasize her accomplishments may lend aid and comfort to those who say the system wasn't (and by implication, isn't today) so bad after all.

(On the question of the provenance and reliability of the troubadour *vidas*, see Riquer, *Los Trovadores*, 26–30. Some of the *vidas* are, as Riquer stresses, more or less reliable; others are clearly no more than fanciful embroidery on suggestions drawn from the poems of the troubadour in question. In the case of Castelloza, the *vida* actually contradicts the picture of the author one would draw from the poems; thus it is not so easily shown to be a fabrication.)

33. See Bernart 15.29–32 and 40.57–64. For an account of this ideal in Giraut, see Sharman, 34–35. Sharman suggests that Giraut might have influenced Bernart on this point, but I see no evidence for this claim.

34. Boris Tomashevsky, "Thematics," in *Russian Formalist Criticism: Four Essays*, trans. Lee T. Lemon and Marion J. Reis (Lincoln: University of Nebraska Press, 1965), 61–98; see esp. 78–84.

35. On the repetition and fracturing of the conventions of the gothic novel in *Jane Eyre*, see the recent and fascinating discussion in Michel A. Massé, *In the Name of Love: Women, Masochism, and the Gothic* (Ithaca: Cornell University Press, 1992), 192–237.

36. On the formal/linguistic transformation in Shakespeare's sonnets of the epideictic tradition in poetry, see Joel Fineman, *Shakespeare's Perjured Eye: The Invention of Poetic Subjectivity in the Sonnets* (Berkeley: University of California Press, 1986). Fineman, however, frames his dazzling and erudite analysis of the originality of Shakespeare's sonnets in almost complete isolation from the classical meditation on desire and death. His analysis of the transition from the "ideal sameness" of the epideictic tradition to the "difference" of the Dark Lady sonnets fails to engage the religious-philosophical context out of which the language of epideixis is carved, a context in which there is an *overwhelming* awareness of the duplicity of love and of what today is called the nonidentity of the subject with herself. Only in a couple of footnote references to Petrarch's *Secretum* does the voice of Augustine intrude as the conscience of what Fineman encapsulates as "Christian orthodoxy" (see esp. 346–47, n. 35).

37. Topsfield does not cite these lines. I cite them from Peire d'Alvernha, *Liriche*, ed. and trans. Alberto del Monte (Torino: Loescher-Chiantore, 1955).

38. *The Seminar of Jacques Lacan: Book VII. The Ethics of Psychoanalysis*, trans. Dennis Porter (New York: Norton, 1992), 150–51.

39. Text and translation from Goldin, *Lyrics of the Troubadours*, 254–61.

40. Cf. the important discussion of Beatrice and the *Petrose* by Regan, who pursues very different ends from my own, in *Love Words*, 134–58.

41. The *Rime petrose* had a considerable influence on Petrarch and, through Petrarch, on much of European poetry. Robert Durling in his rich introduction to Petrarch's *Rime sparse* mentions that there are frequent allusions to the *Rime petrose* in Petrarch, but Durling has in mind mainly references to petrifaction and the Medusa (*Petrarch's Lyric Poems: the Rime sparse and Other Lyrics*, trans. and ed. Robert M. Durling [Cambridge, Mass.: Harvard University Press, 1976], 30–31; citations and translation of the *Rime sparse* from this edition). I suggest that a deeper correspondence between the *Rime sparse* and the *Rime petrose* is indicated by Durling's own analysis of the structure of Petrarch's crucial *canzoni* 125–29.

The persona of these lyrics voices the familiar plaint: I am dying, dying for love of her, and she "stands like ice" (*come un ghiaccio stasse* [125.11]) in the face of my suffering. Here the fantasy is not that of vengeful fucking, however, but its twin, that of the woman's mourning. If I were dead, then she would weep for me as she will not do for me living: "and oh the pity! Seeing me already dust amid the stones, Love will inspire her to sigh so sweetly that she will win mercy for me and force Heaven, drying her eyes with her lovely veil" (126.33–40).

Durling argues that this fantasy of being-mourned triggers a release that is "sublimated and orgasmic, and consciously so" (24), as the image of Laura that was only given in traces in poem 125 now bursts on the poet with great intensity and he sees her in a "rain of flowers" falling on her lap. Durling reads this rain of flowers as a displacement of "the sowing of seed . . . from the lover to the tree" (24), which should scarcely take a Freudian to acknowledge. My main interest, however, is in the indisputable fact that at this turning point in the *Rime sparse* we find the woman's coldness calling forth from the lover the desire to be mourned by her. And if we accept Durling's interpretation of the next stanza, then the entire thing looks like a sublimated or *aufgehoben* version of Dante's fantasy in the fourth of the *Rime petrose,* with Petrarch's lover achieving in a ghostly and passive-aggressive fashion what he cannot achieve in the tumescent flesh. (We will see a variant of this structure in *Heart of Darkness.*)

42. The poem contains the germs of the opening chapters of the *VN*: "the image of 'il libro de la mente' (chap. 1), and the descriptions of the perturbations produced by Beatrice in Dante while he was still a child (chap. 2)." Foster and Boyde, *Dante's Lyric Poetry,* vol. 2: Commentary (Oxford: Clarendon Press, 1967), 88.

43. Robert M. Durling and Ronald L. Martinez, *Time and the Crystal: Studies in Dante's Rime Petrose* (Berkeley: University of California Press, 1990), 199.

Chapter Five: Infidelity and Death in *Hamlet* and *La Princesse de Clèves*

1. I cite *Hamlet* from *The Riverside Shakespeare,* ed. G. Blakemore Evans (Boston: Houghton Mifflin, 1974).

2. For all the vast amount of commentary on this play, only recently, and especially in various feminist readings, has the blatant fact of Hamlet's erotic nausea begun to be placed at the center of analysis. See, for example, the brilliant essay by Margaret W. Ferguson, *"Hamlet:* Letters and Spirits," in *Shakespeare and the Question of Theory,* ed. Patricia Parker and Geoffrey Hartman (New York: Methuen, 1985), 292–309. My own reading of *Hamlet* has a focus very close on some points to Ferguson's. Also insightful on the questions of sex and misogyny in *Hamlet* is Marilyn Butler, *Shakespeare's Division of Experience* (New York: Ballantine, 1981), 140–54. See as well Juliana Schiesari, *The Gendering of Melancholia: Feminism, Psychoanalysis, and the Symbolics of Loss in Renaissance Literature* (Ithaca: Cornell University Press, 1992), 233–67, where, as elsewhere, Schiesari makes observations of the greatest interest for the present study. Another recent discussion of *Hamlet* that I have found of exceptional interest is Ned Lukacher, *Primal Scenes: Literature, Philosophy, and Psychoanalysis* (Ithaca: Cornell University Press, 1986), 198–235.

3. This analogy is explicitly stated in Ulysses' famous "string untuned" speech

in *Troilus and Cressida:* "the glorious planet Sol / in noble eminence enthron'd and spher'd / Amidst the other; whose med'cinable eye / . . . posts like the commandment of a king" (1.3.89–93).

4. The sliding of "sun" in particular manifests an obsessional principle noted by Freud in the case of the Rat Man, "the rule that in time the thing which is meant to be warded off invariably finds its way into the very means which is being used for warding it off." *The Standard Edition of the Complete Psychological Works of Sigmund Freud,* trans. James Strachey (London: Hogarth Press, 1955), 10:225. This principle is also illustrated in the case of the Wolf Man, who became "very pious" at one period but who found that in the midst of his pious ceremonial at the end of the day he recollected "some blasphemous thoughts which used to come into his head like an inspiration from the devil. He was obliged to think 'God—swine' or 'God—shit.' Once while he was on a journey . . . he was tormented by the obsession of having to think of the Holy Trinity whenever he saw three heaps of horse-dung or other excrement lying in the road" (17:16–17). It is not accidental that Hamlet is the only one of Shakespeare's tragic heroes for whom the Christian eschatology is a vivid and present reality and a compelling source of motivation; it would not be far off the mark to call him "pious."

5. G. W. F. Hegel, *Phenomenology of Spirit,* trans. A. V. Miller (Oxford: Oxford University Press, 1979), 271. See chapter 7 for further discussion of this passage in the *Phenomenology.*

6. On the pervasiveness in Shakespeare's plays of references to venereal disease and its effects on the body, see Frankie Rubinstein, "They Were Not Such Good Years," *Shakespeare Quarterly* 40 (Spring 1989): 70–74.

7. Andreas Capellanus, *The Art of Courtly Love,* trans. John Jay Parry (New York: Frederick Ungar, 1941; rpt. 1959), 101, 107.

8. Denis de Rougement called *La Princesse* the last "flame," "tenuous and pure" that would be lit from the fire of the myth of courtly love, whose essential instance Rougement took to be the myth of Tristan and Iseult (*Love in the Western World,* trans. Montgomery Belgion [Princeton: Princeton University Press, 1983], 196). The course Rougement plots from the troubadours to *La Princesse* seems to me plausible in its outlines. For a detailed analysis of the functioning of courtly love conventions within the novel itself, see Jules Brody, "*La Princesse de Clèves* and the Myth of Courtly Love," *University of Toronto Quarterly* 38 (1969): 105–35. An interesting recent book on this novel recasts the question of the courtly rule of distance in Lacanian terms: Jean-Michel Delacomptée interprets the conflict between passion and marriage in terms of "le caractère symbolique de l'alliance confronté à l'imaginaire du rapport passionel" in his *La Princesse de Clèves: la mère et le courtisan* (Paris: Presses Universitaire de France, 1990).

9. Madame de Lafayette, *La Princesse de Clèves et autres romans* (Paris: Éditions Gallimard, 1972), 155.

10. Monsieur de Clèves is also divided, into a husband and a lover—the only man who could be both to the same woman, according to his wife; but as lover he

is subject to a jealousy and lack of candidness with her that annuls the friendship which, as husband, he supposedly shares with her.

11. Absolute or perfect loss and its concomitant pain would thus be the exact converse of absolute possession and its concomitant happiness as eternal proximity to the most perfect object (as in Plato).

12. "I love you, I hate you," Monsieur Clèves tells the princess at one point; "I offend you, I beg your pardon; I admire you, I am ashamed to admire you" (277).

13. According to Veyne, "It was impossible [among the Romans] for a woman to make a fool of her lord and master. Had it been, Cato, Caesar, and Pompey would all have been illustrious cuckolds. A man was the master of his wife, just as he was the master of his daughter and servants. If his wife was unfaithful, the man did not thereby become a laughingstock. Infidelity was a misfortune. . . . If a wife betrayed her husband, the husband was criticized for want of vigilance and for having, by his own weakness, allowed adultery to flourish in the city. . . . The only way for a husband or father to avoid such an accusation was to be the first to denounce publicly any misconduct by members of his family." *The History of Private Life*, vol. 1, *From Pagan Rome to Byzantium*, ed. Paul Veyne (Cambridge, Mass.: Belknap Press, 1987), 39. With all respect to Veyne, whose authority on such a topic I do not dispute, I suggest that some skepticism is in order whenever it is declared that in such and such a culture "it is impossible for a woman to make a fool of her lord and master."

14. It is of course impossible to draw a simple boundary between "inside" and "outside": there is always under way a contamination of each by the other. Even when women are treated in the most extreme fashion as possessions, as they were in classical Athens, the concern with their "interiority" is (in a crude way) necessarily already there. This is indicated in the emphasis Lysias lays, in the speech he wrote for a man accused of killing his wife's seducer, on the "corruption" of a woman's mind as more significant than the violation of a free man's or boy's body—because in her voluntary infidelity lies the possibility of uncertain paternity: "Thus the lawgiver, sirs, considered that those who use force deserve a less penalty than those who use persuasion; for the latter he condemned to death, whereas for the former he doubled the damages, considering that those who achieve their ends by force are hated by the persons forced; while those who used persuasion corrupted thereby their victims' souls, thus making the wives of others more closely attached to themselves than to their husbands, and got the whole house into their hands, and caused uncertainty as to whose the children really were." "On the Murder of Eratosthenes," in the Loeb *Lysias*, trans. W. R. M. Lamb (New York: G. P. Putnam's Sons, 1930), 32–33 (Stephanus, 94–95).

15. Cf. Toril Moi, "Desire in Language: Andreas Capellanus and the Controversy of Courtly Love, in Medieval Literature: Criticism, Ideology and History," ed. David Aers (New York: St. Martin's, 1986), 11–33, esp. 26–27.

Chapter Six: Adam's Choice

1. James Grantham Turner, *One Flesh: Paradisal Marriage and Sexual Relations in the Age of Milton* (Oxford: Clarendon Press, 1987), 79. Turner's book requires to be studied from cover to cover by anyone interested in the problem of eros in *Paradise Lost* or Milton in general, but the crucial theological background may be gleaned from his chapter 2, "The Incorporation of Eros." Turner here presents a detailed conspectus of the evolution of Christian views on sex from Augustine through the Utopian sexual theories of certain seventeenth-century Protestant radicals with which Milton's own vision of marriage has "a complex and troubled relationship" (75).

2. See the discussion of courtly love in chapter 4.

3. F. T. Prince, *The Italian Element in Milton's Verse* (Oxford: Clarendon Press, 1954), 61–63.

4. *Petrarch's Lyric Poems*, ed. and trans. Robert M. Durling (Cambridge: Harvard University Press, 1976), 574–83.

5. The Renaissance preoccupation with the real humanity of Christ and the emphasis on his genitals as the proof of his humanity are documented by Leo Steinberg in his wonderful book, *The Sexuality of Christ in Renaissance Art and in Modern Oblivion* (New York: Pantheon, 1983). On the specific question of the meaning of Christ's circumcision for the Renaissance, see pages 50–72. Steinberg points out that Crashaw's sonnet on the divine circumcision was written in the same year as Milton's poem.

6. I should note, however, that Petrarch's poem itself manifests a quite specific anatomical preoccupation. It is not the guilty sexual parts of the male that absorb Petrarch's attention but the vision of *female* parts whose purity could envelop even the human flesh of a real man (*verace omo* [135–36]):

Virgin unique in the world, unexampled . . . who made Heaven in love with your beauties . . . holy thoughts, merciful and chaste actions made a consecrated living temple of the true God in your fruitful virginity (*tua verginità feconda*). (56–58)

And even more vividly: "Remember that our sins made God take on, to save us, human flesh in your virginal cloister" (*umana carne al tuo virginal chiostro* [78]). Petrarch, in words that resound strikingly in the context of the courtly tradition, refers to Mary as the *donna* of Christ (48). Could Petrarch have been unaware of the erotic joke contained in the reference to the *virginal chiostro* in which the deity takes on *umana carne*? The same image had been used in a Limoges Nativity conductus from the twelfth century that has been identified as the metrical and melodic model for one of Guillaume de Poitou's bawdy songs; Laura Kendrick shows that even those who put together a songbook in which the conductus is found had noticed the joke. "They played with a hole in the leather of the page. . . . The large hole outlined in red appears in a line that describes the Incarnation: . . . In utero virginis·o / carnem sum ( ) sit hominis o·contio . . . ("In the womb of a virgin, O, He took on the flesh of a man. O reunion!") Laura Kendrick, *The Game of Love: Troubadour Wordplay* (Berkeley: University of California Press, 1988), 156.

7. Strikingly, even Robert Durling dismisses Poem 366 as "a tissue of traditional epithets and phrases in praise of the Virgin" (*Petrarch's Lyric Poems*, 574).

8. See the suggestive recent attempt by Sarah Spence to interpret troubadour desire and troubadour rhetoric in relation to the Augustinian tradition: "Rhetorical Anxiety in Troubadour Lyric," in Spence, *Rhetorics of Reason and Desire: Vergil, Augustine, and the Troubadours* (Ithaca: Cornell University Press, 1988), 103–27.

9. On the relation between Milton's Italian sonnets and Petrarch, see the fascinating essay by Lynn E. Enterline, "'Myself/Before Me': Gender and Prohibition in Milton's Italian Sonnets," in *Milton and the Idea of Woman*, ed. Julia M. Walker (Urbana: University of Illinois Press, 1988), 32–65.

10. Cf. lines 53–65 of Petrarch's Poem 126, which read like a more theologically conscious version of Adam's speech than Milton has written, a version that articulates what Adam should, from an orthodox viewpoint, have articulated: the element of illusion involved in the spell cast by the woman.

11. Diane McColley, *Milton's Eve* (Urbana: University of Illinois Press, 1983) and *A Gust of Paradise: Milton's Eden and the Visual Arts* (Urbana: University of Illinois Press, 1993).

12. Cf. the very interesting and very different approach by which William Kerrigan and Gordon Braden link Milton to the *fin'amors* and Petrarchan tradition in their *The Idea of the Renaissance* (Baltimore: Johns Hopkins University Press, 1989) 157–218. Jean H. Hagstrum noted the affinity between Milton and the troubadours in *Sex and Sensibility: Ideal and Erotic Love from Milton to Mozart* (Chicago: University of Chicago Press, 1980), 32.

13. To say that Adam's choice is the crux of Milton's conundrum is not to say that Adam, rather than Eve, is the "hero" of the poem (whatever that might mean). On the contrary, I take it that Eve is by far the most magnificent character in the poem and its real moving force—the arche-pharmakon without which *nothing would happen*. It is the chief virtue of Empson's book that it develops so powerfully the basis for this view of Eve. See William Empson, *Milton's God* (Cambridge: Cambridge University Press, 1961), 163.

More recent criticism, especially by women, has stressed the ambivalence in Milton's portrait of Eve's heroism. Gilbert and Gubar point out that Eve is very similar not only to "Satan the serpentine tempter" but also to "Satan the romantic outlaw," that figure of rebellion and imagination so lionized by romantics since Blake and Shelley; but Gilbert and Gubar are also acutely aware of the difficulties involved in this identification. Sandra M. Gilbert and Susan Gubar, *The Madwoman in the Attic: The Woman Writer and the Nineteenth-Century Literary Imagination* (New Haven: Yale University Press, 1979), 187–212; citation from 201. Lucy

Newlyn has carried further the discussion of the "merging of Satan and Eve" in *Paradise Lost and the Romantic Reader* (Oxford: Clarendon Press, 1993), 153–91; citation from 155. See also Richard Corum, "In White Ink: *Paradise Lost* and Milton's Ideas of Women," in *Milton and the Idea of Woman*, ed. Julia M. Walker (Urbana: University of Illinois Press, 1988), 120–47.

14. Cf. Leopold Damrosch, *God's Plot and Man's Stories* (Chicago: University of Chicago Press, 1985):

> The problem here is to make it seem plausible—or indeed possible—that an unfallen man and woman could fall, a desire for evil entering minds in which evil had as yet no meaning. This issue has excited a good deal of critical controversy, which has proved inconclusive because the participants have been arguing from different premises. One group holds that the idea of a sinless person falling into sin is *psychologically* inconceivable, so that Milton has had to infect his prelapsarian Adam and Eve with fallen characteristics. The other group holds that the idea, whether conceivable or not, is *theologically* authoritative and that Adam and Eve—as Milton repeatedly says—were "pure" and "sinless" until they fell. Both sides are right. Milton did want to portray an Adam and Eve who were sinless yet capable of sin, a paradox which after all is central to Christianity. (106)

15. There is some kinship, but more fundamental differences, between my approach to *Paradise Lost* and that of Herman Rappaport in his *Milton and the Postmodern* (Lincoln: University of Nebraska Press, 1983). Rappaport focuses on "undecidability"; on the allegorical distance between representation and represented; and, in what seems to me an odd turn, on the idea that "traces" (in a sense that Rappaport links to Derrida) point toward "a recuperation of the sacred." "Certainly, it must be in that undecidable space . . . between God's self-concealment and his revelation that man experiences the expectation of an authentic encounter with the Godhead (epiphany) grounded on the experience of loss" (46). My concerns are, by contrast, resolutely naturalistic and textual: my question is whether the textual tradition of Christianity can provide Milton the resources he requires to justify his erotic demand.

16. See the sensitive analysis of Adam and Eve's separation debate by John Reichert in "'Against his better knowledge': A Case for Adam" *ELH* 48 (1981): 83–109, esp. 88–94.

17. McColley delicately refers to "a certain angelic impercipience" (*Milton's Eve*, 70). Other interpreters are less tolerant. David Aers and Bob Hodge refer to Raphael's response as "profoundly ungenerous" and as advocating a "sterile egoism" ("Rational Burning: Milton on Sex and Marriage," *Milton Studies* 13 (1979): 3–33; citations from 26). Turner calls Raphael's judgment on Adam's love a "cynical condemnation" and deems it "appalling" (280).

18. Baldesar Castiglione, *The Book of the Courtier*, trans. George Bull (Bungay, England: Penguin, 1980), 332.

19. Barbara Lewalski, *Paradise Lost and the Rhetoric of Literary Forms* (Princeton: Princeton University Press, 1985), 215.

20. Marsilio Ficino, *Commentary on Plato's Symposium on Love,* trans. Sears Jayne (Dallas: Spring Publications, 1985), 142. Ficino is thought to be the primary source of Bembo's speech in the *Symposium,* but there is a distinct difference of tone and emphasis in their respective treatments of physical beauty.

21. *Paradise Lost* is thus here a development of the project of the divorce tracts, in which, Turner writes, "Milton's chaste hopes, fed by an imagination trained on the *Symposium* and the Song of Songs, did not encourage him to drain erotic energy from any aspect of marriage, but his sense of pollution would not let him celebrate copulation as a good in its own right. . . . He thus develops a theory and practice of Eros which bridges these two extremes, which depreciates the central act of sexuality while extending its peripheral delights into every corner of the relationship" (210). In *Paradise Lost,* "the breach between the affectionate gesture and sexual consummation, once defended with all the disdain at Milton's command, is . . . healed" (258).

22. In fact, as Empson pointed out, the angel too is somewhat tangled in the coils of the problematic of eros; we tend not to notice this because the focus of blame is on Adam. But the angelic lovemaking Raphael describes is not equivalent to the divine eros of the ladder of erotic ascent, much less to the orthodox absorption of self in the love of God. What the angel describes is two individuals absorbed in love of *each other,* and he makes no mention whatever of God as the ultimate object of this act of love. The fact that it is perfectly aetherealized makes angelic interpenetration seem thoroughly "spiritual," but this still leaves open the question of its relation to God because, whereas earthly beings can use eros as an approach to God, the angels are already privy to his presence. As Empson remarked, "Though capable of reuniting themselves with God the angels do not want to, especially because this capacity lets them enjoy occasional acts of love among themselves" (*Milton's God,* 139).

23. Aers and Hodge argue that Raphael's account of angelic merging is "partially aetherealized" but "does not repudiate the physical" ("Milton on Sex," 27), but the repudiation of "restrained conveyance" carries all the force of the classical repudiation. In their enthusiasm for the "rejection of merely genital sexuality in favor of total orgasm, total union," Aers and Hodge manifest that very spiritualizing impulse that drives Milton, too; of course they don't want God involved, but from the present perspective this is a small difference.

24. Castiglione's Bembo, apparently following Pico della Mirandola, describes a more restricted version of what Milton is striving for, not spiritual coition but a spiritual kiss: "The rational lover delights when he joins his mouth to the lady he loves in a kiss, not in order to arouse in himself any unseemly desire but because he feels that this bond opens the way for their souls which, attracted by their mutual desire, each pour themselves into the other's body in turn and so mingle that each of these possesses two souls, and it is as if a single spirit composed of

the two governs their two bodies" (*Book of the Courtier,* 336). Milton's vision of sexual purity is powerful enough to envision the sex act itself in the same terms. Augustine of course had imagined a pure sex life for Adam and Eve, but, as we will shortly see, one without the erotic rapture Milton describes.

25. This obligation is precisely what oppressed Satan in Heaven; turning his thoughts toward his indebtedness for the fund of being that was already his, he *forgot* the perpetual outflow of being toward him from his creator, and fell:

> . . . lifted up so high
> I sdein'd subjection, and thought one step higher
> Would set me highest, and in a moment quit
> The debt immense of endless gratitude,
> So burdensome, still paying, still to owe;
> *Forgetful what from him I still receiv'd,*
> And understood not that a grateful mind
> By owing owes not, but still pays, at once
> Indebted and discharg'd.   (4.49–57; emphasis added)

Temptation is always fundamentally the attraction of the mind away from the consciousness of God; hence Augustine's struggle against even the attraction of the melody of hymns and the beauty of light: "As to that corporeal light, of which I was speaking, it is a tempting and dangerous sweetness, like a sauce spread over the life of this world for its blind lovers. Yet those who know how to praise you for this light . . . are not carried away by it into spiritual sleep" (*Confessions,* trans. Rex Warner [New York: Mentor, 1963], bk. 10, 244). This lust for light would be the most refined form of "that kind of drunkenness in which the world forgets you, its creator, and falls in love with your creature instead of with you" (bk. 2, 43). The general name for the power that draws consciousness away from God toward created things is lust, *concupiscientia:* "In lust, . . . that is to say, in the darkness of affection, is the real distance from your face" (bk. 1, 36).

26. Saint Augustine, *Concerning the City of God against the Pagans,* trans. Henry Bettenson (Baltimore: Penguin, 1972), 14.16.

27. Platonism and Neoplatonism, too, condemn unmeasured pleasure. Milton would have known this condemnation from Plato's *Philebus,* where Protarchus affirms that nothing is "more unmeasured in its character than pleasure and intense enjoyment," and that there is in the experiencing of such pleasures an element of "extreme ugliness" (*The Collected Dialogues of Plato,* ed. Edith Hamilton and Huntington Cairns, trans. R. Hackforth [New York: Pantheon, 1961], 65d–66a). Ficino may have had these remarks from the *Philebus* in mind when he remarked in his commentary on the *Symposium* that "venereal madness leads to intemperance, and therefore to disharmony. Therefore it likewise seems to lead to ugliness, whereas love leads to beauty. . . . Therefore the desire for coitus . . . and love are shown to be not only not the same motions but opposite" (41).

28. *Luther's Works,* vol. 1, *Lectures on Genesis,* chaps. 1–5, ed. J. Pelikan (St. Louis: Concordia Publishing House, 1958), 119.

29. Saint Thomas Aquinas, *Summa Theologiae,* trans. Edmund Hill (New York: McGraw-Hill, 1964), 13:1a, 98, 2.

30. Stanley Fish argues that Adam's original account to Raphael of his love for Eve (8.530–52) was merely careless, and his rephrased account in response to the angels' chiding (8.596–611) is the correct, and unblamable, expression of the nature of his love for her (*Surprised by Sin* [Berkeley: University of California Press, 1971], 229–31). But as Reichert points out, the first words of Adam's inward colloquy when he resolves to fall ("Oh fairest of Creation, last and best / Of all God's works") "contradict, explicitly and directly," the knowledge he had expressed to Raphael in the orthodox portion of his first speech, 8.540–41, "For well I understand in the prime end / Of Nature her th'inferior." Reichert takes this contradiction to show that Adam "knowingly chooses Eve '*against* his better knowledge'" and thus is indeed not deceived, as Milton, following 1 Timothy 2:14, asserts in 9.997–99 ("A Case for Adam," 95). But it also shows that, whatever Adam "knows" about the correct view, in the sense that he is able to parade the right words before his consciousness, his statement that Eve "seems" absolute (8.547) expresses his consistent view.

31. The phrase "so adorn" is Italianate, as Alastair Fowler notes in his edition of *Paradise Lost* (*The Poems of Milton,* ed. John Carey and Alastair Fowler [New York: Norton, 1972], 845); but, more precisely, it is very likely a transcription of the *si adorna* with which Dante describes Beatrice in the *canzone* "Donne ch'avete" in the *Vita Nuova:* "Dice di lei Amor: 'Cosa mortale / come esser pò sì adorna e sì pura?'"

32. Cf. Peter Brown's remarks on Augustine in *The Body and Sexuality: Men, Women, and Sexual Renunciation in Early Christianity* (New York: Columbia University Press, 1988), 419–22.

33. Adam's "resolution is to Die." How is this resolution related to the "resolve," "resolute," and "resolution" by which Macquarrie and Robinson translate Heidegger's *entschliessen, entschlossen, Entschluss*? Resoluteness, says Heidegger, is "the authenticity of care itself" (348), and care "harbours in itself both death and guilt equiprimordially" (354).

Any factical Dasein has been determined by its ownmost Being-guilty both *before* any factical indebtedness has been incurred and *after* any such indebtedness has been paid off; and wanting-to-have-a-conscience signifies that one is ready for the appeal to this ownmost Being-guilty. This prior Being-guilty, which is constantly with us, does not show itself unconcealedly in its character as prior until this very priority has been enlisted in [*hineingestellt*] that possibility which is simply *not to be outstripped*. When in anticipation, resoluteness has *caught up* [*eingeholt*] the possibility of death into its potentiality-for-Being, Dasein's authentic existence can no longer be *outstripped* [*überholt*] by anything. (*Being and Time*, trans. John Macquarrie and Edward Robinson [Oxford: Basil Blackwell, 1980], 354–55; italics in original)

Heidegger of course does not mean by guilt what is normally understood as such in Christian doctrine; yet he is engaged in an elaboration of the traditional meaning. And it is clear that what Adam calls his "resolution" no more satisfies the requirements of Heideggerean authenticity than it does those of Christian righteousness. Adam's "choice" is not "a way of Being of Dasein in which it brings itself to itself and face to face with itself" (357); what it brings him face to face with is, rather, the detour of his being through that of the woman whose own proper nature ensures that she will wander away on her own path.

34. As Fish shows, however, Eve's empiricism is itself thoroughly sinful, a form of belief in oneself instead of in God (*Surprised by Sin*, 248–52).

35. *Marsilio Ficino: The Philebus Commentary*, ed. and trans. Michael J. B. Allen (Berkeley: University of California Press, 1975), 316. On the influence during the Renaissance of the *Philebus* itself and of Ficino's commentary, see Allen's introduction, page 15, and his note 57, page 526.

36. G. W. F. Hegel, *Phenomenology of Spirit*, trans. A. V. Miller (Oxford: Oxford University Press, 1979), 467–68.

37. A radical reinterpretation of Eve might well begin from Christine Froula's revaluation of her "narcissism" as a positive impulse to selfhood. Christine Froula, "When Eve Reads Milton: Undoing the Canonical Economy," *Critical Inquiry* 10 (December 1983): 326–39.

38. I stress the limits of my claim here: I am referring to the moment of Adam's choice and not to the entire architecture of doctrine within which this choice is contained. Adam's choice is by definition the moment of excess, of the irruption of something in Adam that cannot be contained by the economy of Christian doctrine; and Christian doctrine must subsequently be reaffirmed. An important recent essay that tempers enthusiasm about Milton's ideas on equality or mutuality in marriage is Mary Nyquist, "The Genesis of Gendered Subjectivity in the Divorce Tracks and in *Paradise Lost*," in *Re-membering Milton*, ed. Mary Nyquist and Margaret W. Ferguson (New York: Methuen, 1987), 99–127.

39. Edgar Wind has shown that the conjunction of love and death as a figure for spiritual ravishment was a commonplace of Renaissance speculation. Edgar Wind, *Pagan Mysteries in the Renaissance* (New York: Norton, 1968), 152–70. But this death was either merely metaphorical (as in Ficino's *De Amore*, 2:8); or it was the mystical death in which the body is left behind in the soul's ascent to the divine, hence quite the opposite of the death associated with women and copulation.

40. "Those who are noble, magnanimous, and self-sacrificial do succumb to their instincts, and when they are at their best, their reason *pauses*. An animal that protects its young at the risk of its life, or that during the mating period follows the female even into death, does not think of danger and death; its reason also pauses, because the pleasure in its young or in the female and the fear of being

deprived of this pleasure dominate it totally: the animal becomes more stupid than usual—just like those who are noble and magnanimous" (*The Gay Science,* trans. Walter Kaufmann [New York: Vintage Books, 1974], 3).

41. We should recall that "solace" will be the word Milton uses to describe their fallen lovemaking: "the Seal / the solace of thir sin" (9.1043–44). McColley argues that Adam's sexual ardor is "one of the reasons Eve decides later on to leave Adam alone for a while" (*Milton's Eve,* 71):

> In addition to being a real garden really needing care, the Garden is a meta-
> phor for well-tempered passions and pleasures; and Eve, as she tactfully men-
> tions . . . has overheard "the parting Angel" (9.276). . . . What she has heard
> the Angel say to Adam—who has just been wrestling aloud with his passion
> for Eve—is "take heed lest passion sway / Thy judgment" (8.635–36). The
> imagery of her speech is of the tempering of passions in response to what
> Raphael's warnings and, no doubt, her own observations, have told her is
> Adam's greatest need. (146)

42. Critics from both Left and Right have reacted indignantly to Milton's treatment of Eve as sexually modest. "His Eve exhibits modesty too exclusively in sexual contexts," wrote C. S. Lewis, "and his Adam does not exhibit it at all" (C. S. Lewis, *A Preface to Paradise Lost* [New York: Oxford University Press, 1961], 124). From the other wing, Aers and Hodge complain that prelapsarian Eve "does not 'dart contagious fire': she just does not actually refuse. Does she lie there and think of England, as Victorian wives were supposed to do?" ("Milton on Sex," 28). More recently, Kerrigan and Braden have attempted to *validate* Eve's "coyness" as intensifying Edenic eroticism (*Idea of the Renaissance,* 204–6), an argument against which McColley defends both Eve and Milton (*A Gust for Paradise,* 180n).

43. Cf. my discussion of Milton's "On the Circumcision," 110–11 above.

44. Georges Bataille, *Erotism: Death and Sensuality,* trans. Mary Dalwood (San Francisco: City Lights, 1986), 255.

45. The young, chaste Milton dreamed of total delight as dissolution of bound-ary and restraint, but he did so under the figure of music ("L'Allegro"). The *canzone* "On the Circumcision" is formally and temporally paired with "At a Solemn Music," a transparent juxtaposition. In one poem, the infant phallus is scourged in atonement for man's guilt; in the other, perfect delight is imaged as the hearing of the divine music. Because the divine music is to be heard only by the pure, the sublimation involved in the movement from "Circumcision" to "Music" could scarcely be clearer.

But Milton insists on a certain binding of melody as well. There is a chaste, divine music and a bad, Circean music—the latter of course associated with sexual license. Thus in *Comus* the seducer is the son of Circe, and it is he who voices the distinction between the two kinds of music.

46. Augustine's thought concerning sexual libido evolved across time, but the

fundamental point I am making here remains unchanged. For a very thorough account, see Émile Schmitt, *Le Mariage Chrétien dans L'Oeuvre de Saint Augustin* (Paris: Études Augustiniennes, 1983), esp. 90–105.

47. Cf. John Halkett, *Milton and the Idea of Matrimony: A Study of the Divorce Tracts and Paradise Lost* (New Haven: Yale University Press, 1970), 121–22. I think Halkett too quickly dismisses the centrality of sex in the erotic bond that holds Adam to Eve, but his account of the doctrinal situation is correct: "Adam simply chooses Eve over God; he rejects human love as a means and deifies it as an end" (122). See also Damrosch: "Total and unreserved love of another human being, even of Eve the as yet perfect woman, is a disastrous form of self-love, for only God deserves total love" (*God's Plot and Man's Stories*, 110).

48. Even Adam's erotic discourse after the Fall is, with its echoes of the *Iliad,* full of literary refinement; but this refinement serves only to communicate sexual appetite, and its language is thus marked by its difference from that of the earlier speeches as closer to "animal nature."

49. It would seem that the most lawful erection contains an ineradicable residue of carnal lawlessness within it; hence the tortuosities of the Christian interpretation of the relation between sex and sin. (On this topic see C. S. Lewis, *Allegory of Love* [London: Oxford University Press, 1981], 14–17.) The attempt to imagine a completely lustless sex would seem to lead us into Augustine's camp. According to him, it is possible that in Paradise "the sexual organs would have been brought into activity by the same bidding of the will as controlled the other organs" (*CG* 14.26), for "man . . . may have once received from his lower members an obedience which he lost by his own disobedience" (14.24). The possibility of such obedience is evident from the unusual feats of people who can move their ears or sweat at will, or who can "produce at will such musical sounds from their behind (without any stink) that they seem to be singing from that region" (ibid.). These examples show the possibility that in Paradise erection might have been achieved by a "calm act of will" without the "allurement of passion" (14.26).

50. As Juliana Schiesari observes, the medieval nun Hildegard of Bingen criticized Adam as a "melancholic" in terms that have a striking contemporary relevance. Schiesari, *The Gendering of Melancholia: Feminism, Psychoanalysis, and the Symbolics of Loss in Renaissance Literature* (Ithaca: Cornell University Press, 1992), 154–59.

51. For certain Gnostics, "Eve is the spiritual principle in humanity who raises Adam from his merely material condition"; Elaine Pagels, *The Gnostic Gospels* (New York: Random House, 1979), 31. This Gnostic doctrine inverts the valuation of the woman while leaving intact the split between body and spirit that Gnosticism not only shares with the orthodox tradition but indeed heightens.

Chapter Seven: Inflicting/Mourning

1. The most extensive discussion of the style and narrative technique of *Heart of Darkness* is to be found in Ian Watt, *Conrad in the Nineteenth Century* (Berke-

ley: University of California Press, 1979), 168–214. See especially the discussion of the influence on Conrad of Henry James, 200–214.

2. The edition I will cite is Ford Madox Ford, *The Good Soldier* (New York: Vintage Books, 1989).

3. Joseph Conrad, *Heart of Darkness*, ed. Robert Kimbrough (New York: Norton, 1988), 20. All quotations of *Heart of Darkness* will be from this edition.

4. The incident during which the allusion to *Heart of Darkness* occurs concerns Dowell's sense that beneath Nancy Rufford's gaiety "there lurked some terrors." One day when they are "chattering away" together they hear the voice of her father, a voice that brings her bad dreams, from the arcades behind them: "He was walking away with an Italian baron who had had much to do with the Belgian Congo. They must have been talking about the proper treatment of natives, for I heard him say: 'Oh, hang humanity'" (141).

5. "The Return" cited from Joseph Conrad, *Tales of Unrest* (New York: Doubleday, Page & Co., 1924), 118–83.

6. Other similarities between the concluding scene of "The Return" and *Heart of Darkness* were noted by Thomas Moser in his *Joseph Conrad: Achievement and Decline* (Hamden, Conn.: Anchor Books, 1966), 79. Moser's discussion first called my attention to "The Return," but he greatly understates its resonance with *Heart of Darkness*.

7. The woman in "The Return" is not given a great deal more substance by Conrad than is the Intended; yet, despite the waverings in his portrayal of her, Conrad does manage, at least at moments, to give us some sense of "the spiritual and tragic contest of her feelings" (185). In reply to her husband's demand, she says, "I have a right—a right to—to—myself" (ibid.). Such a remark is far beyond anything one could conceive in the mouth of the Intended.

8. On the tone of "nervous anxiety and overassertiveness" in Marlow's remarks on women, see Walter J. Ong, "Truth in Conrad's Darkness," *Mosaic* 2 (1977): 162.

9. For a feminist reading that focuses on this and similar passages see Johanna M. Smith, "Too Beautiful Altogether: Patriarchal Ideology in *Heart of Darkness*," in *Joseph Conrad, Heart of Darkness: A Case Study in Contemporary Criticism*, ed. Ross C. Murfin (New York: St. Martin's, 1989), 179–95.

10. On the fundamentals of the light/dark imagery see Eloise Knapp Hay, *The Political Novels of Joseph Conrad* (Chicago: University of Chicago Press, 1963), 134–39.

11. The emaciated, enfeebled Kurtz displays the symptoms that Victorian medicine (following the ancient tradition documented by Foucault) interpreted as the effects of sexual excess, specifically as the consequence of the loss of vital force in ejaculation—the state Doctor William Acton referred to as "spermatorrhea." I am relying here on Steven Marcus's discussion of Acton's 1857 book (reprinted repeatedly in the following decades) *The Functions and Disorders of the Reproductive Organs*. "Along with tuberculosis," Marcus comments, spermatorrhea "appears to have been one of the virtually universal afflictions of the time" (Steven

Marcus, *The Other Victorians: A Study of Sexuality and Pornography in Mid-Nineteenth-Century England* [New York: New American Library, 1974], 27).

> What then [Marcus asks] is the prevention, cure, or solution for all these dangers? Acton's one recommendation is continence which consists not only in sexual abstinence "but in controlling all sexual excitement." True continence [Acton writes] "is complete control over the passions, exercised by one who knows their power, and who, but for his steady will, not only could, but would indulge them." (23)

Marlow's discourse on restraint and Acton's are clearly variations on the same theme, but with sex strangely absent from Marlow's account of Kurtz's lawless passions.

12. Conrad may have had somewhere in mind Nietzsche's description in *The Birth of Tragedy* of the Dionysian "phenomenon that pain begets joy, that ecstasy may wring sounds of agony from us. At the very climax of joy there sounds a cry of horror or a yearning lamentation for an irretrievable loss" (*The Birth of Tragedy and the Case of Wagner,* trans. Walter Kaufmann [New York: Vintage, 1967], 40).

13. See note 11.

14. It is, however, true that Conrad's period is marked by an explosion of interest in pornography, much of it by "gentlemen," and often, apparently, satisfied at the British Museum under the cover of an interest in "anthropology." See Ronald Pearsall, *The Worm in the Bud: The World of Victorian Sexuality* (Harmondsworth, Middlesex, England: Penquin, 1971), 454–56. It is perhaps also worth mentioning Bernard Meyer's argument that Conrad's story "The Arrow of Gold" is strongly influenced by Sacher-Masoch's *Venus in Furs.* Bernard C. Meyer, *Joseph Conrad: A Psychoanalytic Biography* (Princeton: Princeton University Press, 1967), 310–16.

15. G. W. F. Hegel, *Phenomenology of Spirit,* trans. A. W. Miller (Oxford: Oxford University Press, 1979), 275.

16. Jean Hyppolite, *Genesis and Structure of Hegel's Phenomenology of Spirit,* trans. Samuel Cherniak and John Heckman (Evanston, Ill.: Northwestern University Press, 1974), 282–84.

17. *The Lustful Turk,* too, registers in its grotesque way the necessity of the woman's mourning memorialization. When one of his victims cuts off the Turk's penis, he "calls upon his physician to complete the castration, and has 'his lost member preserved in spirits of wine in glass vases.' He then sends for Emily and Sylvia [his established slave-lovers], gives them each one of the vases, and has both girls shipped back to England" (Marcus, 203).

18. W. Thomas McCary, *Childlike Achilles: Ontogeny and Phylogeny in the Iliad* (New York: Columbia University Press, 1982), 22–25.

19. The original cry of the natives also comes through a shutter, this time a metaphorical one; but the repetition of the signifier seems a consequence of the coherence of the chain the links of which we have been tracing: "a white fog, very

warm and clammy. . . . At eight or nine, perhaps it lifted as a shutter lifts. . . . and then the white shutter came down again." It is then that we hear the "very loud cry, as of infinite desolation" that comes from the bush (41).

20. Cf. Judith Butler on "the mute facticity of the feminine, awaiting signification from an opposing masculine subject." Judith Butler, *Gender Trouble: Feminism and the Subversion of Identity* (New York: Routledge, 1990), 37.

21. For a Freudian reading of sexual anxiety in *Heart of Darkness* that remains of interest, see Frederick Crews, "Conrad's Uneasiness—and Ours," in Crews, *Out of My System* (New York: Oxford University Press, 1975).

22. On the way in which the Intended is described as maneuvering Marlow into his lie, see Bruce R. Stark, "Kurtz's Intended: The Heart of *Heart of Darkness*," *Texas Studies in Literature and Language* 16 (1974): 535–55.

23. Cf. Butler's caution that "any theory that asserts that signification is predicated upon the denial or repression of a female principle ought to consider whether that femaleness is really external to the cultural norms by which it is repressed. . . . Indeed, repression may be understood to produce the object it comes to deny" (93).

24. For an analysis of *Heart of Darkness* in terms of the ideology of "separate spheres," see Smith, "'Too Beautiful Altogether.'" I have benefited from Smith's criticism in this article of the earlier version of the present essay that was published in *Critical Inquiry*.

Chapter Eight: The Bride Stripped Bare

1. My account of Lacan considers his work between 1948 and 1964 and includes only the *Écrits* and the five seminars from this period that had been published at the time of this writing. I will cite the following works of Lacan, parenthetically giving first the page number of the English translation and wherever I cite the French, that of the original text after the solidus: *Écrits* (Paris: Seuil, 1966) and *Écrits: A Selection*, trans. Alan Sheridan (New York: W. W. Norton, 1977), cited as *E*; *Le Seminar I: Les écrits technique de Freud* (Paris: Seuil, 1975) and *The Seminar of Jacques Lacan: Book I. Freud's Papers on Technique*, trans. John Forrester (New York: Norton, 1988), this and the other seminars cited by the corresponding arabic numeral; *Le Seminaire II: Le moi dans la théorie de Freud at dans la technique de la psychanalyse* (Paris: Seuil, 1978) and *The Seminar of Jacques Lacan: Book II. The Ego in Freud's Theory and in the Technique of Psychoanalysis*, trans. Sylvia Tomaselli (New York: Norton, 1988); *Le Seminaire III: Les psychoses* (Paris: Seuil, 1981) and *The Seminar of Jacques Lacan: Book III. The Psychoses*, trans. Russell Grigg (New York: Norton, 1993); *Le Seminaire VII: L'éthique de la psychanalyse* (Paris: Seuil, 1986) and *The Seminar of Jacques Lacan: Book VII. The Ethics of Psychoanalysis*, trans. Dennis Porter (New York: Norton, 1992); *Le Seminaire XI: Les quatre concepts fondamentaux de la psychanalyse* (Paris: Seuil, 1973) and *The Four Fundamental Concepts of Psychoanalysis*, trans. Alan Sheridan (New York: Norton, 1977).

2. Jacques Derrida, "To Speculate—On 'Freud,'" in *The Post Card: From Socrates to Freud and Beyond,* trans. Alan Bass (Chicago: University of Chicago Press, 1987), 257–409.

3. Jacques Lacan, "Desire and the Interpretation of Desire in *Hamlet,*" in *Literature and Psychoanalysis,* ed. Shoshona Felman (Baltimore: Johns Hopkins University Press, 1982), 11–53; citation from p. 30.

4. Mikkel Borch-Jacobsen, *Lacan: The Absolute Master,* trans. Douglas Brick (Stanford: Stanford University Press, 1991). Borch-Jacobsen's is in my view the most searching and illuminating reading of Lacan since Derrida's "Le Facteur de la Verité" (in *The Post Card,* 411–96). Very schematically, I would say that Derrida overstresses the fullness of authenticity and full speech in Lacan, whereas Borch-Jacobsen too univocally stresses the emptiness of the transcendent subject. In this essay I attempt to define the matrix of *empty fullness* that generates both Derrida's and Borch-Jacobsen's readings.

5. There is, as often, extreme compression here in Lacan's language, but not necessarily confusion. Because of the identification that takes place between subject and object and because of the transitivity of relations between subject and Other ("even his demand originates in the locus of the Other" [*E* 269]), Lacan can in many passages slip legitimately from one side to the other of the relations between these terms; as Borch-Jacobsen notes, the *aufgehoben* object in the passage cited is an object "in which the subject loves himself" or "a signifier in which he signifies himself" (208).

6. Cf. Borch-Jacobsen, who says, citing the unpublished Seminar 5, that "the symbolic father" in Lacan enjoins the mother "not to reintegrate her product (much more than he forbids the child to possess the mother, as in Freud)" (226; see also 220).

7. When Lacan refers to Augustine's observation in the 1948 "Aggressivity in Psychoanalysis," he vaguely gestures at a historicizing justification: Augustine "foreshadowed psychoanalysis" because he "lived at a similar time" (*E* 20). But elsewhere, as in Seminar 1, Lacan refers to the same passage without any qualifications as to the generality of its truth (1.171).

8. This hatred, which is that of God for men, is the "correlative" of the structure of destructive aggressivity that Lacan himself describes, which involves the relation between "the law" and *das Ding* (7.97).

9. On this aspect of Nietzsche, see Henry Staten, *Nietzsche's Voice* (Ithaca: Cornell University Press, 1990), esp. chap. 6, 108–21.

10. See, for example, Elizabeth Grosz, *Jacques Lacan: A Feminist Introduction* (London: Routledge, 1990), 70.

11. Marcelle Marini, *Jacques Lacan* (Paris: Pierre Belford, 1986), 85–86.

12. Arnaut's poem, along with the other three pieces in this debate, are gathered, with commentary, in Pierre Bec's invaluable *Burlesque et obscenité chez les troubadours: Pour une approche du contre-texte médiéval* (Paris: Editions Stock, 1984), 138–53.

13. I reproduce the translation of Freud's text by Patrick J. Mahony given in the English version of Seminar 2, 148–49. The original was published in Mahony, "Towards a Formalist Approach to Dreams," *International Journal of Psychoanalysis* 4 (1977), 83–98. (Cited in the bibliography of Seminar 2 as *International Review of Psychoanalysis*; rest of citation identical.)

14. For a defense of Lacan's claims to overleap the established sciences, see Shoshona Felman, *Jacques Lacan and the Adventure of Insight: Psychoanalysis in Contemporary Culture* (Cambridge: Harvard University Press, 1987), esp. 154–58. For a closely argued critique of these claims, see François Roustang, *The Lacanian Delusion: Why Did We Follow Him for So Long?*, trans. Greg Simms (Oxford: Oxford University Press, 1990).

15. The concept of the being of the subject that is at stake here, as well as the distinction between the imaginary and symbolic dimensions of love, is consistent with Lacan's later work; yet it seems that the definition of love on the symbolic plane is already fundamentally reconfigured in Seminar 2. The imaginary relations of libidinal investment are now distinguished not from love of the other's true being but from the "symbolic pact." Love on the symbolic plane, married love, is now said not to be directed toward the individual person in question "but at a being beyond"—not the "being beyond" of the absolute particularity of the spouse but toward a "universal function," "the universal man, the universal woman" (2.260–61). In the "primitive form" of marriage, which best manifests the nature of love on the symbolic plane, the universal man is a "god," in the sense that he embodies the transcendent function of the symbolic organization that exchanges women between "androcentric lineages" (262), and it is to this god that a woman is given in marriage. In the decayed state of our own culture, however, men and women have ceased to embody universal functions and have become merely imaginary rivals (263).

Even though Lacan describes the "universal man" of the symbolic pact as "both the most concrete and the most transcendent man," his terminology here would seem difficult to reconcile with the notion of the "absolute," "opaque" particularity of the loved being in Seminar 1.

16. This particularity is in Seminar 11 linked to the notion of the "primary" signifier, the signifier that cannot be substituted for, which is "unary" and thus does not signify for another signifier (11.251). As such, it is "pure non-sense" and becomes "the bearer of the infinitization of the value of the subject, not open to all meanings, but abolishing them all," constituting the subject "in his freedom in relation to all meanings" (252). The "particular value" of the relation of the subject to the unconscious that contains this primordially repressed signifier is, nevertheless, made possible, as in Lacan's other accounts, by the "dialectized significations in the relation to the desire of the Other" (ibid.).

Index

Acton, William, 156–57
agape, 11, 189n. 11; in Lacan, 184
akhos 'grief', 33, 38, 42–43
Anaximander, 63
apoina 'ransom', 'reparation', 25, 28–32,
 39
Aquinas, Thomas, 121
Arnaut, Daniel, 11, 76, 88, 177–78
ascent to ideal, 3, 6
attachment. *See* cathexis
Aufhebung 'sublation': of body, contrasted with natural dissolution, 62;
 body transfigured by beauty, 116–17;
 of individual, in attainment of pleasure, 160; in Lacan, 169
Augustine: on blameworthy desire, 11,
 15; *City of God*, 121, 131; *Confessions*, 2,
 6–7, 75–132; on edenic sexuality, 109;
 On Free Choice of the Will, 8–9, 11;
 and Lacan, 172, 175; on libidinal
 investment, 6–7; on love of creature/
 creator, 75, 132; on mourning, 2; and
 Neoplatonism, 2, 73; on sexual passion, 121, 124, 131; and troubadour
 rhetoric, 82
automourning: in Dante, 96–97; in

Heart of Darkness, 15–16; and heteromourning, 10–11, 38–44, 70; in *Iliad*,
 9–10, 21, 35, 161–62

Barrett, C. K., 68
Bataille, Georges, 131
Bec, Pierre, 178
Benveniste, Emile, 22
Bernart de Ventadorn, 11; and Capellanus, 103; compared with Dante, 97;
 and denigration of women, 86, 88;
 and fear of women's treachery, 88, 91;
 and formalism, 81–84; and sexual
 desire, 77–81
body: of death, 15, 70, 102–3, 165, 181;
 dissolution of, 11, 59–61, 99–102, 181;
 evaded by Gnostics, 136; female, in
 Lacan, 180; of love, 49, 70, 102–3, 165;
 love of, in Platonic doctrine, 74; and
 Milton's monism, 120; and nature of
 Eve's beauty, 118; as object of concupiscence, in Augustine, 131; resurrection of, 51–52; transfigured by beauty,
 116–17. *See also sarx* 'flesh'; *sōma*
Borch-Jacobsen, Mikkel, 167, 173
Boyde, P., 95

LIBRARY OF CONGRESS CATALOGING-IN-PUBLICATION DATA

Staten, Henry, 1946–
    Eros in mourning : Homer to Lacan / Henry Staten.
        p.   cm.
    Includes bibliographical references and index.
    ISBN 0-8018-4923-3
    1. Desire in literature.   2. Loss (Psychology) in literature.   3. Mourning in literature.
4. Literature—History and criticism—Theory, etc.   I. Title.
PN56.D48S83   1995
809'.93353—dc20   94-16559